BRITISH NEWS MEDIA AND THE SPANISH CIVIL WAR

International Communications
Series Editor: Philip M. Taylor

This is the first comprehensive series to tackle the fast-expanding subject of International Communications.

This multi-disciplinary subject is viewed as a field of enquiry and research that deals with the processes and impact of the transfer of information, news, data and cultural products as well as other forms of transborder communication between nation-states within the wider context of globalization. As such it is not only a field of study in its own right but also directly connected to international history, international politics, international affairs and international political economy.

Most writers in these more 'established' fields are agreed that communications have come to play an ever more significant part in relations between states at the political, economic, diplomatic, military and cultural levels. This series will show how communications serves to influence those activities from the points of transmission to those of reception.

Enormous breakthroughs in communications technologies – satellite communications, computer mediated communications, mobile personal communications – are now converging, and the possibilities which this might present are forcing a reconsideration of how established patterns of inter-state relations might adapt to, or be influenced by, this latest phase of the information age.

Debates relating to international regulation, censorship, public diplomacy, electronic democracy, cross-cultural communications and even information warfare all reflect the sense that communications are transforming the nature and practice of government, education, leisure, business, work and warfare. Information has become the lifeblood of this globalizing set of patterns.

Books in the series reflect this phenomenon but are rooted in historical method, even when tackling more contemporary events. They are truly international in coverage. The range of books reflects the coverage of courses and teaching in international communications and they are carefully aimed at students and researchers working in this area.

British News Media and the Spanish Civil War

Tomorrow May Be Too Late

David Deacon

Edinburgh University Press

To Luke, Jack and Jo, with love

Edinburgh University Press Ltd
22 George Square, Edinburgh

Typeset in Ehrhardt by
Servis Filmsetting Ltd, Stockport, Cheshire, and
printed and bound in Great Britain by
CPI-Antony Rowe Ltd, Chippenham, Wilts

A CIP record for this book is available from the British Library

ISBN 978 0 7486 2748 6 (hardback)

Contents

Acknowledgements

The production of this book would not have been possible without the help of many people. My grateful thanks to: Ben Oldfield for his major contribution to the media analysis; Patricia Marshall for her meticulous copy-editing and checking; John Entwisle (The Reuters Archive), James Peters (Manchester Guardian Archive), Nicholas Mays (Archives & Record Office News International) and Tracey Weston (BBC Written Archive Centre) for generously sparing their time and expertise to guide me around their archives; Shen Liknaitzky for helping me to make some extremely useful contacts; Sam Lesser, Jack Jones and David Marshall for sparing time to share their experiences with me; Jo Aldridge and Simon Cross for their proofreading and encouragement; my colleagues at the Department of Social Sciences, Loughborough University, in particular Michael Billig, John Downey, Mike Gane, Peter Golding, Emily Keightley, Jim McGuigan, Sabina Mihelj, Graham Murdock, Michael Pickering, John Richardson, Peter Riley-Jordan, Ann Smith, James Stanyer, Ian Taylor and Dominic Wring for their support; Felix Delmer, Gerald Seiflow, Llewellyn Howland III, Sarah Monks, John Monks and Dina Monks for providing photographs of their relatives; Philip Taylor, Sarah Edwards, Máiréad McElligott, James Dale, Esme Watson, Roda Morrison and all at Edinburgh University Press for their patience, encouragement and work in producing this book; June Deacon, Malcolm Deacon, Pamela Eve, Brian Aldridge, Kathleen Aldridge, Paul Smith, Julian Jeffery, Nicola Jeffery, Marc Jeffery, Natalie Jeffery, Jason Allen, Julie Allen, John Ferris, Carol Ferris, Chris Codman and all my other friends and family for their support and encouragement; and the Economic and Social Research for funding the research that forms the basis of this book (RES-000-22-0533). Any errors are, of course, entirely my responsibility.

I imagine in the year A.D. 2000 the young journalist who arrives in Madrid will glide into the Norte Station in a luxurious motor-train which will have whirled him down from the frontier in four or five hours. Or he will land at Barajas Airport after a speedy stratosphere flight from London. He will be primed with data on Spain prepared by the Learned men to whom I have referred above and the study of which will enable him to judge with fair accuracy the conditions in the country before his arrival. Doubtless my young colleague of the future will have been examined and certified by some international body as a fit and competent person to undertake the highly delicate work which reporting on international affairs comprises if it is done intelligently and honourably. Such at least are my hopes for the future which seems very distant indeed in these days when Europe is in a fair way to return to the Stone Age in its customs.

Henry Buckley, *The Life and Death of the Spanish Republic*, p. 15

An Emblematic Editorial

The subtitle of this book is taken from an editorial published by the *News Chronicle* on 19 January 1937 about the Spanish Civil War. The article occupied most of the fifth page of the paper and under its headline, 'TOMORROW MAY BE TOO LATE', was a map of the Iberian peninsular, North Africa, Western France and Southern Britain superimposed with a photograph of a deranged-looking Adolf Hitler. The caption underneath invited readers to '[i]magine a regime benevolent to Hitler and Mussolini on the Spanish mainland, in the Balearics, in Spanish Morocco, in the Canaries, in Rio de Oro'.

The article was unequivocal about which side in the civil war deserved Britain's support. It said of the Republican government besieged by the military rebellion that started on 17 July 1936:

> The Government of Spain was freely elected. It was democratic. If it has since become more extreme, more autocratic, that is not the fault of the democracy that elected it but of the rebels who by wantonly attacking it forced it to extremes in defence of its existence.

It remarked of the Nationalists:

> General Franco fights with a few Spaniards, but chiefly with Moors, foreign legionaries and a host of German and Italian conscripts, aided by an armada of German and Italian aeroplanes with German and Italian pilots . . . [Germany and Italy] will have the power in Spain, and in the Spanish possessions, a man who has been placed there by their connivance, who owes his very existence to their support, who is tied to them body and soul.

There are several reasons why the headline from this editorial seemed an appropriate choice for inclusion in this book's title. The most banal is that it offers an example of its subject matter, which examines how the Spanish Civil War was represented by the British news media of the day. I explain why this is a topic worthy of serious consideration in the concluding section of this chapter.

The tone of the editorial and its headline also highlights how the engagement of particular news media was often infused with deeply politicised views of the conflict and its wider significance, and one of the themes of this analysis will be to show how these had an impact upon the way they interpreted and reported events. Furthermore, there is something in the poetic and subtle internal alliteration of the editorial's headline that captures the spirit of its time, in particular an anxious awareness of what Churchill would later term 'the gathering storm' (1948). As the article put it: 'This is not a fight for Spain alone; it has become a fight for the soul and body of human freedom everywhere.'

Despite this bold declamation, the content of the editorial also reveals uncertainty and confusion, which again was emblematic of many media responses to Spain and international events more generally (Graves and Hodge, 1940: 341). At the start of the war, the *News Chronicle* endorsed the international non-intervention agreement authored by the French government and supported unstintingly by the British government (for example, 'DEMOCRACY AND THE EMPIRE ARE AT STAKE', 6 August 1936: 8). The editorial of 19 January 1937 shows that, five months later, the paper's faith in the policy had diminished, mainly because of the flagrant contravention of the agreement by the Fascist states, but the *Chronicle*'s editorial didn't follow through the logical implications of its analysis and urge the British government to abandon non-intervention. Instead, it concluded with a request for clarification as to when the British government would 'give assurances of support to France to enable the Quai d'Orsay to say to the Fascist powers: "Thus far and no farther"?' Within three months, the paper recovered some belief in the non-intervention agreement (for example, 'A Welcome Change', the *News Chronicle*, 23 April 1937: 10), only to have it dashed days later by the destruction of Guernica. By the end of the war, its disillusionment was complete and it had no qualms about campaigning for Britain to permit the Republic to acquire the weapons it needed to prevent Franco's victory (for example, 'Let Spain Buy Arms', 18 January 1939: 8; 'Arms for Spain!', 19 January 1939: 10; 'Not Too Late', 27 January 1939: 10). Changes of this kind again highlight a major aspect of the analysis I develop in this book. Media responses to Spain were not as static and unyielding as some historical commentary appears to assume. Moreover, these shifts in opinion were not just restricted to matters of foreign policy. As will be shown, several news organisations also changed their opinion about the legitimacy of the warring parties.

A further reason for selecting the *News Chronicle* headline is its dramatic irony. We now know that the hopes it expressed for a principled and assertive response from the democracies to events unfolding in Spain never materialised and that Franco captured Madrid on 1 April 1939 and commenced a period of dictatorial rule that continued until his death in 1975. Because of this, it is, perhaps, tempting to see the *Chronicle*'s demands in patronising terms – as naive and ill-informed for failing to appreciate that it was already 'too late' for the Republic. There are several reasons why this is unfair. To treat journalism as bad history is to misunderstand its function. Journalism contributes to historical understanding but that is not its principal raison d'être. Journalism seeks to engage with the here and now and, where it is politically motivated, to influence developing social and political events. In January 1937, there were grounds for optimism about the Republic's chances: Madrid had successfully resisted the Nationalist advance in

November 1936; the extent to which France and Britain would be willing to tolerate Italian and German contraventions of the non-intervention agreement had not yet become clear; the Nationalists' devastating attack on the Basque region was still two months hence. There was, therefore, much that was uncertain and much to play for when the *Chronicle*'s editorial appeared. To assume that, because events subsequently resulted in the Republic's defeat, this was an inevitable result is to mistake history for destiny. The *News Chronicle*'s intervention of 19 January 1937 may have been in vain but, judged in the specific context of its publication, it was neither naive nor futile.

Of course, I cannot avoid using the lessons of history to assess the interventions du jour of the British media but I want to avoid an imperialistic application of hindsight. This is not just to be fair to the news-makers of the day who did not have the same perspective and knowledge at their disposal but because it can create some distorted assessments of journalists' performance in Spain. This point is best illustrated by way of an example.

Since its first publication in 1975, Phillip Knightley's study *The First Casualty* has gained a deserved reputation for its panoptic and highly critical view of journalists' performances in reporting international conflicts. One of its chapters assesses the performance of foreign correspondents in Spain, excerpts from which formed a major feature item in the *Sunday Times* magazine that marked the publication of the book ('The Spanish Civil War: How Truth Lost to Propaganda', the *Sunday Times* Magazine, 20 September 1975: 14–26). The crux of Knightley's critique in both book and article was that many British and American correspondents let their hearts rule their heads in reporting the civil war to such an extent that these sympathies made them both wittingly and unwittingly complicit in the dissemination of pro-Republican propaganda (1975: 202, 215–16). As an example of the latter, Knightley discusses 'the Guernica myth' that gained wide currency following British press reports of the destruction of the Basque town by German bombers on 26 April 1937. The complexities of the reporting of this incident are dealt with later in this book but a general summation of the events is as follows. Guernica became an international cause célèbre because of the chance proximity of four foreign journalists (George Steer of *The Times*, Noel Monks of the *Daily Express*, Christopher Holme of Reuters and Mathieu Corman of *Ce Soir*)[1] who provided eyewitness accounts of the immediate aftermath of the carnage. Two claims in their initial reports provoked controversies that raged for decades afterwards – that German aviators were responsible for the attack and that Guernica had been targeted solely because of its symbolic significance as the spiritual home of the Basque nation. Because of these conclusions about the mode and motivation for the destruction, the event instantly 'passed into the traditions of the Left as a symbol of everything hateful about Fascism, a turning point of history' (Knightley, 1975: 203).

The immediate response of the Nationalists to the international furore provoked by these press reports was initially to deny that any planes had been in the area at the time but, when this was readily refuted, they claimed that the destruction had been wrought by incendiary devices planted by retreating 'Red' forces.

Noel Monks (the *Daily Express*)

Christopher Holme (Reuters)   **George Steer (*The Times*)**

Three of the journalists who brought Guernica to the attention of the world.

Nationalist supporters and some historians persisted with the self-destruction argument for many years after the war (for example, Bolín, 1967; Hart, 1973; Crozier, 2001). But any vestige of credibility in the lie was effectively ended on 24 April 1998 when the German parliament issued a formal apology to the inhabitants of Guernica for the destruction their bombers had wrought (Simons, 1998).

However, Knightley's criticism of the initial reporting of Guernica mainly concerned the conclusions that were drawn about the motives for the air raid. Drawing on recently published historical assessments by two esteemed civil war historians, Hugh Thomas and Herbert Southworth, he rejected the imputation that Guernica had been targeted for symbolic rather than military reasons and concluded:

> [I]t is clear that the correspondents made Guernica. If Steer, and, to a lesser extent, Holme, Monks, and Corman, had not been there to write about it, Guernica would have passed un-noticed, just another incident in a brutal civil war. Yet the conclusion must be that Steer, with understandable professional, political, and personal ardour, overreacted to the story. (Knightley, 1975: 209)

Whilst I concur with Knightley's point that Guernica was, in essence, a media event, I believe his criticisms of Steer and the other journalists are harsh and crucially misconstrue what were the core issues at stake when the reports were initially filed. First, he glosses over a major difference in the actions of the parties involved in the initial public communication of the event. Of the Nationalists' response to the journalists' reports, he commented:

> On all the evidence available, Guernica was bombed for tactical military reasons. Then the Nationalists, instead of saying that war is hell and it is sometimes necessary to bomb towns for military reasons, became apprehensive about the reaction abroad, especially in the United States and Britain . . . They panicked and committed themselves first to outright denials that there had been any bombing, and then to the untenable Basque-self-destruction stance. (ibid.)

This invites the view that both journalists and propagandists were guilty of hasty and mistaken responses but this equivalence is unjustified. The journalists' error was one of interpretation, whereas the Nationalists' was one of active deception, manifestly a greater transgressive act. Second, Knightley's phrase 'On all the evidence available' ignores the fact that this evidence and perspective only became available well after the end of the war and that, even then, Southworth and Thomas's judgements about the military motives for the attack were qualified, 'on-balance' judgements rather than definitive assessments.[2] Third, Knightley overestimates the significance of questions about motive in the political controversy that followed the attack. The critical question at the time was that of culpability and Steer's categorical identification of German bombing planes, in particular, sparked a diplomatic storm in which the German government vilified *The Times* newspaper for publishing these claims, much to the discomfort of the British government and the paper's editor, Geoffrey Dawson. But, despite these denials and dissembling, history has proven that Steer was absolutely right about the matter of culpability. Moreover, his identification of the perpetrators in the face of powerful political pressures to do otherwise, deserves more credit than is apportioned by Knightley.

Knightley's critique of journalists in Spain is on firmer footing in its identification of those occasions when they knowingly falsified or distorted information for partisan purposes – although others (for example, Inglis, 2002: 141) have argued there is even a case here for greater tolerance. There were certainly plenty of liars and fantasists in the international press corps that covered Spain and, on occasions, the level of their deception could astound. Some three years after the war's end, George Orwell reflected:

> Early in life I have noticed that no event is ever correctly reported in a newspaper, but in Spain, for the first time, I saw newspaper reports which did not bear any relation to the facts, not even the relationship which is implied in an ordinary lie. I saw great battles reported where there had been no fighting, and complete silence where hundreds of men had been killed. I saw troops who had fought bravely denounced as cowards and traitors, and others who had never seen a shot fired hailed as the heroes of imaginary victories; and I saw newspapers in London retailing these lies and eager intellectuals building emotional superstructures over events that had never happened. I saw, in fact, history being written not in terms of what happened but of what ought to have happened according to various 'party lines'. ([1943] 2001: 352)

However, the identification of active falsehoods is not always a straightforward matter. For example, the most sensational suggestion made by Knightley was that the photojournalist Robert Capa's iconic photograph of a loyalist militiaman at the moment of death – the famous 'falling soldier' image – might have been staged. The basis for his suspicions lay in the testimony of some of Capa's associates who noted his evasiveness about the origins and context in which the image was taken and the fact that, when it appeared in the French magazine *Vu* on 23 September 1936 and then *Life* magazine on 12 July 1937, it became clear that it was one of a set of related photographs, some of which were manifestly posed for the camera. Knightley's suspicions have evidently strengthened over the years (Whelan, 2002) and others have since elaborated upon them, paying particular attention to a second picture of a *fallen* soldier that was published alongside the image of the *falling* soldier in its original presentation in *Vu*. At first sight, the two pictures seem to be sequential images of the same man but detailed analysis of the clothing of each figure suggests they are not the same. Furthermore, it is clear from the similarities in light and shadow, the cloud formations in the background and distinctive foliage in the foreground that both photographs were taken in the same location within moments of each other. If they are images of two different men dying in the same location at a similar time, how can one explain the absence of the first body in the second image? And, even if the two photographs were sequential images of the same person, how can one explain that the figure in the first is in the process of dropping his rifle but in the second has retrieved hold of it? On the basis of these and other concerns, the author of a major study of news photography in the Spanish Civil War concluded that 'the *Death of a Republican Soldier* provides no documentary record of any moment of death; indeed its relationship with the truth in its most orthodox sense is at best heavily undermined' (Brothers, 1997: 183).

However, such scepticism has not remained unchallenged and there are those who still insist the picture is genuine. One of the abiding mysteries surrounding the image was Capa's failure to give details about where and when he took the picture and the identity of the man in the photograph. Capa's official biographer recently claimed to have identified all these details (Whelan, 2002). Through close cross-referencing of new and existing sources, Whelan identified the man as Federico Borrell García who was killed in battle at Cerro Muriano on 5 September 1936. Furthermore, through his own detailed analysis of both images (which he accepts are of different men), Whelan explains the absence of the first body in the second image by reference to a third photograph in the set of images published by *Life*, which suggests Capa was sheltering in a deep trench when taking the picture. This afforded an opportunity for the militia to recover Borrell's body before the second man fell. Whelan also recruited expert forensic opinion which highlighted a hitherto unnoticed detail in the falling man image. Underneath the man's left thigh one can see his left hand is curled inwards, showing his muscles were limp rather than stressed at the time of his collapse. Whelan concludes:

> Hardly anyone faking death would ever know that such a hand position was necessary in order to make the photograph realistic. It is nearly impossible for any conscious person to resist the reflex impulse to brace his fall by flexing his hand strongly backward at the wrist and extending his fingers out straight.

In January 2008, *The New York Times* reported that three suitcases containing Capa's negatives from the Spanish Civil War had been discovered in Mexico many years after their disappearance in Paris during the Nazi occupation. This raises the possibility that the controversy may be resolved definitively, particularly if the cache contains the image's negative in its original sequence. However, my suspicion is that an absolute resolution is unlikely and we're just going to have to accept that the militiaman, like the cat in Erwin Schrödinger's thought experiment, will forever remain superpositional, at once dead and alive.

This example demonstrates the difficulties in separating the reality of events from their representation. But this is not to suggest that questions of truth are pointless or futile – to surrender any attempt to appraise the validity and reliability of historical claims means one has to treat all competing and contradictory accounts as equally legitimate social constructions. The politics of despair in this relativism is addressed and dismissed by Pierre Vilar in his introduction to Southworth's Guernica study:

> I am told such a search [for certainty] is chimerical and that history is an artificial construction just as a painting is not a photograph. But every passionate quest for a concrete truth is in effect a spontaneous critique of false constructions, of fake compositions. The true naïf never has the ambition to achieve reality. On the contrary, he begins with the images imposed upon the public by bad painters and photographers, and because he cannot accept these images, he draws nearer – and draws us along with him – to the inaccessible 'truth' . . . I now know that there are two 'memories' of any Spanish event. But this does not mean that the lie is as strong as the truth. (quoted in Southworth, 1977: ix–x and xvii)

Respecting ultimate distinctions between lies and truth does not mean abandoning consideration of processes of social construction. If there is one cumulative lesson to be learnt from years of sociological research into news reporting, it is that reality construction is an inevitable facet of journalists' work. As Gilles Gauthier remarks:

> The realist theory proposed here is not to say that the world viewed by news journalism – which is essentially a social world – is a given. On the contrary, this realism readily admits that journalistic reality, and more importantly, social reality, are constructed realities. This perspective simply attempts to demonstrate how this construction depends on a reality that is not constructed. (2005: 59)

Journalists have no choice but to select and prioritise issues, people and events as there is always far more that could be news than can be news. Moreover, research has also shown that structural and cultural factors have a far more significant role in this construction process than deliberate political bias – that is, the tendency to privilege people, issues and perspectives because they fit more effectively into the cycles and demands of the news industries, because they have greater cultural significance and proximity and because they do not confound broadly accepted normative values.

For this reason, this book is mainly concerned with media representation rather than deception. At times, this discussion also addresses questions of misrepresentation, thereby re-engaging with questions of truth, but in the main this study seeks to understand the nature of British news constructions of the war and the factors that shaped them. To do this, the analysis goes beyond the news texts themselves to locate the various factors and stages that contributed to their creation and draws on a wide range of primary and secondary sources. Some estimable research has already been conducted into the mediation of the Spanish Civil War and one of the purposes of this book is to collate and combine what is still a rather dispersed literature. My analysis also makes extensive use of the dozens of accounts published by journalists, both during and after the war, which related their experiences of reporting in Spain and provide insights into the challenges they confronted and, often in spite of themselves, the values and mind-sets that informed their work. Furthermore, I have analysed in detail various official and media archives and uncovered much new evidence about the hidden editorial politics that framed British news coverage.[3] With the assistance of my colleague Ben Oldfield, I have also analysed more than ten thousand news and commentary items published about Spain between 1936 and 1939.

There are two reasons why I believe all this effort has been warranted. The first is the contribution a comprehensive analysis of the role of the British media makes to historical understanding of the Spanish Civil War and its political and cultural dynamics. Despite being dwarfed by the carnage of the Second World War, it was by any measure a significant war on its own terms. Advances in air-craft technology produced a qualitatively new mode of warfare and, as news spread of the bombing of civilians in Madrid, Barcelona, Guernica and else-where, citizens across Europe began to quail at what this might portend. Although labelled a 'civil war', it was a conflict that implicated all the major inter-national powers of the day.

But the war was about more than global power politics. From the beginning, it was recognised as a battle of ideas, of ideals and of ideologies and, seventy years since the war's conclusion, two types of representation related to the conflict retain considerable currency in popular memory. The first is the pro-paganda produced during the war, in particular the vivid posters, whose 'bright hard primary colours' (Lee, 1991) became 'an essential part of the visual land-scape in which individuals living the tragedy of the war went about their daily business of survival . . . a conspicuous and inescapable reminder that a new reality was upon them' (Vergara, 1999). The second is the profusion of artistic work stimulated by the conflict; much of which was intended as direct political interventions but has remained treasured for their intrinsic artistic merits.

Both of these representational forms expressed political and moral certainties about the conflict and it is interesting to speculate how this impassioned advo-cacy may have influenced subsequent perceptions of the conflict. For, with the Spanish Civil War, it would appear that history has been written by the defeated (Beevor, 2003: 250). From our contemporary vantage point, claiming a moral equivalence between the antagonists seems specious and it no longer seems difficult to identify where the moral obligations and strategic interests of the British nation lay. However, this contemporary collective certainty had no equiv-alent existence in British society in the 1930s. At the time, the conflict fractured political and public opinion in unpredictable ways, manifesting itself as much in divisions within left-wing and right-wing politics as between them (Buchanan, 1997: 36; Watkins, 1963).

The root of these conflicts lay in profound disagreements about what the war constituted. Did the mobilisation of the various Socialist, Anarcho-syndicalist, Liberal and Communist groups in defence of the Popular Front government in 1936 auger a genuine social revolution or was the war principally about protecting democracy from Fascist aggression? Did it expose the threat posed by the rising tide of Communism across mainland Europe? Or was it just an ebullition of ancient local enmities? Our appreciation of these complexities may have receded with time but they were at the very heart of public debate as the war unfolded.

In this context, the coverage given to the war by the mainstream news media was seen by all participants to have great influence in the management of public perceptions and attitudes (Buchanan, 1997: 21–4). Although impassioned advocacy was a feature here too, so was dispassionate arbitration (albeit often masking advocacy). Significantly, interest in the disposition of the British media extended far beyond the nation's shores, revealing international recognition of the pivotal influence that Britain's stance on intervention could play in the outcome of the conflict.

The second justification for this analysis of British media coverage of the Spanish Civil War is the historical perspective it can lend to many contemporary debates about the role of the news media, particularly during international crises. It is frequently claimed that recent changes in media structures, values and practices have transformed the nature and conduct of politics in capitalist democracies. Mazzoleni and Schulz (1999) discuss recent claims that we have witnessed a shift from the 'mediation' of politics to their 'mediatisation' – a situation where all political processes are exposed to the remorseless force of media logic. In a similar vein, Hargreaves claims the media are now the first rather than fourth estate of democracy – they are 'the primary agency for determining public questions, from decisions on war and peace to the fate of individual politicians and other public figures' (2003: 19).

The reference to military conflict here is significant because it identifies this as one area where the intrusive and central presence of 'our global, always-on media' (ibid.) has supposedly become most evident. Richard Keeble asserts, 'Major, high profile wars are no longer fought as merely military events . . . Major wars are now fought as media spectacles for largely non-strategic purposes' (1997: 5–6). According to Combs, we have entered the era of 'a new kind of war, war as performance. It is a war in which the attention of its *auteurs* is not only the conduct of the war but also the communication of war' (1993: 277 quoted in ibid.).

If there seems a widespread consensus about the growth of 'mediatisation' and 'promotionalism' (see, for example, Wernik, 1991; Leys, 2001; Davis, 2001; Miller and Dinan, 2000), there seems less agreement as to which agencies are driving the process. For some, the principal cause is the increasing aggressiveness, acuity and cynicism of political elites in their media management strategies: capturing and co-opting journalists in a vortex of spin. For others, these are essentially defensive strategies, necessitated by a voracious, hydra-headed media, whose powers are becoming ever greater and less accountable (see, for example, Straw, 2003; Oborne, 1999; Blair, 2007).

This book is mainly a historical case study but it also has relevance to these contemporary concerns. For, although assertions about a recent epochal shift in political communication are widespread and it is clear that media institutions and technologies are developing and changing with increasing rapidity, these facts alone do not provide a sufficient basis for proving the mediatisation thesis. It may be that some of the characteristics taken as evidence of the recent mutagenic impact of the media on political processes have deeper historical roots than is appreciated. Significantly, some recent commentators contend that many contemporary analyses of the media–politics interface underestimate the sophistication and extent of earlier political marketing and news management and overestimate the docility, deference and lack of reflexivity of media professionals during these periods (see, for example, Negrine and Lilleker, 2003; Wring, 1996).

The structure of the book

The substantive investigation of the mediation of the Spanish Civil War begins in the next chapter with an examination and comparison of the international news management and censorship activities of Republican and Nationalist authorities in Spain. Chapter 3 discusses the attitudes, actions and experiences of the foreign correspondents that covered the war directly. Chapter 4 focuses specifically on women correspondents and the distinctive nature of their contribution. Chapter 5 examines how the British government sought to manage British media responses to Spain and how these activities linked to the commercial and political interests of senior news proprietors and editors. Chapter 6 analyses the interpretative and evaluative features of British daily newspaper coverage of the war, from its start through to its conclusion. Chapter 7 examines representations of the war in newsreel coverage, photojournalism and the editorial responses of weekly news periodicals. Chapter 8 summarises the findings of the research to draw wider conclusions about the continuities and discontinuities between this historical case study and contemporary conditions concerning the communication of international conflicts.

Notes

1. The very first British report of the attack on Guernica was published by the London *Star* newspaper on the evening of 27 April 1937. Until recently, the author of this piece was unknown but research by Tom Buchanan (2007) has identified the author as Keith Scott-Watson. Watson was a sculptor who first went to Spain at the start of the war and fought with the Tom Mann Centuria, which was the first group of British volunteers to fight in Spain on behalf of the Republic. After some initial military action he offered his services to the *Daily Express* and worked with Sefton Delmer in Madrid for a brief period. According to Delmer (1961: 304–7), Watson had to flee Madrid because he was under-threat of arrest for desertion, which, if true, makes his reappearance in Bilbao a matter of months later remarkable in itself (Watson's own account [1937] is somewhat evasive on the manner of his departure from Madrid). Watson returned to Spain again in 1938, when he reported on the war from Barcelona for the *Daily Herald*.
2. Knightley's use of cool historical analysis to condemn hot-headed journalistic responses is also not as straightforward as it appears in this instance. First, Herbert Southworth's dedication of his book on Guernica to the memory of Steer, Corman,

Monks and Holmes validates rather than repudiates their contribution. Second, Knightley overstates the extent to which Southworth and Thomas agreed on the Nationalists' and Germans' motives for destroying the town and their respective responsibility. See, for example, Thomas's review of the Spanish edition of Southworth's book on Guernica ('If we assume that Guernica was destroyed by the Germans, it is still not absolutely clear, even after reading these 500 absorbing pages, exactly why it happened' – 'Heinkels over Guernica', *The Times Literary Supplement*, 11/4/1975).

3. The main archives accessed for this study were: The Times Newspaper Limited Archive (Wapping); Guardian (formerly Manchester Guardian) Archive, John Rylands University Library, University of Manchester; The Reuters Archive (Canary Wharf); the BBC Written Archive Centre (Reading); British Library Newspapers, Colindale Avenue, London, NW9 5HE; and The National Archives (Kew).

The Ground Rules – Republican and Nationalist International News Management

The Spanish Civil War was a domestic conflict in name only. It attracted the attentions and interventions of many foreign governments, political parties, activists, workers, artists and intellectuals, most of whom engaged in propagandistic activity intended to influence attitudes, policies and outcomes related to the war. I examine some of this activity in a British context in Chapter 5 but the discussion here focuses solely on the propaganda of the local combatants in Spain. This is because, for all the geopolitical significance of the war, it is appropriate to conceive of the local antagonists as both the principal sources and preliminary mediators of the conflict. It was their actions, values, interests and ideologies that were the root referents for all other interventions and representations.

Furthermore, the discussion concentrates mainly on their internationally targeted propaganda, as opposed to their efforts to win, or terrorise, local hearts and minds. This is not to suggest that the local dimension is unimportant or that there is a neat and absolute distinction between these levels. News from abroad could sometimes stimulate hope or despair to those directly affected by combat, just as local rhetoric could resonate internationally and, indeed, through history. For example, when Dolores Ibárruri Gómez, 'La Pasionaria', delivered the first of her famous oratories in defence of the Republic on Madrid radio on 19 July 1936, her main concern was to exhort local 'workers, peasants, anti-fascists and patriotic Spaniards' to resist the rebellion (Thomas, 2003: 233). However, her rallying cry '¡No pasarán!' ('They shall not pass') quickly acquired international fame as a clarion call for anti-fascism in Spain and beyond (ibid.). Nevertheless, there were major differences in the messages these warring parties sought to communicate at home and abroad.

Additionally, this discussion will concentrate on propaganda activities that were geared towards managing, controlling and influencing foreign media coverage. Such media-centrism is justified by the principal concerns of the book but it does mean that many locally initiated cultural and political activities that fulfilled propagandistic functions are excluded from discussion. (For a valuable review of the range of political and cultural propaganda produced in Republican and Nationalist sectors during the war, see Holguín, 2002: 168–94.)

One final point to explain concerns my use of the term 'propaganda' in this and subsequent chapters. To the extent that the term retains contemporary currency, it is in a provocative capacity (see, for example, Herman and Chomsky, 1988; Pilger, 2005) and there are those who reject its usage, because of its pejorative connotations and lack of conceptual precision (see Corner, 2007). However, I have used it here for two reasons. First, it is the term that would have been employed at the time to label the matters under discussion. Second, although the term had started to acquire negative connotations from the end of the First World War (Taylor, 1999), it still had a more ambiguous quality in the 1930s than it does today and it was as commonly used descriptively to label promotional communication of any kind as it was to stigmatise particular forms of public discourse.[1]

This chapter is structured around two sections. The first outlines the broad themes that guided the communication and propaganda activities of the combatants in Spain. The second examines how these translated into the practical arrangements for foreign journalists on both sides of the war.

Propaganda themes

It is easier to identify the core themes in the propaganda of the forces that rebelled than it is to precis the equivalent goals of the government they attacked. This is because of their different political structures. It is an oversimplification to characterise the Nationalists as a completely cohesive political and ideological force. Nevertheless, under Franco's centralised and hierarchical leadership, the different demands and disaffections of the constituents of the Nationalist rebellion were quickly contained and controlled. In contrast, the Republic was politically and geographically heterogeneous, particularly during the first year of the war, containing political elements with very different beliefs and objectives. At times, this affected the coherence of the messages they communicated.

Nationalist themes

Three related themes dominated all Nationalist propaganda. The first was a visceral anti-Communism in which all creeds and factions on the left, and indeed political centre, were vilified as 'Reds' who threatened Spanish values and unity. As one foreign correspondent noted:

> The Nationalist propaganda was concentrated exclusively on the fight against Bolshevism . . . I found, however, that Bolshevism was an elastic word, for it included democrats as well as Communists; in fact, everyone who did not support a totalitarian regime was lumped together as Red. (Cowles, 1941: 72)

The second theme was a self-conscious religiosity that characterised the Nationalist rebellion as a Catholic 'crusade' against atheistic hordes. This proved highly effective in mobilising support internationally for Franco, both domestically and among Catholic institutions and congregations across the world (Thomas, 2003: 495; Flint, 1987). The final theme drew on reactionary conceptions of Spanish nationhood, which repudiated regional separatism and sought to associate Franco 'with the great heroes of Spain's past' (Preston, 1993: 290). Although dependent on the military and political support of Germany and Italy, the Nationalist leaders were sensitive to suggestions that they were mere clients of these fascist powers and conduits for their ideologies.[2]

Nationalist propagandists also had to attend to questions of self-legitimacy, particularly as the conflict extended and attracted more international attention. The military rebellion was always intended to be a coup rather than a civil war, achieving its political objectives through force of arms rather than ideas. It was only in the face of the Republic's enduring resistance that the Nationalist leadership had to grapple with explaining and justifying actions that could claim no 'objective legitimacy' (Ellwood, 1994: 78).

One of the initial means by which they did so was through atrocity propaganda, which highlighted the violent excesses of the Republic and thereby inverted the question of culpability. Writing at the time of the conflict, the pro-Republican journalist Arthur Koestler, argued that the Nationalists had no option but to dramatise and exaggerate the scale of the Red Terror as this was the only message likely to secure international support among general political and public opinion, internationally:

> The rebels are fighting for a military dictatorship, for a corporate state, for clericalism – causes which are very unpopular in France and England . . . Genuine political arguments, therefore, with the exception of the Communist bogey, were of no use as propaganda to Franco in Western Europe. So he deliberately chose a form of propaganda that from the time of the ritual murder myths of the Middle Ages until the time of the Reichstag fire and the Abyssinian campaign has always proved an unfailing standby, whenever it has been essential to avoid awkward political discussions and to justify one's own terroristic acts by pointing to the other side . . . This was intended specially for English consumption . . . He preferred to tell them stories of mangled corpses, of the putting out of eyes, and of Red cannibalism. (1937: 128–9)

Alongside the atrocity propaganda, the Nationalists publicised documents said to prove that a radical takeover of the Republic was being planned at the time the rebellion occurred. Historical analysis has definitively exposed these documents as forgeries (Southworth, 2001) but they provided valuable ammunition for Nationalist apologists at the time, particularly internationally (see, for example, Gerahty, 1937: 214–9).

A clear indication of the Nationalists' concerns about their legitimacy was their sensitivity about the labels applied to them by foreign commentators. For example, a special correspondent for the *Daily Mail* recounted a conflict between a Nationalist censor, Captain Rosales, and John Whitaker of the *New York Herald Tribune* at the start of the war:

[I]n John's stories they are the 'rebel' armies and in fury Rosales tells him he will not stand for it. He will forbid the word 'rebel' to be used in stories hereafter. 'Patriot' armies, 'Nationalist' armies, 'White' armies – any man who used the term 'rebel' will have his passes revoked and will leave the country! (Davis, 1940: 131)

These semantic concerns were far more than just an idiosyncratic fixation of an overzealous press officer. Rather they were an abiding and strategic concern to Franco's forces throughout the war. The British Foreign Office was lobbied repeatedly on this matter and relayed the Nationalists' concerns to other British organisations with interests in the region, including the BBC.[3]

The international impression that the Nationalists sought to convey – that their rebellion was an act of legitimate reaction and that they represented a force for moderation in a tumult of extremism – contrasted markedly with their local propaganda, which was highly polemical and threatening in tone. Drawing on their experiences in Spanish Morocco, the Nationalist generals often sought to inculcate terror amongst their opponents through both their actions and pronouncements. For example, Franco sometimes decreed that official executions conducted by garrottes were publicised in Nationalist papers ('*garrote y prensa*') to traumatise and demoralise the enemy 'with evidence of inexorable might and implacable terror' (Preston, 1993: 227). At the start of the war, General Queipo de Llano captured Seville for the Nationalists recruiting the assistance of military forces already based in the area. Establishing the city as something of a personal fiefdom, he became known as 'The Radio General' on the basis of his nightly broadcasts in which he both raged against Republican atrocities and threatened Nationalist atrocities in the future. One threat he often mentioned was the prospect of mass rape by African mercenaries fighting on the Nationalists' behalf.[4]

Republican themes

As noted, summarising the core themes in Republican propaganda is complicated by the political diversity of the Popular Front government, which 'ran the gamut from "new Deal"-type republicans to revolutionary socialists, communists, and anarchists' (Jackson, 1972: 4). As Beevor comments, 'The Nationalists defended a common view of the past; the Republican coalition, in contrast, had widely different visions of the future' (2003: 411). An added complication is that the prominence of these themes changed over time, as the political balance of the Republic altered as military defeats and internal conflict took their toll.

At the start of the war, two competing discourses vied for prominence in Republican propaganda. The first advanced a revolutionary vision of Spain's future and characterised the rebellion as the beginning of a genuine social revolution in Spain, in which centuries of injustice would be swept away through the redistribution of land and industries to unions and workers syndicates. This was the view of Anarchists, Syndicalists and revolutionary Communists and it was particularly prominent in Catalonia, which had been a stronghold of anarcho-syndicalism for many years prior to the war. The second was effectively counter-revolutionary and emphasised the democratic legitimacy and bourgeois credentials of the Republic. This was the view advanced by a coalition of liberals, left Republicans, Basque Separatists, right-wing Socialists and, crucially, the pro-Stalinist Communists whose transformation into social conservatives 'was partly in response to the policies of Stalin searching for support from Popular Fronts in respectable democracies' (Carr, 2001: 139).

These tensions were particularly evident and significant because of the greater communications dependency of the Republic. Whereas the Nationalist rebellion was not reliant fundamentally on popular mass organisation, the Republic could only sustain effective resistance by convincing local citizens of the need to fight. Internationally, too, 'the cause of the Republic depended on the world knowing the facts' (de la Mora, 1939: 288), particularly in trying to persuade democratic nations to intervene in support of the Republic. However, this created contradictions in the messages the Republic conveyed locally and internationally. As Hugh Thomas notes:

> In republican propaganda, two pictures were counterposed as if there were always potentially a civil war within the civil war: one picture, for foreigners, depicted constitutional democracy struggling against international fascism; the second picture, for consumption at home, showed the Spanish people at one pace away from a new world: victory would lead to *la vida nueva*. (2004: 525)

To cover these contradictions, directives were issued by the central government to suppress news about any social revolution in Spain. On taking over as Republican Prime Minister in August 1936, Largo Caballero set aside his radical principles and instructed it was 'necessary to sacrifice revolutionary language to win the friendship of the Republic' (quoted in Conlon, 2001: 9). As one former minister noted at the time:

> During the three months that I was director of propaganda for the United States and England under Alvarez del Vayo, then Foreign Minister for the Valencia Government, I was instructed not to send out one word about this revolution in the economic system of loyalist Spain. Nor are any foreign correspondents in Valencia permitted to write freely of the revolution that has taken place. (quoted in Chomsky, 1968: 96)

As the war progressed, the problems of reconciling the different visions of national and international communication became less acute for the Republic following the centralisation of political control by the more conservative forces and the active suppression of revolutionary advocates and discourses.[5]

However, there was one recurrent and consistent theme evident in all Republican propaganda, regardless of its level, source or timing. This was the theme of anti-Fascism that disregarded any political and ideological differences within the rebellion and cast the Nationalists and their supporters as indistinguishable from Fascist regimes elsewhere in Europe. Anti-Fascism had resonance at both local and international levels. Locally, it fed fears that all the tenuous social and political gains made since the declaration of the Second Republic in 1931 would be lost as 'the champions of the dark past of ignorance and illiteracy' reasserted their command (Ministry of Public Information leaflet, 1937, quoted in Holguín, 2002: 177). Internationally, it provided a common ground for radical and liberal opinion to unite in support of the Republican cause.

From this discussion some parallels are evident in Nationalist and Republican propaganda, despite their ideological differences. Both sides stigmatised their enemies simplistically. Both sides had to communicate competing and essentially contradictory messages – local messages of radicalism or ruthlessness were never intended for international consumption where both sides sought to promote an image of moderation, responsibility and restraint. In the sections that follow, the discussion focuses on the international news management activities of both sides and their role in achieving these complex tasks in impression management. As will be shown, the respective strategies of control that emerged revealed the different political cultures from which they originated. However, these activities were also affected by technological factors and it is necessary to consider these material constraints first.

International news management

Table 2.1 identifies the location and control of the key elements of the Spanish telecommunication structure during the war involved in *international* communication, which depended on four channels – telegraphy, telephony, radio and mail services. (Note that details of facilities used for internal communication within Spain are not included in Table 2.1.)

The first international cable connections to Spain were established in the nineteenth century and the three main international cable heads were located at Vigo, Bilbao and Malaga. Before the war, international mail was mainly routed from Barcelona, which meant the Nationalists had to improvise new routes by rail, by air to Rome and by sea to Genoa and Marseilles (Shelley, 1960). Prior to the 1920s, the Spanish telephone system was one of the most antiquated in Europe. However, a rapid process of expansion and modernisation began in 1923 under the military dictatorship of General Primo de Rivera. The following year, the Compañía Telefónica de España (CTNE) was established. A subsidiary of International Telephone and Telegraphy (ITT), the company had monopolistic control and, by 1929, 71,800 kilometres of local and long distance lines had been constructed and the number of telephones in the country had trebled (Little, 1979: 453). Nevertheless, international phone connections in 1936 were still tenuous, being limited to the main telephone exchanges in Madrid, Barcelona and Valencia.

Table 2.1 Principal international communication and news censorship arrangements

	Republican sector		*Nationalist sector*
Madrid	For the entire war: • International Telephone • International Cable • Short-Wave International Radio Broadcasting • Foreign News Censorship offices	**Salamanca**	For the entire war: • Foreign News Censorship offices
		Vitoria	For the entire war: • Foreign News Censorship offices
Valencia	For the entire war: • International Telephone • International Cable • Short-Wave International Radio Broadcasting • Foreign News Censorship offices	**Vigo**	From September 1936: • International Cable
Barcelona	Until January 1939: • International Telephone • International Cable • Short-Wave International Radio Broadcasting • Foreign News Censorship offices	**Burgos**	For the entire war: • Foreign News Censorship offices
Bilbao	Until June 1937: • International Cable • Foreign News Censorship offices	**Malaga**	From February 1937: • InternationalCable
Malaga	Until February 1937: • International Cable	**Zaragoza**	From September 1936: • Foreign News Censorship offices
		Bilbao	From June 1937: • International Cable
		Barcelona	From February 1939: • International Telephone • International Cable • Short Wave International Radio Broadcasting

Radio was the newest technology on the scene. Indeed, the Spanish Civil War has been labelled the first 'radio war' because it was the first conflict where the technology had a significant impact as a means of information transmission and of mass communication (Davies, 1999). However, the significance of radio mainly resided at local level.[6] For example, wireless telegraphy alerted sailors of the rebellion and prevented the navy from falling under insurgent control but it was never a significant means for the transmission of international journalists' copy during the war.[7] This was because of its unreliability over long distances and the concerns of authorities on both sides to avoid the unregulated transmission of information from their zones of control. In terms of broadcast programmes, the Republic transmitted foreign language programmes from Barcelona and Madrid throughout the war, recruiting help from volunteers from the International Brigade and, occasionally, foreign correspondents. But even those involved in these broadcasts remained uncertain about how clearly they were received overseas and whether they attracted an audience (Graham, 1999: 49). The Nationalists' international broadcasting was principally organised through The Radio Club of Tenerife, based in the Canary Islands, which was unreliable and often needed supplementing with amateur radio transmissions (Davies, 1999: 493).

The details in Table 2.1 reveal four points about the distribution of international communication resources in Spain during the war. First, the Republican side had considerable advantages over the insurgents at the outset. They controlled two of the three main international cable heads in Bilbao and Malaga, had the most powerful radio transmitters and also sole access to the international telephone lines. It took several weeks for the Nationalists to get the cable head at Vigo operational which meant that, at the start of the war, foreign news reports had to be couriered by car to France, Gibraltar and Portugal for dispatch (Davis, 1940: 154). The Republic also had advantages in its mail services. As Robert Shelley explains, apart from controlling the main international mail routes:

> [t]he Republicans, because they possessed the printing works at Madrid and large supplies of stamps, were not philatelically embarrassed. Not so with the Nationalists, who in many cases had to improvise. It is not uncommon, therefore, to find during the early part of the war that some covers had the 'Mayoral mark' and words to the effect: 'I certify that there are no stamps, (signed) the Mayor.' (1960: 1)

Second, the transmission advantages of the Republic eroded as the war progressed. In December 1936, the headquarters of the new Nationalist radio network, Radio Nacional de España, based in Salamanca, took delivery of a 20kW transmitter from Germany, which meant Nationalist broadcasts could be heard clearly across Spain for the first time (Thomas, 2003: 504). This capacity was enhanced further by their acquisition of a 30kW station in Zaragoza the following year (Davies, 1999: 484). By mid 1937, the international cable facilities in Malaga and Bilbao were also in Nationalist hands, with their tie-ups to Italcable and Eastern Cable Services.

Third, despite these changes, the Republic retained significant advantages in telecommunication throughout the conflict because of the Nationalists' failure to capture any international phone lines in Spain until the last months of the war. Telephony was a superior technology to wireless and cable telegraphy for a range of reasons. It was a far more stable and reliable means of transmission (Knoblaugh, 1937: 133). It offered the opportunity for verbal communication, thereby avoiding the labour intensive and time-consuming tasks of encoding and deciphering messages in Morse code. It was far cheaper on a word-cost basis than cable and offered the potential for greater freedom of expression.[8] It could also be used for telegraphy. However, the principal advantage of telephony was the speed with which information could be dispatched. Telephone contact provided instantaneous communication between journalists in the field and their newsrooms, whereas telegraphic contact involved substantial time delays (see Bolín, 1967: 221).

Fourth, the mechanisms for the censorship and dispatch of foreign correspondents' copy were more closely integrated in the Republican sectors, which further increased the efficiency of their international news management. In Madrid, foreign journalists, censors and telephonists all worked in the imposing Telefónica building. Built in 1929, it was the city's first skyscraper and its location at the top of the Gran Via provided an excellent view of the front lines to the west and protection from Franco's artillery. In Barcelona, too, journalists and censors worked in close proximity in the Telefónica building. In contrast, the Nationalists' international press and censorship offices were distant from the international dispatch points, which meant they depended on local telegraphy and telephone services that were notoriously unreliable and added further delay to international news flows from Franco's Spain (Bolín, 1967: 221). To give an example, in March 1937, Ralph Deakin, the foreign news editor of *The Times* conducted an internal audit of the thirty-two cables sent by the paper's main correspondent in the Nationalist zone between 22 February and 5 March 1937. The results showed the cables took an average of eleven hours to reach the news desk in London. Deakin initially surmised that the Nationalist censors were obstructing their dispatch, but eventually concluded that it was the inefficiency of the land connections that was the major reason for the delays (Deakin Papers, The Times Newspaper Limited Archive (TNL Archive), March 1937).[9]

One of the solutions used by foreign correspondents to deal with the limited international communication facilities available in Spain was to travel over surrounding borders to transmit copy from France, Portugal, Gibraltar and Tangiers. Indeed, this was the only means of transmitting copy during the earliest stages of the war (Fernsworth, 1939; Delmer, 1961) and journalists continued to exploit the opportunities for sending uncensored copy throughout the war. However, authorities on both sides moved quickly to regulate over-the-border communication and this was just one aspect of the controls they imposed. It is to these matters that the discussion now turns.

(From the author's own collection.)

The Telefónica building, Madrid

Built in 1929 by Compañía Telefónica de España (CTNE), a subsidiary of International Telephone and Telegraphy (ITT), this was one of only three international telephone exchanges in Spain during the Civil War. It became a crucial hub in the dissemination of news from the Republic internationally.

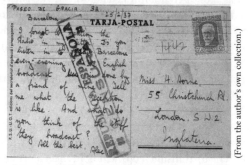

(From the author's own collection.)

A postcard from Barcelona, February 1937

The full text reads:

I forgot to mention the radio in my letter. Do you listen in to Radio Barcelona every evening? The English broadcast is done by a friend of mine. Tell me what the reception is like. And what do you think of the stuff they broadcast?

The Spanish Civil War has been called 'the first radio war' but radio played only a minor role in international communication and publicity.

Nationalist news management

A considerable amount has been written about the policies and personalities involved in Franco's news management. Much of it was published during the war and its immediate aftermath in the personal testimonies of journalists who experienced these controls directly (for example, Cardozo, 1937; Davis, 1940; McCullagh, 1937; Cowles, 1941; Whitaker, 1943; Knickerbocker, 1936). These accounts have, in turn, provided the foundation for historical reviews of this subject (see, for example, Southworth, 1977: 45–59; Preston, 2004).

Although the eyewitness testimonies of the foreign correspondents in Nationalist Spain provide valuable insights, they have limitations when taken in isolation. The tour of duty for a journalist in Franco's Spain was typically shorter than for their colleagues in the Republic partly because of the propensity of the Nationalists to expel foreign correspondents on the slightest of pretexts and partly because the pressures of working in a controlled and often intimidating environment.[10] Thus, many accounts offer only brief snapshots of the Nationalist arrangements rather than lengthy perspectives. Furthermore, most journalists' accounts describe arrangements for the first year of the conflict, which invites a presumption, but not a demonstration, that news management remained constant throughout the conflict. However, if one looks closely at the specific temporal location of foreign journalists' written testimony, it is clear that there were three distinct phases to the foreign news management of the Nationalists.

Phase 1: confusion (July–September 1936)

The first phase was the briefest in duration and was a period where the supervision and censorship of international media activity was weak and disorganised. Once the borders were opened, foreign journalists made regular and unsupervised forays into Nationalist territory from France, Gibraltar and Portugal and were free to return to send their uncensored reports.[11] Sefton Delmer of the *Daily Express*, Louis Delapreé of *Paris Soir* and Hubert Knickerbocker of the Hearst Press chartered a plane and landed in Burgos without even knowing who controlled the city. Although arrested on their arrival, they were allowed to remain to report the rapidly developing events. Delmer recalled:

Delapreé and I went into it in a spirit of whoopee that first day while Knickerbocker was away in Bordeaux transmitting our dispatches. We had no passes, no papers of any kind from the army. We were supposed to stay in our hotel. Instead we hired a taxi in Burgos and told the man to drive us up the road to Madrid. 'Arriba España!' we roared, waving our straw hats to everyone we met, including the men on the road blocks. And the sentries thinking we were señorito volunteers shouted back 'Arriba España' and waved us through. It was wonderful fun. (1961: 275)

The laxity of this situation revealed the confusion and chaos of the first weeks of the rebellion, when it became apparent that the coup had failed. As discussed, the rebels had not anticipated the need to explain themselves and the absence of any co-ordinated system of press accreditation and supervision was symptomatic of their broader failure to develop contingency plans to deal with communication matters.

Phase 2: control (October 1936–late 1937)

Inevitably, this situation did not last. As the insurrection developed into a protracted conflict, the Nationalist leadership began to appreciate the need for effective control of foreign journalists. As one military officer put it to Frances Davis of the *Daily Mail*, '[t]he press will have their place in the war but they will not move as they want. They will move as the army says they may. They will no longer cross the frontier carrying stories that are not permitted' (1940: 98; see also Knickerbocker, 1936: 50).

A particularly significant figure in this imposition of control was Luis Bolín. Prior to the war, Bolín had been London correspondent for the Spanish monarchist daily *ABC*. He was one of the conspirators who organised for a plane to be flown from Croydon airport to deliver Franco and General Emilio Mola from the Canary Islands to Spanish Morocco in preparation for the revolt. In the first few weeks of the war, Bolín was based in Seville with General Queipo de Llano and, despite ongoing uncertainties about the leadership of the rebellion, he urged that tighter and more effective press controls be imposed urgently:

> I spoke to General Franco. Unless we acted promptly to establish our case, I said, the blame for what was happening might eventually fall on us . . . Meanwhile, not all correspondents attached to us were submitting their writings to censorship, as is customary and usual in all wars. In certain cases we could not even find their contributions in the papers they allegedly represented, which were printing stories with the dateline 'Seville' signed by names we had never heard of. It took time to sift credentials, the genuineness of which could not be doubted, from others, undoubtedly false, but we got to know that some of these journalists, after spending a few days with us, were taking advantage of the freedom which they enjoyed to file their pieces under other names in Tangier or Gibraltar, with complete disregard for the rules of fair play. I recalled the restrictions imposed on War Correspondents with the British during World War I. Measures similar to these, though far less strict, were rapidly introduced, and in Seville a Press Office was established, which I directed for a brief period. (Bolín, 1967: 186–7)[12]

In October 1936, Franco gained uncontested command of the rebellion. He moved his general headquarters to the Episcopal Palace in Salamanca and appointed General José Millán Astray as head of *La Oficina de Prensa y Propaganda* (The Office for Press and Propaganda), which was also located in the building.[13] Millán Astray was already renowned as founder of the Spanish Foreign Legion and had lost an arm and an eye during military campaigns in Spanish Morocco in the 1920s, where his ruthlessness and fanaticism had started to coalesce into a distinctive 'ideology of death' that proved influential in shaping right-wing military conceptions of national identity during that period (Jensen, 2002: 147). Millán Astray was fiercely loyal to Franco and gave full vent to his enthusiasm and belligerence in his role as propaganda chief. He harangued and bullied the foreign press contingent on regular occasions and encouraged his senior press officers to do likewise. Bolín was placed in charge of the Nationalists' foreign press bureau and was bestowed with the honorific title of Captain of the Legion; and Captain Gonzalo de Aguilera, a retired cavalry officer and wealthy landowner, became a prominent figure in the organisation of foreign press relations in Northern Spain, working under General Mola's staff.

Both men shared Millán Astray's extreme and reactionary views and their free articulation of these opinions shocked many of the foreign correspondents under their supervision. Noel Monks, correspondent for the *Daily Express*, witnessed Bolín spit on the corpses of executed Republican prisoners on several occasions, disdaining them as 'Reds' and 'vermin'. Monks concluded that Bolín 'had a cruel streak in him that was essentially Spanish' (1955: 73). Aguilera famously bragged to international journalists that he had shot six of his workers on the day the rebellion occurred 'pour encourager les autres'. John Whitaker, correspondent for the *New York Herald Tribune*, recollected several others of Aguilera's more memorable statements:

> 'We have got to kill and kill and kill, you understand' . . . 'You know what's wrong with Spain?' Aguilera used to demand of me. 'Modern plumbing! In healthier times – I mean healthier times spiritually, you understand – plague and pestilence could be counted on to thin down the Spanish masses.' . . . 'It's our program, you understand, to exterminate one third of the male population of Spain. That will purge the country and we will be rid of the proletariat.' (1943: 108)

Similar sentiments were also voiced by other Nationalist press officers – indeed, correspondents soon realised that these opinions were entirely typical of the officer classes on the Nationalist side (Preston, 2004). Noel Monks noted how openly officers boasted 'of what *they*'d done when they took over from the Reds. But they weren't *atrocities*. Oh no, señor. Not even the locking up of a captured militia girl in a room with twenty Moors. No, señor. That was fun' (Monks, 1955: 79). However, this candour was intended for private consumption only as journalists were prohibited from making any reference to these views or actions in their editorial copy (ibid.).

Consideration of the major personalities involved in Nationalist news management is important because it demonstrates how this activity was rooted in a military culture that was instinctively suspicious and antagonistic towards journalists. Of the senior press officers, only Bolín had any previous journalistic experience which he chose to play down, revelling instead in his *faux* military status, which invited derision from genuine soldiers and foreign correspondents alike. Foreign journalists were expected to work in the service of the Nationalist authorities and convey their propaganda uncritically. Legitimate journalistic inquisitiveness was readily cast as espionage and independence of thought and action construed as insubordination – both heinous sins to the military mindset. The new stringent restrictions aimed to control these aspects. As René MacColl of the *Daily Express* recalled:

> A new British correspondent turned up from London and requested credentials. The suspicious Franco H.Q. man subjected him to a long questionnaire. Finally, the Englishman produced a letter from his head office, which set forth his qualifications. The letter described him as being a 'strictly objective reporter'. When he came to this passage, the Franco official started and looked up in horror. 'Objecteeve!' he cried. 'But that is inadmissible!' Those who were not with Franco were against him. (1956: 82–3)

Once the cable head at Vigo became operational in late August 1936, correspondents were discouraged from couriering their copy by hand for transmission at locations beyond the Nationalists' control. Although they could never completely stop this outlet, copies of international papers were scoured to identify any transgressions and transgressors. Strict censorship rules were imposed forbidding any reference to the presence of German and Italian forces or Nationalist atrocities. At times, the authorities could display a neurotic sensitivity about the nature of their representation. For example, Sefton Delmer of the *Daily Express* was expelled from the Nationalist sector in October 1936 because of a story he filed about a civilian plane that had been mistakenly fired upon by anti-aircraft gunners as it approached Burgos. He reported that the British pilot only became aware of the danger after he landed which, in the Nationalists' opinion, both encouraged aerial attacks on Burgos and made their air defences seem inefficient.[14]

Strict accreditation of foreign journalists was also introduced. Correspondents could no longer gain retrospective permission for their presence and were required to obtain clearance formally from Franco's representatives located on the Spanish borders. Journalists could be denied accreditation for a range of reasons. Any evidence that a correspondent had previously visited the Republican sector was normally sufficient grounds for a refusal, although some correspondents – Virginia Cowles and Denzil Batchelor, for example – managed to get around this prohibition (see Cowles, 1941; Batchelor, 1961). The Nationalists also began to proscribe news organisations deemed unsympathetic to their cause. For instance, in the earliest days of the war Arthur Koestler had interviewed General Queipo de Llano in Seville on behalf of the *News Chronicle* but, in October 1936, Bolín rejected the paper's request for permission to send a further representative and threatened that, if one of their correspondents was found in Nationalist territory, 'it would be the worst for him' (Weaver, 1939: 111). Other liberal papers that were banned included the *Manchester Guardian* and the

(Reprinted with the permission of the estate of Frances Davis Cohen.)

A Nationalist press tour, Northern Spain, September 1936

After an initial chaotic period, a strict censorship regime was introduced by Nationalist authorities and foreign correspondents were only permitted to go to the front on collective visits organised and chaperoned by Nationalist press officers. Harold Cardozo, Special Correspondent for the *Daily Mail* is third from the left and Frances Davis (the *Daily Mail* and *Chicago Daily News*) is fifth from the left.

Chicago Daily News. The consequences for entering Nationalist territory without official clearance could be severe, even for those sympathetic to Franco. For example, Hubert Knickerbocker of the Hearst Press reported extensively from the Franco's side during the first months of the war and wrote approvingly of the Nationalists' cause (see Knickerbocker, 1936) but this did not prevent his imprisonment when he was caught entering Northern Spain without authorisation in early 1937 (Preston, 2004: 299).

Gaining entry was just the first barrier. There were no blanket passes for foreign correspondents and every major trip required special permission from the military authorities specifying points of departure and destination. Many journalists became extremely frustrated at these bureaucratic procedures and the amount of time they wasted chasing paper, getting nowhere (see Davis, 1940: 130–1, 165, 171; McCullagh, 1937: 111–12; Cardozo, 1937: 220–1).

The Nationalists authorities not only sought to control what journalists said but also what they saw. Even when permission was granted, foreign correspondents were not allowed to travel unchaperoned. The fact that so few Nationalist press officers feature so frequently in so many journalists' accounts reveals the strict pool system that was introduced. Foreign correspondents were billeted around the main Nationalist press offices in Salamanca, Burgos, Seville, Vitoria or Zaragoza and their visits to the front were collective affairs led by press officers who arranged transportation, offered translation support and censored their copy. These trips were often anodyne exercises involving tedious journeys, although Aguilera in particular gained a reputation for recklessness in approaching the front which meant that the correspondents in his company often saw more of the action than they were prepared for or comfortable with. On 31 December 1937, three journalists' luck ran out on a Nationalist press visit to the front at Teruel when their car was hit by shrapnel from a Republican shell. The blast killed Bradish Johnson of *Newsweek* outright and mortally injured Richard Sheepshanks of Reuters and Edward Neil of the Associated Press. Kim Philby, who was then Nationalist correspondent for *The Times*, escaped with minor injuries.

The intimidation of foreign journalists was systemic in the Nationalist sector during this period. Threats ranged in severity from reprimands to execution threats, expulsions, imprisonment and worse (Millán Astray encouraged his press officers to threaten to shoot correspondents who transgressed rules). In the early days of the war, Guy de Traversay, correspondent of *L'Intransigeant*, was killed in Nationalist-held Majorca and several other journalists nearly shared his fate. In September 1936, René Brut of the *Pathé Gazette* was imprisoned for three weeks after pictures were released of the Nationalist massacre at Badajoz. Bolín repeatedly threatened to shoot him but was unable to prove that Brut was responsible for the footage (he was). The following month, Denis Weaver of the *News Chronicle*, 'Hank' Gorrell of the United Press and James Minifie of the *New York Herald Tribune* inadvertently strayed from Republican territory and were captured by Nationalist forces. For several days, they too feared execution but were eventually ejected over the French border. The most notorious case involved the imprisonment of Arthur Koestler in early 1937. Koestler and Bolín had met earlier in the war in Seville, before Koestler was forced to flee after being spotted by an ex-colleague from a German newspaper who denounced him as a Communist. Bolín said he would shoot Koestler should they ever meet again and fate delivered this opportunity when he arrested Koestler as the Nationalist forces entered the Malaga. The presence of another British national at the scene stayed his hand but Koestler was imprisoned for several months afterwards and only escaped execution after concerted international pressure.

The intimidation of journalists was not restricted to those working in areas under Nationalist control. In late 1936, Franco issued a decree that any journalists who had reported from the Nationalist side ran the risk of execution if they were subsequently captured on the Republican side (editorial department memo, Reuters, 4 May 1937, Christopher Holme's Personnel File, the Reuters Archive). Specific personal threats were also made to individual journalists working in the Republican sectors. In November 1936, Lester Ziffren, Madrid correspondent for United Press, reported that Franco's forces failed to capture the capital because of weaknesses in their military intelligence. A month later, he was informed by his London office that Franco had told the UP representative in Salamanca that he would be 'taken care of' once they captured Madrid (Wurtzel, 2006). Similar threats were issued to Ernest de Caux, the Madrid correspondent

Catastrophe at Caude

On 31 December 1937 a car carrying foreign journalists on a Nationalist press tour was hit by artillery fire. Richard Sheepshanks of Reuters (top left), Edward J. Neil of Associated Press (top middle) and Bradish Johnson of *Newsweek* (top right) died of their injuries. Kim Philby of *The Times* (not pictured) escaped with minor head injuries.

of *The Times*, Christopher Holme of Reuters, George Steer also of *The Times* and Noel Monks of the *Daily Express*.

Holme, Steer and Monks were specifically targeted because of their involvement in the international controversy caused by the destruction of the Basque town of Guernica by Luftwaffe pilots on 26 April 1937. All three journalists were dining in nearby Bilbao when news came through of the attack in the early evening, and, accompanied by Mathieu Corman, correspondent of *Ce Soir*, they rushed to the scene to find the town still ablaze. On returning to Bilbao they immediately filed accounts of what they witnessed and their interviews with survivors and identified German aviators as responsible for the attack. Their reports appeared in the later editions of the British newspapers on 28 April 1937 and caused an immediate international outcry. George Steer's account in *The Times* was particularly influential because of the authoritative international status of the paper and the fact that the article was reprinted in *The New York Times*, a title of equivalent repute.

It is clear that the Nationalists were unprepared for the 'world wide eruption of indignation caused by the original news stories' (Southworth, 1977: 32), no doubt assuming that their tight control of the activities of foreign correspondents in the region would prevent any coverage of what was originally deemed a very successful military exercise. However, they had not bargained for the presence of the British and Belgian journalists in Bilbao and, although it may seem distasteful to refer to such an iconic atrocity as a 'media event', that is precisely what it was. As Southworth notes, had it not been for the chance witness of these international journalists:

> the Guernica story the world knows would never have existed. There would have been delayed news stories; the press services from the frontier would have sent their telegrams, but the story would never have had the same impact . . . The bombing of Guernica was a lot like the tree that falls in the forest. If nobody hears it fall, does it make any noise? (ibid., 374)

Bolín was the main architect of the Nationalists' response to the escalating diplomatic storm and its contradictions belied the haste of its construction. At first, it was claimed that no Nationalist planes had flown on the day of the attack due to bad weather but this assertion was dropped when it became clear that many had witnessed substantial air activity on that day. It was then conceded that some Nationalist planes had bombed the town but that these were attacking legitimate military targets and had not been responsible for the devastating conflagration in the town centre. Nationalist estimates of the proximity of their forces to the town at the time of the attack were adjusted from fifteen kilometres to six kilometres, to increase the plausibility of this new emphasis on the town's military significance. The crux of the Nationalists' defence, however, remained constant throughout. This was that the town was burnt to the ground by retreating Republican forces, replicating the destruction of Irun by Anarchist forces earlier in the Basque offensive. As soon as Guernica fell to Nationalist forces, select groups of foreign journalists were given guided tours of the town, closely chaperoned by Aguilera, and some of their censored dispatches lent support to the Nationalists' version of events by raising the possibility that the aerial attack had not been the principal cause of the destruction.

A lengthy cablegram sent by Bolín to Franco's representative in London on 23 May 1937, which, until recently, was held in the archives of the Cervantes Institute in London, provides further insight into how he elaborated the defence over the following weeks. The cable claimed to represent both elite and general Nationalist opinion and Bolín urged that it be circulated as widely as possible. It began with a denial of the presence of any foreign troops in Nationalist territory and expressed concern at the 'GULLIBILITY [of] PUBLIC OPINION'. Bolín claimed confidently that the 'GUERNICA MYTH HAS NOW BEEN BURIED ABROAD AND FRAUD PRACTISED ON HONEST FOREIGN OPINION BY MERCENARY JOURNALISTS SHOWN UP STOP NUMEROUS AUTHORITATIVE FOREIGNERS NOW HAD TIME EXAMINE RUINS GUERNICA ESTABLISH TOWN WAS DELIBER-ATELY BURNT'. The cable then referred to Republican attacks on civilian areas, including the shellings of Zaragoza, Cordoba and Toledo, which failed to excite equivalent media outrage. It continued:

> LATEST OUTRAGE DASH WHICHLL PROBABLY BE PATIENTLY WITNESSED BY SAME FOREIGN OPINION WHICH EXALTEDLY PROTESTS AGAINST MYTHS AND LEGITIMATE ACTS WARFARE DASH IS BOMBARDMENT GIRLS SCHOOL AT PAMPLONA WHERE THREE GIRLS KILLED.

The cable concluded:

> PUBLIC OPINION NATIONAL SPAIN PERPLEXEDLY ASKS WHETHER ABROAD THERES TENDENCY ACCEPT ANY BASE-LESS CALUMNY SPREAD BY RED PROPAGANDA WHETHER ABROAD THERES INABILITY DISTINGUISH LIES FROM TRUTH WRONG FROM RIGHT STOP

The reference to 'mercenary journalists' is significant as it shows how the Nationalists sought to defame the reputations of the journalists who had first reported the attack on the town as well as to intimidate them. Noel Monks was condemned by Bolín as a drunkard, despite being teetotal, and a regrettable error in the Reuters newsroom in London gifted the Nationalists an opportunity to question Holme's credibility. On 29 April 1937, Reuters filed a further report from Holme rebutting Nationalist denials of the attack in which he identified the types of German aircraft involved (Heinkel He-111 and Junkers Ju-52 bombers and Heinkel He-51 fighters). Unfortunately, a subeditor misread these as indi-cating the number of planes. As Holme's namesake explains:

> The mistake was corrected within an hour but it was nonetheless a gift to the German Press. The *Frankfurter Generalanzeiger* called Holme an idiot and the Nazi *Völkischer Beobachter* called for his dismissal claiming he was in the direct pay of the Bolshevists. (Holme, 1995: 275)

In addition to this, Nationalist sources told the British ambassador in Hendaye that Holme had fought for the Basques in the last phases of the battle for Bilbao. According to Reuters' own report of the claim:

> The ambassador emphasized that he could not control the truth of this report, but he felt bound to pass it on for the information of the Foreign Office and ourselves, as Holme being already far from *persona grata* to General Franco, such conduct on Holme's part, if true, would doubtless

lead to a disagreeable incident, were he to fall into the insurgents' hands. The Foreign Office suggest we should warn Holme to be careful. (Foreign Office Report, 22 June 1937, Holme Personal File, the Reuters Archive)

But the main journalist the Nationalists sought to discredit was George Steer of *The Times* and the smears against his integrity, frequently championed by Franco-supporters based in Britain, continued for years. In 1939, he took legal action against an author who claimed that he had only been a minor freelancer with *The Times* when he filed his Guernica report and that he had been sacked because of the report (see Rankin, 2003: 142–7).

Phase 3: conciliation (mid 1937 to April 1939)

The months after the Guernica controversy there was an intensification of significant changes in Nationalist news management that had first became apparent at the start of 1937 with the deposition of Millán Astray as head of the Propaganda and Press department.[15] As the Basque offensive concluded in mid 1937, Aguilera became sidelined and Bolín fell into active disfavour with his political superiors. In June 1937, he was sent to London and had three meetings with the foreign news editor of *The Times* in which he denied making any threats against the newspaper's Madrid correspondent, Ernest de Caux. When informed of this, de Caux replied to the foreign news editor:

> What you say about Bolín is most interesting and not a little intriguing. Do you know that he was finally turned out of Salamanca, given £300 and told to go and travel the world? Nobody there wants to see him again. It was not easy to get rid of him.' (letter from Ernest de Caux to Ralph Deakin, 15 June 1937, Deakin Papers, TNL Archive)

The sidelining of these controversial figures reveals Franco's growing appreciation that their actions and rhetoric were bringing the Nationalist cause into disrepute (Preston, 1993: 190). Around this time, a pamphlet was published in Britain that highlighted the plight of 'Foreign Journalists Under Franco's Terror' ('A Journalist', 1937). The author, 'a bona fide journalist' whose anonymity spoke of the culture of intimidation that existed, catalogued the humiliations and threats meted out to foreign journalists by the Nationalist authorities and Bolín in particular during the first year of the war. Bolín's reputation suffered further damage as the international scandal about Guernica persisted and his role in Koestler's detention and death sentence became internationally publicised. Around the same time, Hubert Knickerbocker of the Hearst Press exacted revenge for his detention by the Nationalists by publishing an article in the *Washington Times* that outlined the extremism and bigotry of a 'Captain Sanchez', a thinly disguised reference to Aguilera, whom he blamed for his incarceration. The article was quoted in detail in the US congress in May 1937 and represented 'a significant propaganda blow against the Francoists, coming as it did shortly after the bombing of Guernica' (Preston, 2004: 299).

The new personnel who assumed control of the Nationalists' press and propaganda operations in Salamanca were different characters from their predecessors. Pablo Merry del Val was promoted to head of Propaganda and Press and, as the Oxford-educated son of a senior diplomat, he conveyed an altogether more urbane impression, although the whiff of menace remained. Alan Dick of the *Daily Telegraph* recalled his first meeting with him in July 1937:

> Outwardly he was the complete Spanish aristocrat. A stiff red Requete beret – insignia of the Royalists of Navarre – sat like a pancake on his small, oiled head. His lean face rarely abandoned its expression of tolerant hauteur. His voice was clipped and precise. 'I think we understand one another,' he said as we paced slowly round the external balcony overlooking the academy quadrangle. The voice was friendly, but the words sounded to me remarkably like a threat. I could imagine the friendliness fading abruptly if we ever failed to 'understand' one another. (1943: 109)

Other new appointments in the Nationalists' press operations during this period included Manuel Arias Paz and Francisco de Buis, editor of the Spanish newspaper *El Debate*.

The promotion of individuals with more diplomatic demeanours marked a distinct shift away from the rigid militarism evident in the previous phase and a greater willingness to accommodate the professional needs of the foreign journalists. For example, Bolín's visit to *The Times* in June 1937 was followed soon after by a visit from Arias Paz, who replaced Vicente Gay as the head of the Delegation of Press and Propaganda, which was responsible for controlling print and broadcast media within Spain (Southworth, 1977: 33). Whereas Bolín's attempts to build bridges with the paper amounted to little more than blatant lies about his earlier actions, Arias Paz offered some significant concessions and reassurances on the part of the Nationalist authorities. Further details of the meeting were included in a letter sent by the acting foreign news editor in Deakin's absence to the paper's Madrid correspondent:

> He was obviously anxious to do anything he could for *The Times*. He indicated that Salamanca would not object to your remaining in Madrid 'after it fell', if your messages until then had been 'objective'. They were quite willing to understand the limitations that the Madrid censorship would impose. I pointed out that if they wanted to get an idea of what your messages from Madrid would be like they might as well look back and see what they had been like. The Director of the Salamanca Press Bureau then admitted he had never read any of your uncensored dispatches. I immediately sent for the cuttings book and showed them to him and it was almost impossible to get him out of the building.' (letter from Burn, the acting foreign news editor, to de Caux, 4 July 1937, de Caux Papers, TNL Archive)

A symbolic example of the Nationalists' less confrontational approach to foreign journalists came in their response to the death of Richard Sheepshanks,

Edward Neil and Bradish Johnson on an official press tour of the front at Teruel on New Year's Eve 1937. Whereas months before Bolín and Aguilera had been freely threatening to execute foreign journalists, *La Oficina de Prensa y Propaganda* provided a detailed ten-page report of the incident and the medical treatment given to Neil before he succumbed to his injuries. Merry del Val personally escorted Sheepshanks's coffin over the French border and Kim Philby of *The Times*, the only journalist to survive, received a medal from Franco.[16]

In noting the emergence of a more conciliatory approach to the foreign media, it is important not to overstate the changes. Essentially, these represented a shift in style rather than content. The censorship restrictions remained in place, journalists were still chaperoned and their movements continued to be restricted. They could also be debarred on the flimsiest pretexts. For example, Hessell Tiltman of the *Daily Express* arrived in Zaragoza in December 1938 but was prevented from witnessing the Nationalists' entry into Barcelona and accompanying their advance to the French border. He was then summarily expelled and only received an explanation from Franco's envoy when he arrived in France:

'My government instructs me to inform you that they have no complaint to make concerning your personal conduct in Nationalist territory. Nor with any of the despatches you have written. Apparently the difficulty arose owing to something published in your paper from another source for which, of course, we had to hold you responsible. Burgos desires me to state, further, that if you will sign a written statement guaranteeing not to write anything for the *Daily Express*, you may at once be readmitted to Spain.' (quoted in Tiltman, 1940: 187)

Republican news management

Whereas, in the Nationalist sector, foreign correspondents were barely tolerated, in the Republic, they were encouraged. As noted, to some extent this accommodation was necessitated by the material needs of the loyalists and their recognition that the recruit of international support would be essential for resisting Franco and his Italian and German allies. However, this greater receptivity also revealed the political sensibilities and professional background of major figures in the administration, particularly during the early part of the war. As Southworth comments:

Despite the discontent expressed by certain correspondents concerning the conditions of work and the censorship rules in the Republican zone, relations between the foreign reporters and the Republican authorities were much closer than those between the foreign pressmen [sic] and the Nationalists. Men in the Spanish government like Alvarez del Vayo, Pietro, Zugazagoitia, and others were former newspapermen themselves and sympathized with the problems of the press. (1977: 54)

The greater acceptance of journalists' presence and needs in the Republican sector manifested itself in several ways. Journalists were granted more freedom of movement than they were in the Nationalist zones. Although *salvoconductos* were required, their monitoring and use was often haphazard. Virginia Cowles, who was a freelance journalist working for *The New York Times* and *The Sunday Times*, was surprised by the ease with which she was able to visit the military front at Madrid in April 1937:

> Although journalists were supposed to get a proper authorization, few of the Spanish sentries could read and almost any bit of paper (no matter how far out of date) would do. When you wanted to go to the front, you just got into a car and went. (1941: 21)

Foreign journalists were not routinely accompanied by press officials on their news-gathering trips and there was no formal pooling system. When journalists worked together, as they often did, it was out of choice as they engaged in the kind of 'relations of mutual benefit' so frequently noted among specialist correspondents (Cottle, 2007: 9). One factor that encouraged such collectivity was the limited availability of cars and petrol which hindered the mobility of the foreign press corps. The Republican authorities provided press cars and chauffeurs but demand always exceeded supply and many journalists became extremely frustrated at the way these resources were reserved for the more senior and sympathetic correspondents (Herbst, 1991). However, differential allocation of this kind was inevitable given the severe transport and petrol shortages in the Republican sector.[17]

The Republic was also willing to tolerate journalists who had reported from Nationalist sectors and representatives from newspapers ideologically antipathetic to their cause. For example, journalists from the *Daily Mail* were present in the Republic throughout the war, despite the paper's ardent support of the Nationalist rebellion and uncritical reproduction of their atrocity propaganda during the early stages of the war. Some foreign journalists, particularly those with strong personal and political affiliations to the Republican cause, found this indulgence bewildering. Claud Cockburn, who reported the war for the *Daily Worker* under the byline 'Frank Pitcairn', described the bemusement of a Republican press officer at the publication of a string of specious atrocity stories in the British press:

> Like innumerable Spaniards on the Government side who ought to have known better – it was one of their great weaknesses – he found it quite impossible to take the British right-wing newspaper propaganda seriously. He shrugged and laughed 'Funny people,' he said, shaking his head and re-reading the newspaper story in front of him, 'Very funny people.' (Pitcairn, 1936: 65–6)

Republican news management was also more internationalised in its structure than that of the Nationalists. Scores of foreign volunteers were involved directly in Republican propaganda activity – sometimes to such an extent that their involvement occasionally caused a degree of local resentment. As Constancia de la Mora, a senior Republican censor who worked for the Foreign Press Bureau of the Republic, retrospectively remarked:

> Our office was over-run with well-meaning foreigners of distinguished reputation who had come to help us counteract the campaign of lies and slander the British Foreign Office and the Nazis were spreading about the Spanish Government. Actually, we needed no outside advice. (de la Mora, 1939: 285–6)

Foreign volunteers were also involved in censoring journalists' copy, which proved an effective means of preventing foreign correspondents from using slang phrases and colloquialisms to evade censorship. Republican press provision also extended physically beyond Spanish borders. For example, the press office of the Spanish Embassy in London provided a considerable amount of pamphlets and briefings promoting the Republican case throughout the war (see, for example, de los Rios, 1937). In Paris, the Agence Espagne was created as a pro-Republican news service and it recruited the services of several renowned foreign correspondents, including Claud Cockburn, Arthur Koestler, John Langdon-Davies and William Forrest.[18] Although a front organisation for the Comintern and constituted by international sympathisers, the Spanish news agency worked closely with the Republican authorities and, in 1937, Rubio Hidalgo, Chief Censor and Head of the Foreign Press Bureau in Valencia, went to Paris to work within it.

Of course, foreign journalists were not given carte blanche in the Republic. Their activities were monitored and it was said that the secret police kept personal dossiers on all of them. Several journalists reported occasions when they were followed, threatened and detained but expulsions and incarcerations were never as defining a feature of Republican press relations as they were in the Nationalist sector. Generally, intimidation was intimated rather than stated.

Control was principally achieved through close monitoring and censorship of all material dispatched by the journalists. As with the Nationalist authorities, certain topics were forbidden – in particular, sensitive military information, references to foreign military involvement, speculative political conjecture, references to internal political factionalism and division, and any discussion of revolutionary developments within the Republic. As discussed earlier, the Republic's exclusive access to the international telephone lines gave them considerable advantages in terms of the speed with which news could be disseminated internationally. But foreign correspondents were never allowed to use the flexibility of the technology to extemporise or digress in their calls to their news desks. Prior to its dispatch, their copy had to be submitted to censors who then listened in to the phone calls to ensure that there was no deviation from the cleared text. Even slight transgressions led to the immediate mechanical termination of the call.

Among the foreign correspondents who worked in the Republic opinion is divided as to whether the censorship restricted their professional practices. Herbert Matthews of *The New York Times* never felt that the restrictions

(Reprinted with the permission of the *Daily Telegraph*.)

Foreign correspondents with Republican forces on the Ebro, 1938

British and American journalists often collaborated closely and several submitted copy to newspapers on both side of the Atlantic. This picture was taken by Henry Buckley of the *Daily Telegraph* and features, from right to left, Vincent Sheean (the *Chicago Tribune*), Herbert Matthews (*The New York Times*) and Ernest Hemingway (the *North Atlantic News Alliance*).

impeded his work to any significant extent. Claud Cockburn even suggested that the censorship procedures were too relaxed (Pitcairn, 1936). In contrast, Edward Knoblaugh of the Associated Press railed against the 'censorship barriers' in Madrid (1937: 137) and Ernest de Caux of *The Times* repeatedly complained to his foreign news editor about the constraints that he had to contend with. It is noticeable that correspondents' opinions about the censorship rules often correlated closely with their general political opinions about the Republic. As is shown in the next chapter, Matthews developed a considerable admiration for the Republic and Cockburn was an active propagandist on its behalf. In contrast, Knoblaugh and de Caux, whilst publicly dispassionate about the conflict, were privately unsympathetic to the Republican cause.

It may be that correspondents simply exaggerated or underplayed the significance of the censorship practices for ideological purposes to highlight the democratic or illiberal qualities of the Republican government. Alternatively, it could be that they had qualitatively different experiences that developed through their ongoing interactions with Republican press officers. Correspondents sympathetic to the Republic were more likely to submit palatable and unthreatening copy to the censors, which, in turn, would generate greater official trust and co-operation. In contrast, sceptical, even hostile, journalists would be more inclined to test the censors' tolerance through their work thereby increasing the authorities' suspicion and obstructiveness.

The memoirs of Constancia de la Mora, who replaced Rubio Hidalgo as head of the Foreign Press Bureau, are instructive on this point. Published just after the end of the war, her account describes the close working relations the Bureau had with individual correspondents and the strong opinions that were held about them. Many, such as Ernest Hemingway, Herbert Matthews, Henry Buckley, Lawrence Fernsworth and Vincent Sheean, were held in high esteem whereas others, such as Sefton Delmer of the *Daily Express*, were 'disliked and distrusted' (de la Mora, 1939: 290). What is clear is that these judgements were based on close observation of the personal conduct and editorial copy of the correspondents rather than the ideological orientations of the news organisations they represented. De la Mora's comments on Henry Buckley of the *Daily Telegraph* offer a case in point:

> He knew Spain inside out from years of work and study here . . . He had lived the war from the very outset, Madrid, Valencia, Barcelona. His dispatches appeared under a Valencia dateline – his stories always carefully described the Spanish Government as mildly liberal. But the editorials in the same edition of the paper called the Spanish Government 'communist' and the fascists 'religious crusaders'. It was a case of the left hand not knowing what the right hand doeth. (de la Mora, 1939: 291)

As with Nationalists, Republican news management did not remain static throughout the conflict although the transitions were not as clear-cut. In the first few weeks, journalists enjoyed considerable freedoms in the Republic although travel was not without risks and they regularly travelled over the Spanish borders to transmit their uncensored copy (see, for example, Fernsworth, 1939). Restrictions were soon imposed when the authorities became alarmed at the sensitivity of the information that was being publicised freely abroad. However, the establishment of a centralised and cohesive system of control was often confounded by the political heterogeneity of the Republic, especially during the first year of the conflict. Regional autonomy in the Basque country and Catalonia, in particular, meant that political factions had separate propaganda and press arrangements which overlapped with, and occasionally challenged, official directives. In Barcelona, this created a highly bureaucratic censorship system that inhibited the flow of foreign news. The Madrid correspondent of *The Times* described the arrangements in Barcelona in 1937:

> There are two censors in different offices in Barcelona. One has to submit messages to each in turn. They close down at 9pm so any news breaking after that hour must remain over until the next day. Then, sometimes another censor intervenes. On August 3rd I was just about to begin dictating when a listener in the telephone building cut me off and further revised my message . . . I have discussed the stringency with both censors here.

They are intelligent men, with enough knowledge of journalism to realise where the shoe pinches, but they are held down by their instructions. (letter to Ralph Deakin, 21 August 1937, Deakin Papers, TNL Archive)

In contrast, in the Basque country, journalists were permitted considerable freedom of action. For example, George Steer of *The Times* was astounded by the candour and openness of the Basque government. Here he describes an occasion when prisoners in Bilbao were massacred by citizens enraged by the air attacks:

> At this time, it should be remembered, true stories of killings in Madrid could only be smuggled out as uncensored articles by unknown correspondents: with Franco, the situation was even worse. If a foreign newspaper dared to publish any statement about atrocities in his territory, its correspondent – whether responsible or not – was immediately expelled.
>
> For the Basques, the word conscience was possessed of dynamic meaning. They had, as best they might, to expiate the horrible crime committed by the air maddened population of Bilbao. Though they were at war, they gave orders to the censor to let all truthful descriptions pass.
>
> Leizaola, at his Ministry of Justice and Culture, affixed a list of all the dead. At the bottom he admitted eight names 'mutilizados' – the dead who had also been mutilated. The representatives of the foreign press were allowed to broadcast all these facts, and so was Bilbao radio. (Steer, 1937: 119)

In Steer's opinion, such openness was both a great virtue and failing of the Basque state. Although the Basques perceived no need for 'a new fangled hortatory organisation' that would 'lay down the lines of each day's press', Steer believed their failure to fortify public morale through effective propaganda in the face of the Nationalist military onslaught fostered a sense of defeatism that contributed to the capitulation of the Basque republic. In his view, the lessons of their defeat stand 'as a warning to democracy – that some freedoms should not be tolerated in war' (Steer, 1937: 182).

These regional and political variations were reduced by the start of the second year of the war as a consequence of military defeat in the North and the political suppression of radical groups in Catalonia. Indeed, the decision of the Valencia government to place major elements of the telecommunications system in Barcelona under the control of the *Ministerio de Propaganda* was the catalytic event that started the fighting between the central government and anarchist and radical groups (Davies, 1999: 484). (Until May 1937, the telephone exchange in Barcelona was controlled by a joint committee of the anarchist Confederación Nacional de Trabajo (CNT) and the socialist Unión General de Trabajadores (UGT).) However, political and regional sensitivities did not disappear completely. For example, when the main Republican Foreign Press Bureau was moved from Valencia to Barcelona in 1938, there were concerns that this could encroach on the operation of Catalonia's own censorship office and, hence, 'the privileges granted to the Catalans by the Cortes' (de la Mora, 1939: 339).

Concluding remarks

This chapter has examined the political and propaganda objectives of the main combatants in the Spanish Civil War and how these affected their international news management arrangements. It has also considered the technical constraints that affected their ability to communicate internationally.

Inevitably, questions arise as to which side won the propaganda battle for international opinion and which news management regime was most effective. Answering the first question raises a wider range of issues than can be addressed in a media-focused book of this kind. To answer the second question requires the consideration of more evidence – in particular, closer analysis of the opinions, actions and responses of the foreign correspondents themselves and of the terms of international media representation. These are all considered in subsequent chapters. However, evidence presented in this chapter suggests that any answer to this question is unlikely to be straightforward and that it is only appropriate to talk of degrees of success rather than outright victory. For example, the rigid and aggressive news management of the Nationalists in the first year of the war alienated many foreign correspondents and began to damage the reputation of Franco's regime internationally. Nevertheless, it proved crudely effective in preventing foreign journalists from witnessing and testifying to the full brutality of Nationalist forces in action. In the Republic, by comparison, the greater preponderance of journalists and their greater freedom of movement meant that news about killings and atrocities could not be so easily suppressed, which, in turn, led to their relative over-reporting in foreign news coverage (Beevor, 2007: 272). Having said this, the Republic's more permissive approach also offered salvation, most dramatically in the case of the destruction of Guernica where, had it not been for the freedom and mobility of a small number of foreign journalists, the world would never have received news of the event so swiftly nor had the perpetrators identified so convincingly. It is difficult to overestimate the damage the event did to the Nationalists' cause at the time.

However, there is one fundamental point that needs to be appreciated in any assessment of who won the propaganda war in Spain. This is that the criteria for victory were not the same for both sides. The Republicans had the most daunting challenge as they had to convince international opinion of the need to intervene in their defence. The Nationalists, in contrast, merely needed to maintain the status quo and ensure the democracies stayed out of Spain. Thus, while the Republic needed to win arguments, the Nationalists only needed to relativise them. And even in the case of Guernica, where their actions seemed so indefensible, the evidence against them so strong and their political defence so inconsistent and unconvincing, managed, with the assistance of ideological sympathisers abroad, to do just enough to cloud the issue and thwart a growing momentum in international opinion that such actions were intolerable and that something needed to be done in the Republic's defence.

Notes

1. For example, throughout the 1930s the British Foreign Office unselfconsciously discussed the need for 'cultural propaganda' to promote British values and interests internationally.
2. From the start of the war, foreign journalists were aware of tensions between the Nationalist leadership and their Italian and German allies. For example, in December 1936, Christopher Holme, then Reuters correspondent in the Nationalist sector, briefed the British Embassy in Hendaye, France that '[r]elations between the Spaniards on the one hand and the Germans and the Italians on the other are not too cordial . . . General Franco definitely does not want the foreigners there for ever and intends to be master in his own house one day' (The National Archives (TNA), FO 371/20553, Paper W17655/62/4). This message was reiterated the following year in a further Foreign Office briefing by another Reuters correspondent, Richard Sheepshanks (TNA, FO 371/21301, paper W19746/1/41). Also in 1937, a correspondent for the *Daily Telegraph* was encouraged by the Nationalist high command to write an uncensored dispatch exposing the falsity of Italian claims about their military successes. He declined the opportunity because he feared retribution from Italian authorities (Dick, 1941: 131).
3. For example, in November 1937 the Foreign Office advised the British Chamber of Commerce for Spain to use 'Nationalist' rather than 'Insurgent' in describing Franco's authorities (TNA, FO 371/21382, Paper W20044/40/41). See also the confidential meeting between Sir Robert Vansittart, Permanent Under-Secretary of State for Foreign Affairs and Lord Reith, the Director General of the BBC, which is discussed in Chapter 5.
4. Another famous example of the use of local communication to spread alarm and fear is a radio speech delivered by General Emilio Mola in 1936 in which he claimed that pro-Nationalist supporters within Madrid would rise up as 'a fifth column' to support his four army columns that were then converging on the capital. The term 'fifth columnist' quickly passed into general usage as a term for any clandestine agents who assist invading forces.
5. One aspect of this involved placing the major elements of the telecommunications system under the control of the Ministerio de Propaganda (Davies, 1999: 484).
6. Before the war, the government had kept control of high-powered transmission services and spectrum allocation but encouraged the installation of low power transmitters by independent operators to provide the basis for local radio services (MBC, 2007). This meant that a wide variety of small and large radio stations engaged in propaganda activities at the start of the war but, by early 1937, both sides started to centralise control of their radio networks to increase the coherence and effectiveness of their propaganda activities and to suppress dissident voices within their rank.
7. Davies (1999) mentions that US journalists occasionally used shortwave radio to transmit messages in Morse to the US but, as I have only identified two reference to wireless telegraphy in the dozens of journalist memoirs written about Spain, it was evidently a peripheral method of communication (Knoblaugh, 1936; MacColl, 1956).
8. Foreign correspondents were often urged by their editors to use cables sparingly and only prioritise messages when it was strictly necessary. To economise further, journalists also wrote in 'cable-ese', a form of writing that compressed essential words, omitted non-essential words and ignored conventions of punctuation. These messages were then 're-inflated' when received by home news desks.

9. Nationalist censorship practices of domestic and international mail were also more stringent than those of the Republic, which would have further delayed their dispatch. According to Robert Shelley:

> There was a rigid censorship throughout the war, in fact nearly every Nationalist town and village had its own censor office manned from an officer and several men in the larger towns to a sergeant or corporal in the villages. The village censor office probably dealt with only internal mail and sent letters written in a language other than their own to the larger offices in the Provincial capitals . . . The Republicans did not have such a rigid censorship. Letters for abroad were censored at their port of departure and internal ones, in the main, passed uncensored. (1960: 3–4)

10. The personnel files of Richard Sheepshanks held in the Reuters' archive provide testament to the pressures of reporting from the Nationalist side. He was sent to Salamanca as Reuters' 'Special Correspondent with General Franco's forces' in June 1937. In late August he cabled Sir Roderick Jones, head of Reuters, expressing concerns about his ability to fulfil his brief. The precise details of his worries are unknown as neither his original cable nor Jones's response have survived but they were clearly severe. In a subsequent letter to Jones he wrote:

> I must thank you for your very charming letter of September 6, which has just reached me here. Of course, I entirely agree with everything that you say, and I can only repeat that I do sincerely regret the momentary loss of nerve-control that made me send so unnecessary a telegram. Please be reassured that I will do my utmost to prevent such a thing happening again. (letter from Sheepshanks to Roderick Jones, 27 September 1937, Sheephanks file, the Reuters Archive)

He briefly returned for home leave in October of that year but returned to report the fighting on the Teruel front and was killed on an official press tour on 31 December 1937.

11. Journalists required passes (*salvoconductos*) to travel in Nationalist Spain even at the start of the war but the permissions process was often conducted retrospectively after journalists had arrived and was organised on a piece-meal basis (see Taylor, 1939: 56).

12. International press exposure of the Nationalists' massacre of more than a thousand defenceless prisoners held in the bullring at Badajoz in mid August 1936 was a specific catalyst for the change in the Nationalists' strategy.

13. In January 1937, the Nationalist high command established 'The Delegation of Press and Propaganda' headed by Vicente Gay. The Delegation's responsibilities solely concerned printed and broadcast media within Spain (Southworth, 1977: 33).

14. Delmer claimed the real reason he was expelled was because of the arrival of the Germans, who believed he was a British spy.

15. The most serious propaganda disaster Millán Astray presided over was a public ceremony organised in Santander on 12 October 1936. Titled the *Día de la Raza* (the 'Day of the Race'), the celebration commemorated Columbus's discovery of America and sought to demonstrate the credentials of the emerging Nationalist state. The ceremonies concluded at the local university where a succession of intemperate speeches vilified the Republic and Basque and Catalan nationalism. Caught up in the

excitement, Millán Astray stood to echo the foreign legion battle, *!Viva la Muerte!* (Long Live Death!), that was being chanted by sections of the crowd. At that moment Miguel de Unamo, the rector of the university and a famous Basque philosopher, started to speak. To the growing apoplexy of the General and the audience, he castigated the previous speakers and directed particular scorn towards the propaganda chief:

> It pains me to think that General Millán Astray should dictate the pattern of mass psychology. A cripple who lacks the spiritual greatness of Cervantes is wont to seek ominous relief in causing mutilation around him. . . You will win because you have more than enough brute force. But you will not convince. For to convince, you need to persuade. And in order to persuade you would need what you lack: reason and right in the struggle. (quoted in Thomas, 2003: 113)

It is said that only the presence of Franco's wife prevented Unamo from being summarily executed for this extraordinary act of defiance. He was subsequently dismissed as rector of the university and died several weeks later, an isolated and broken man.

16. There has since been speculation that Philby caused the explosion by placing a grenade in the car boot because he feared that Sheepshanks was about to expose him as a Soviet agent (see, for example, 'Was Philby Guilty of Murder?', *The Evening Standard*, 21 October 1991: 6). However, the evidence to support this claim is not strong. First, there were four Nationalist press officers on the scene at the time, supervising four cars of journalists. Second, there was more than one explosion during the attack. In the Nationalists own official report on events they testify that a first shell fell a few hundred yards away from the car, before the second explosion hit the car. Third, photographs held in the Reuters Archive show that the car in which the journalists were sitting when the bomb hit was extensively damaged down the entire nearside. The car boot, however, remained intact. Fourth, the injuries that killed the journalists were entirely consistent with a shrapnel explosion to the side rather than the rear of the car. Fifth, Bill Carney of *The New York Times* arrived at the scene of the accident just after it had occurred and confirmed to the foreign editor of *The Times* that Philby had a significant scalp cut and other minor injuries contradicting claims that he had faked his injuries.

17. On occasions, the services offered to high-profile journalists and celebrities were abused. In 1937, the film star Errol Flynn flew to Valencia and demanded that the press office provide him with immediate transport, guides and passes to go to Madrid, promising the donation of a substantial amount of aid and publicity for the Republic. Despite an acute petrol shortage, he was granted a car and a chauffeur and, when he arrived in Madrid, he sent a pre-arranged message to Paris that prompted a series of hoax reports stating that he had been killed on the Spanish front and then that he had been seriously injured. The Valencia government frantically wired the Madrid authorities to find out what had happened to Flynn (de la Mora, 1939: 297–8). It transpired that the Hollywood star had spent no time at the front, preferring instead to visit a local brothel and that his 'injuries' amounted to no more than a self-inflicted scratch. He flew out from Barcelona, thereby avoiding the irate Valencian authorities, and his promise of delivering substantial aid to the Republic never materialised. The American press corps were scandalised by his actions. The journalist

George Seldes later described him as 'one of the most despicable human beings that ever lived' (1987: 325).

18. Agence Espagne was established at the start of the war to promote the Republican cause. Headed by Otto Katz and principally based in Paris, it was heavily controlled by Communists (Cesarani, 1998: 123).

3

Eyewitnesses and 'I' Witnesses – Journalists in Spain

But of late, observers with sensitive ears report
Recalcitrant undertones, rustles of defiance
   Geoffrey Parsons, 'Europe a Wood', 1938 (quoted in Skelton, 1964: 99)

War begets many things, among them journalist memoirs. In this respect, the Spanish Civil War was a paradigm case. Dozens of European and North American journalists who reported the war described their experiences in book form, many of which were published before the war ended. This professional literature offers an obvious resource for the subject matter of this chapter, which is an exploration of the activities, experiences and perceptions of the foreign journalists who reported directly on the events in Spain as the civil war unfolded. But what status should we attribute to these sources of evidence?

In an introduction to a reprint of Franz Borkenau's contemporaneous account of the war and its origins, *The Spanish Cockpit*, the historian Hugh Thomas compares its worth to other accounts published by the many journalists, artists and politicians who rushed to Spain and then to their typewriters:

> I have many of their books in my library and occasionally one falls from the wall, crumbling with dust for it has been too long unconsulted . . . I cannot think of one which has stood the test of time. (Borkenau, [1937] 2000: xi)

As Thomas is one of the most esteemed historians of the conflict, this seems a damning indictment of the historical worth of these testimonies but what factors may have compromised their value? The first factor may be their partisanship. As will be shown, many correspondents harboured or developed strong opinions about the war and its antagonists. Consequently, dispassionate analysis is hardly a defining characteristic of this literature. In some cases, journalists' accounts were intended as direct propagandistic interventions in the war. For example, Claud Cockburn's book *Reporter in Spain*, published under the pseudonym 'Frank Pitcairn' in late 1936, was written in a weekend under the orders of Harry Pollitt, General Secretary of the Communist Party of Great Britain (Cockburn, 1967: 167). Arthur Koestler's *Spanish Testament*, published in late 1937, deliberately wove Popular Front and Communist propaganda into a personal account of his traumatic incarceration by Nationalist forces when reporting the war for the *News Chronicle* (Cesarani, 1999: 137).

A second limitation to the journalistic literature may be the extent to which the correspondents foregrounded their personal experiences and observations in their analysis of events. There were several reasons why journalists came to 'write themselves into the story' so significantly (to borrow a phrase from Matthew Kerbel, 1999). For all the political engagement of many of these correspondents, most remained concerned about demonstrating the integrity of their accounts. Lacking the cool analysis of history to sift claims and counterclaims, personal experience became the bedrock for their testimony. As Herbert Matthews, who reported the war from the Republican side for *The New York Times*, later put it, 'No news that is not first-hand is worth any more than the source to which it is ascribed' (1946: 37). In addition, journalists were encouraged by their editors to emphasise their personal experiences as witnesses to the first total war on European soil. Reportage was a cornerstone of British and North American news coverage of the conflict. This is a term that is often conflated with 'reporting' but is actually a distinctive form of journalistic discourse. Reporting is 'a fact-centred discursive practice' (Chalaby, 1998: 5) rooted in the empirical traditions of Anglo-American journalism. Reportage has its foundations in French journalistic culture and represents, in the words of Egon Kisch, 'a form of literary art in which accuracy of observation and fidelity to facts combine with creative narrative' (Segel, 1997). Whereas reporting requires 'the eradication of the reporter's position' (Durham, 1998: 119), in reportage, the author occupies centre stage. As Noel Monks, writing almost two decades after he reported on the conflict for the *Daily Express*, observed:

> These were the days in foreign reporting when personal experiences were copy, for there hadn't been a war for eighteen years, long enough for those who went through the last one to forget and for a generation and a half who knew nothing of war to be interested. We used to call them 'I' stories, and when the Spanish war ended in 1939 we were as heartily sick of writing them as the public must have been of reading them. (1955: 95–6)

But if this reliance on personal testimony was deemed to lend veracity and integrity to these journalists' accounts, it inevitably limited them. Many correspondents were only able to report the war from one side of the conflict, many were restricted to particular theatres and some only stayed in Spain for a brief period. None of these factors were conducive to the development of a panoptic perspective. Additionally, few of the correspondents who published books on Spain could be described as area specialists, conversant with the culture, history and, indeed, languages of the region. There were some exceptions but, in the main, these professional eyewitnesses garnered their understanding of the Spanish labyrinth 'on the job' and in the white heat of battle.

If all these factors undermine the value of these accounts as historical analyses – which is, I believe, the crux of Thomas's dismissal – they do not detract from their value as historical evidence. As Fred Inglis remarks:

> If culture at large may be temporarily defined as the ensemble of narratives we tell ourselves about ourselves, then journalism is the everyday

domestic conversation of a society as it first devises, disputes and circulates those stories – as it tries out their *grip* . . . [O]ne reason for the uncertain status of journalism in the conversation of humankind is its preliminary and provisional air, its inevitably hasty contrivance out of the unsatisfactory bits of information which are its origins. (2002: 98–9)

It is precisely the engagement and immediacy of these journalistic accounts that make them so valuable as material for historical analysis. As interventions of their time, they can be seen as discourses that convey the 'structures of feeling' (Williams, 1977) that pervaded the journalistic and political fields of that period – that is, '[t]he culture of a specific place and time, the actual day-to-day interactions of a particular class or society, which corresponds to the dominant social character' (Brennen, 2003: 115). They also have value as an information resource. For, however deficient their macro-analyses may have been, these accounts are a treasure trove of details about journalistic practices and perceptions that, through collation and triangulation, can help construct an understanding of the challenges journalists faced in Spain.

I begin this discussion by examining the configuration of the news net in Spain during the conflict. In the analysis that follows, I do not draw distinctions between the attitudes and experiences of UK- and US-based journalist, a conflation which may seem contentious to those who argue that there are greater professional and normative differences between the two journalistic cultures than is allowed for in the influential definition of journalism as an 'Anglo-American invention' (Chalaby, 1998). This is because I could discern no differences in the political and professional responses of journalists to the conflict on the basis of nationality. For example, American journalists could be as passionate and partisan about the war as British correspondents – just as British journalists could as readily invoke professional obligations to balance, impartiality and neutrality to defend their actions. Furthermore, British and American journalists co-operated closely together in their news gathering, sometimes out of choice and sometimes out of necessity, and some worked coincidentally, sequentially or interchangeably for British and North American newspapers. On several occasions, identical copy from them was published on both sides of the Atlantic. If national differences were evident in press reporting of the war, which is a moot point, then their principal manifestation would probably have been 'up line' in the strategic editorial planning of the news organisations themselves.

The news net in Spain

The 1930s have been labelled a 'golden age' of British and American foreign correspondence (Hamilton, 2005: 64; Cox, 1999: 249). As the Spanish Civil War was one of the biggest international stories of that period, it is not surprising that some of the most prestigious journalistic figures of the twentieth century reported on the war directly. Despite their presence, the Anglo-US news net in the conflict was constructed in haste, limited in reach and of dubious tensile strength.

To understand why this was so, there is a need to appreciate the marginality of the Iberian peninsula on the international news beat before the war broke out. In the 1920s and 1930s, Spain was perceived in Britain as a backwater of Europe – 'remote and insignificant, her glory a thing of the past' (Shelmerdine, 2002: 367). This meant there was limited allocation of foreign media resources in the region before the war. For example, by the 1920s, *The Times* had established an unparalleled network of international correspondents but its coverage of Spain was threadbare. Ernest de Caux, who was the paper's Madrid correspondent during the war, was first recruited to cover Spanish news in 1910. In his letter of appointment, he was instructed:

> All we would ask of you is that you keep us advised so far as lies in your power of the progress of any movement in the country which may necessitate our sending out a special correspondent and to keep us so advised by occasional letters, not necessarily for publication. (letter from Moberly Bell to de Caux, 8 April 1910, de Caux Papers, TNL Archive)

In 1920, de Caux was asked to take responsibility for the whole Iberian peninsular for *The Times* but, two years later, his retainer was reduced due to financial retrenchment. It was only in the following year that the paper's editor began to accept that they 'ought to have a whole time correspondent in a place like Madrid' (Geoffrey Dawson letter to William Lints Smith, 2 July 1923, de Caux Papers, TNL Archive), largely as a result of the quality of the copy sent by de Caux.

His permanent appointment, however, was atypical of the region in that period. In the early 1930s, international coverage of the Spanish news beat was mainly provided by freelancers who had travelled to Spain on their own initiative. Henry Buckley, who reported on the Civil War for the *Daily Telegraph*, first arrived in Spain in 1929 and, by his own admission, started freelance work with only 'the vaguest knowledge of what was going on' (Buckley, 1940: 15). Lawrence Fernsworth, Barcelona correspondent for *The Times* and *The New York Times* during the war, first visited Spain in 1930 on a sabbatical. He reported the proclamation of the Second Spanish Republic for *The New York Times* in 1931 and remained in Catalonia until the end of the Civil War (Fernsworth, 1939).

The armed rising of workers in Asturias and Catalonia in 1934 and the victory of the Popular Front in the 1936 election created brief created ripples of interest across the international news beat (see, for example, Delmer, 1961: 259; Buckley, 1940: 163; and Knoblaugh, 1937: 31) but did not lead to a structural deployment of editorial resources to the region before the rebellion occurred. When the storm did break, even Reuters was caught napping. Despite having a staff correspondent on the scene, when the correspondent sent the pre-arranged message 'Uncle Charlie Dies Tonight' to signal an uprising had started, the London desk initially assumed he was drunk (Read, 1999: 237–8).

The news net that was quickly improvised to cover the Spanish Civil War was an amalgamation of freelancers, stringers, special correspondents and staff reporters. 'Freelancers' and 'stringers' were those who had only tenuous and temporary contractual relationships with news organisations (freelancers provided written copy to news organisations; stringers provided factual information and leads). Many were inexperienced in news gathering and their principal value was their serendipitous proximity to matters of international interest. 'Special correspondents' were also employed on a freelance basis but were more likely to be seasoned foreign correspondents with considerable experience in reporting international affairs and conflicts. They often worked for more than one news organisation at a time and their established reputations and experience meant that their analyses carried considerable weight (Reed, 1938: 211–15). 'Staff correspondents' were directly employed by news organisations and had most internal status within their organisation.

In the early stages of the war, freelancers and stringers played an important role in providing coverage of events in Spain. Their significance receded as special correspondents and staff correspondents started to arrive in numbers and the Republicans and Nationalists started to rationalise their accreditation and censorship practices. For example, *The Times*' coverage of the Nationalist sector relied very heavily on the contributions of William Stirling until March 1937. Stirling had been in Spain completing a doctoral thesis on phonetics for a London university (the thesis was subsequently destroyed when the Nationalists captured San Sebastian). In July 1936, he was employed as a lecturer at the International University of Santander but, when the war broke, he was recruited as a temporary correspondent for the paper in the October. His experiences over the next few months were traumatic. He struggled with the oppressive Nationalist censorship, endured patronising reproaches from the London desk for his professional inexperience, contracted paratyphoid, was injured in a crash that wrote off the paper's staff car and was arrested as a spy by the Nationalist authorities. One can sense the relief in his letter to the foreign news editor of *The Times* in February 1937 when he heard the paper was sending out James Holburn, its Berlin correspondent, to assist in covering the Nationalist sector:

> I am very glad that you are sending out a Senior Correspondent and hope to learn much from him since I fear my ignorance of journalism must be proving a great handicap to *The Times* and I would like to learn more so as to be better equipped for the job. (letter from Stirling to Ralph Deakin, 13 February 1937, Deakin Papers, TNL Archive)

For all his difficulties and inexperience, Stirling fulfilled a vital role for *The Times* in maintaining coverage of the Nationalist sectors during the early stages of the war, visiting the Madrid front and witnessing the bloody aftermath of Franco's victory in Toledo. However, his services were quickly dispensed with once the senior correspondent was in place – 'inexperience was against him, and we feel we must liquidate the commitment as soon as possible' (letter from Ralph Deakin to James Holburn, 16 March 1937, Holburn Papers, TNL Archive).

The collective presence of international journalists in Spain was at its apex in late 1936 and 1937. On the Nationalist side, large numbers of foreign

Sefton (Tom) Delmer of the *Daily Express*, Madrid, 1937

Delmer reported from both sides of the war. Although he was antipathetic politically
to the Republic, he came to admire the defenders and citizens of Madrid.

correspondents massed in anticipation of the capture of Madrid by Franco's forces in November 1936 (see Buckley, 1940: 269). At the same time, many foreign correspondents reporting from the Republican side fled the city out of fear of reprisals but soon returned after its successful defence and formed a loose professional cadre based around the Hotel Florida on the Gran Via (see Cowles, 1941: 30–3; Herbst, 1991: 135–41; Moorehead, 2003: 140–1; Cox, 1937: 156; Matthews, 1938: 194). This presence was not sustained and, from mid 1937 onwards, many foreign correspondents left Spain. Other major international crises broke out and attracted their attention. The Japanese attack on China in mid 1937 and Munich crisis of 1938, in particular, displaced Spanish news considerably. Furthermore, one senses from the accounts that many journalists began to run out of new angles to take on the conflict. As Gramling notes in his early history of the AP news service, 'The Spanish Civil War, like so many stories of long duration, temporarily had become a matter of routine interest by mid-December, 1937' (1940: 452). However, the major reason for the reduction in journalists was financial cost. For example, Reuters was the most prestigious and widely used British news agency in the war (see Chapter 6) but, between January and October 1937, its expenditure on its Spanish Service exceeded revenue by 59 per cent (Documents P27a–P2710, The Reuters Archive).

As well as this temporal unevenness, there was also an imbalance in the number of journalists in Republican and Nationalist sectors. In researching this book, I collated all references to British or North American journalists who reported directly from Spain at some stage of the conflict. This count included all types of journalist – the sole criterion was that named individuals received payment for the provision of editorial copy or information for one or more UK or English language news organisation. The final total of 179 correspondents is undoubtedly an underestimation of the actual number of reporters that reported in Spain. Even so, it can be claimed to contain the most important figures in the field and, therefore, does reveal something significant about the relative distribution of the editorial resources of the UK and US media in the war.

Of the 146 correspondents where it has been possible to establish which side of the war they had reported upon, far more reported from the Republic than from Nationalist held zones (eighty journalists compared with forty-six). A further twenty journalists reported from both Republican and Nationalist sides, of which most visited Nationalist zones before entering the Republic. Only six of these journalists first experienced the war from the Republican side.

These unequal distributions demonstrate the effect of the structural and political differences in Republican and Nationalist news management practices discussed in the previous chapter – that is, the more repressive nature of Nationalist news management and the Republic's technical advantages. The combination of these factors also explains the tendency for journalists to cluster in particular areas. In Republican Spain, most journalists were based in Madrid, Barcelona, Bilbao and, to a lesser extent, Valencia while, in Nationalist Spain, they were concentrated in Salamanca, Burgos and Vigo. These were the locations for the censors and the telegraphic and telephonic links and journalists could not afford to stray too far from them. As Herbert Matthews of *The New York Times* remarked:

> Neither side was equipped for transmission from the front. A correspondent on the Republican side had to return to Madrid, Valencia or Barcelona to cable or telephone his despatches. This cut down on the number of stories one could write and the continuity of a particular coverage. It also meant that despatches were often written under conditions of extreme fatigue. (1972: 21)

There was only one period when journalists' dependence on Republican and National channels of communication was limited and that came at the beginning of the war. When news of the rebellion broke in July 1936, large numbers of journalists congregated around France's south-western borders with Spain, around Hendaye and Saint-Jean-de-Luz, partly because of the confusions and uncertainties about gaining entry and accreditation to Spain but also because major fighting was underway around Irun. Journalists made daily forays into Spain to observe the action and then returned to transmit their uncensored dispatches. Due to the topography of the border, they were also able to observe the battle from the freedom and relative safety of French territory. This opportunity led to the first ever live radio broadcast from a battlefield on 30 July 1936, when Hans von Kaltenborn of CBS ran a cable out from a telephone in Hendaye to a haystack close to the battle for Irun and delivered his news talk live to US audiences with an accompaniment of artillery and gunfire (Kaltenborn, 1937: 14).

Reporters on the border remained part of the news net for the rest of the war but their importance reduced. First, because Republican and Nationalist censors clamped down on the free movement of journalists across the border to send dispatches, recognising that this compromised their control over the content of the material sent. Second, because, as the war intensified, the key military action moved to other regions in Spain and the border points became an increasingly unreliable font of supposition and rumour.[1]

A key question is whether this statistical imbalance in the Republican and Nationalist news nets had any parallels in other aspects of foreign journalists' engagement with the war, in particular their attitudes towards the combatants. It is to these matters that the discussion now turns.

Going Red? Journalists and their elective and experiential affinities

In March 1937, Virginia Cowles, a freelance reporter for *The Sunday Times* and *The New York Times*, was completing the last leg of a lengthy car journey from Valencia to Madrid. Reflecting on her first impressions of the country, she later claimed, 'I had no "line" to take on Spain as it had not yet become a political story for me' (1941: 55). Among her companions in the car was a Catholic priest who had been recruited to make propaganda lectures in France repudiating claims of religious persecution in the Republic. During the journey he pressed Cowles about her political views and reacted with scepticism to her noncommittal responses. ' "It is impossible to be nothing," he retorted. "No-one comes to Spain without an *idée fixe*." ' (ibid.).

Cowles's neutrality must have seemed strange to an active propagandist in a war whose gravity and polarity seemed to provide little room for moral or political equivalence. However, many correspondents, like Cowles, initially went to Spain for the story rather than the struggle. For example, Frances Davis rushed to Spain at its outbreak as an inexperienced freelancer and became an accredited correspondent for the *Daily Mail* almost by accident (see Chapter 4). She also had 'no line to take' at the start and was more interested in the dramatic news value of the rebellion. As she later conceded, 'In this preoccupation with how to get to Spain, I had not asked myself who was at war' (1981: 138).

It was not long before both women began to develop strong opinions about the antagonists. Writing of her experiences in Madrid, Cowles confessed, 'I took a great liking to the Spanish people' (1941: 35). She later reported from the Nationalist side, witnessing the end of Franco's Basque offensive, and spoke of her 'revulsion' at what she witnessed on a press trip organized by the military to the front at Gijon (ibid.: 85). Although Frances Davis only reported the civil war from the insurgent sector – and therefore had no equivalent opportunity for making direct comparisons – she, too, came to dislike the Nationalists and their supporters. The politics of the war are entirely absent from the first half of her first and lengthiest account of her experiences in Spain (1940), and it is only mid-way through her account that she begins to express her disdain for the Nationalists' rhetoric (ibid.: 137), and the complicity of her paper in their propagandistic activities: 'I don't like the stuff I send. I don't like the stuff the *Daily Mail* likes. The *Daily Mail* calls these "Patriot" armies' (ibid.: 131). Of her relationship with Captain Gonzalo de Aguilera, who was in charge of press relations in the north, she later wrote, 'I know him for my enemy, and I am his. Everything that has made me is death to him; everything that has made him is death to me' (1981: 159).

That both women came to sympathise with the Republic is perhaps not surprising, given their shared liberal backgrounds and their gender (see Chapter 4). But the Spanish arena produced other, more dramatic, damascene conversions. Herbert Matthews of *The New York Times* arrived in Madrid in December 1936 as an 'admirer' of Fascism having witnessed the Italian invasion of Abyssinia. He later wrote:

> I know, as surely as I know anything in this world, that nothing so wonderful will ever happen to me again as those two and a half years I spent in Spain. And it is not only I who say this, but everyone who lived through that period with the Spanish Republicans. (Matthews, 1946: 67)

Noel Monks of the *Daily Express* first reported the civil war from the Nationalist side in the Basque region and then from Republican held territories in Bilbao and Madrid. As a Catholic, he was initially sympathetic to Franco but he later said, 'My six months in Franco Spain deeply shocked my religious sensibilities. And they were to receive further shocks when I went to Government Spain, but for totally different reasons' (Monks, 1955: 84). So transformative were these experiences that he later acted as press agent for Katharine Stewart Murray, 8th Duchess of Atholl, who was fighting a by-election having resigned her Conservative parliamentary seat in protest at the British government's failure to support the Republic (see Thomas, 2003: 591).

Other journalists with clear elective affinities at the start of the war may not have had their politics altered so dramatically but do also attest as to how their experiences affected their perception of the war. Sefton Delmer of the *Daily Express* first visited Spain to report on the armed rising of workers in Asturias and Catalonia in October 1934. In April 1936, he travelled to Madrid and interviewed all the major Spanish politicians of the day, professing a particular admiration for José Antonio Primo de Rivera and his Falangist movement. This fitted with his general worldview at the time, which was vehemently anti-Communist and sympathetic to aspects of the Nazi regime.[2] For all his right-wing proclivities, he later reflected:

> Despite all I had seen of the brutality and contempt for justice of the Reds, despite my own antipathy to Marxism as a demagogic fraud, despite all this and much more, I nevertheless found I was being swept along in the exhilaration of Madrid's refusal to abandon the fight. I found myself sharing the thrill of the reverses with which the Reds were inflicting on the side I would certainly have chosen had I been a Spaniard and forced to decide between the ugly alternatives of Franco and Caballero. (Delmer, 1961: 299)

As will be shown, there was also no shortage of idealists and ideologues among the international press corps on both sides who had their preconceptions and predispositions reinforced by their experiences. Even so, it is important to consider why it was that, when journalists' convictions did change as a result of their experiences, their sympathies tended to incline towards the Republic. Or, as a bemused *Daily Telegraph* correspondent reporting from the nationalist sector put it more bluntly to his colleague, ' "How is it, Mac, that there's a tendency on the part of newspaper reporters to go Red?" ' (McCullagh, 1937: 109).[3]

A range of factors explains the development and direction of these experiential affinities. The different treatment accorded journalists in Nationalist and Republican zones discussed in the previous chapter undoubtedly affected journalists' attitudes. The repressive news management of the Nationalists, in particular, angered many correspondents and they were often appalled by the harsh opinions and actions sanctioned by senior Nationalists. In contrast, the greater freedom journalists had 'to see things for [them]selves' (Bartlett, 1941: 263) in Republican sectors confounded many of the simplistic caricatures of 'Red Spain' they had arrived with. Noel Monks was surprised to discover he was freely able to celebrate Catholic Mass in all the Republican sectors he visited. Vernon Bartlett of the *News Chronicle* struggled to meet any Russians in Madrid, despite widespread media reports that they had flooded into the city (ibid.). Herbert Matthews arrived in Madrid in a state of high anxiety:

Nobody had told me that I would find anything but a ruined and terrorized capital, ruled by Red gangsters and ready to fall prey to the army of Generalissimo Franco. All that I saw in the succeeding days and weeks was a revelation to me, so much so that the very first night here I wandered the streets almost desperately for an hour and a half, trying to find the American Embassy and not daring to ask for fear I should immediately be arrested because I still had no night pass. It was some days before I realized that all I had to do was walk up to a guard, explain my predicament, and he would not only direct me, but with true Spanish courtesy as like as not accompany me to the Embassy to be sure I did not get lost. (1938: 185–6)

Time and again in their accounts, foreign journalists in the Republic eulogise the bravery, hospitality, optimism and stoicism of the ordinary people they encountered. To Matthews, 'the nonchalance of the Madrileños was a staggering thing to behold' (ibid.: 186). Virginia Cowles marvelled at how, '[e]ven in their darkest hour, they retained a sense of humour and a zest for living' and, in observing the stark contrast between the grinding poverty of many and the opulence of the local cathedrals, she 'began to understand the grievance against the Church' (Cowles, 1941: 35). Vincent Sheean of the *Chicago Tribune* believed the citizens of Madrid had 'turned the brothel and shop window of feudal Spain into this epic . . . In this one place, if nowhere else, the dignity of the common man had stood firm against the world' (1939: 199). And Henry Buckley's admiration for and allegiance to the citizens of the Republic remained undimmed to the end: 'By and large the individual man and woman was showing a fierce, vital courage. These people vibrated with life and blood. They were human beings that fought and battled, not worn-out robots' (Buckley, 1940: 227).

For those journalists who witnessed the war from both sides, the contrast between the humanity of the ordinary people and the hauteur of the military was stark. As Sefton Delmer remarked:

Madrid in those frosty days of November and December 1936 was to me infinitely more Spanish and therefore infinitely more lovable than the theoretically Super-Spanish Nationalist H.Q. in Burgos with its British-educated señoritas and its hoards [sic] of solid bourgeois. About Red Madrid there was a sharp sincerity and peasant earthiness I never felt on the Franco side. (1961: 300)

British and American journalists often invoked conceptions of 'Spanish-ness' in their appraisals of the warring factions and these characterisations connected with powerful cultural stereotypes about Spain and its people that were prevalent in Northern Europe and North America at the time. The actions and rhetoric of the Nationalists corresponded to the so-called 'black legend', which originated in the sixteenth century and the struggles between Spanish Catholicism and Northern European Protestantism (Moradiellos, 2003). This trope depicts the Spanish as vain, intolerant, violent, acquisitive and fanatical – qualities which were said to be exemplified by those involved in the Spanish

Inquisition in Europe and the conquistadors in South America. The 'black legend' may have informed some journalists' perceptions of certain Republican factions (see below) but the admiration of others for the ordinary people of the Republic corresponded more closely to the 'romantic legend', a discourse that emerged in the nineteenth century and celebrated the exotic, fatalistic, passionate, bucolic and chaotic aspects of Spanish society.

A further factor that increased some journalists' identification with the Republic was their relationship with the British and American volunteers who fought in defence of the Republic. The correspondents were fascinated by the activities of these fighters because of the local news angle they offered. Although some of the volunteers had reservations about consorting with the press (see, for example, Romilly, [1937] 1971: 131), they met journalists and even socialised with them on several occasions – Delmer kept an open bar in one of his hotel rooms in Madrid which was frequented by many international volunteers. This physical and cultural proximity allowed journalists to gain insights into the personal biographies and motivations of these volunteers and many correspondents were moved by the idealism and selflessness of the brigaders. Geoffrey Cox of the *News Chronicle* stated, 'It would be hard to find a body of British men to equal these first volunteers in the International Column' (1937: 145). Sefton Delmer spoke in paternalistic terms about his first sight of British volunteers: 'They stood out from the Germans like a schoolboy team from the Blues. Their cheerfulness was magnificent' (1961: 310). In the view of Vernon Bartlett:

> They talked with the same enthusiasm, the same readiness to sacrifice themselves, the same desire to kill as a matter of duty as we showed in 1914 when we were fighting for the independence of gallant little Belgium, for justice, for freedom, for decency . . . I admired and liked these volunteers. (Bartlett, 1941: 277)

Herbert Matthews described the Internationals as 'the finest group of men I ever knew or hope to know in my life' (1946: 92) and Vincent Sheean said their 'courage and generosity' offered 'the hope of the world; I think the only hope' (1939: 70).

Which Republic?

To observe that the direct experiences of foreign correspondents in Spain often fostered sympathy towards the Republic begs the question of which aspects the correspondents identified with most closely. As discussed in Chapter 2, the Popular Front government of 1936 was a complex amalgam of revolutionary and liberal factions that held very different political visions of the purpose of the war and how it should be conducted.

It is striking that, although many correspondents were unconditional in their admiration was for the ordinary people of the Republic, they were very discriminating in their support for its different political factions. Unsurprisingly, those journalists working for pro-Communist newspapers or with formal Communist allegiances adhered to the party line. Joseph North, who reported from Spain on behalf the US *Daily Worker*, praised the Communists and Socialists and criticised the anarcho-syndicalists and 'the traitorous intrigues and subversive impeachments of the Partido Obrero de Unificación Marxista (POUM), the Trotskyist formation which assailed the goals of the Popular Front by their vociferous insistence upon and immediate socialism' (North, 1958: 140). Louis Fischer, another correspondent working for the Communist press in the US, wrote in glowing terms about the new government headed by Juan Negrín that came to power after the suppression of the Anarchists and the POUM in Barcelona in May 1937. Elsewhere he dismissed the Anarchists in Catalonia as 'romantic revolutionists' who 'never got anywhere' (1941: 404) and accused them of shirking their responsibilities in defending the Republic. Arthur Koestler, who in 1937 was both a special correspondent for the *News Chronicle* and a covert member of the Communist Party, had no compunction about labelling the POUM 'Trotskyist' and, along with the Anarchists, deeming them responsible for the 'agitation' in Barcelona (1937: 178).

But what of the views of journalists not operating, either overtly or covertly, as Communist Party members or fellow travellers? In *Tree of Gernika* (1938), George Lowther Steer, Special Correspondent for *The Times*, expressed his deep respect and empathy for the Basque nationalists and a grudging regard for the discipline of the socialist UGT. In contrast, he was bemused and alienated by the revolutionary fervour of the Anarchists. For example, his description of the destruction of Irun by Anarchist forces prior to its capture by Franco's forces is laced with deeper political metaphors:

> The whole day, from sunrise to sunset, they poured Benzine and threw dynamite over the little town of Irun, which once housed sixteen thousand Spaniards . . . There a ravenous and pulsing furnace swallowed up their individual life, obliterated their frailer, more sensitive, and volatile existences in universal fire . . . Against it one could sometimes see moving darkly the tormented and violent people who created it. (1938: 53)

Noel Monks, like Steer, connected most strongly with the Basque nationalists and Henry Buckley shared Steer's antipathy to the Anarchists:

> They could be terrible with that kind of blind passion of the illiterates with all the hatred of a feudal regime burned into their souls by centuries of sufferings and without leaders or a programme capable of turning this hatred into something more or less constructive, as was the case with Socialists and Communists. (1940: 275)

Herbert Matthews lauded 'the realism and discipline' of the Communists and welcomed the suppression of the POUM and the Anarchists and the rise of 'the better and more moderate elements – the Republicans, Socialists, small shop-keepers and landowners' (1938: 286).

What is striking from all these accounts is the common ground that most liberal and left-wing journalists shared in their factional affiliations. The radical components of the Popular Front were variously attacked as impotent, misguided, lawless and deceitful and the assertion of Communist control from mid 1937 onwards was welcomed as making the Republic more effective in resisting Franco, more ordered and, even, more democratic. Even Ernest de Caux, Madrid correspondent for *The Times*, who had been highly critical of the Republic in the early stages of the war, wrote approvingly of the Negrín government and the imposition of centralised control, claiming in a message to the London news desk 'The sympathy of the people is today with the agent of authority not against it . . . The Negrín cabinet represents the Frente Popular bereft of its extremist components' (5 September 1937, de Caux papers, TNL Archive). This counter-revolutionary consensus contrasts with an Orwellian orthodoxy that has gained prominence in modern historical analyses of the war and which tends to see the suppression of the Anarchists and POUM in April 1937 as signalling the point at which political idealism and revolutionary optimism were crushed by Communist control (Buchanan, 1997: 201).

Pressures on professionalism

If many journalists found it difficult to be dispassionate about the Spanish Civil War, what implications did these opinions have for their professional conduct in reporting the war? Schudson observes that journalists do not fake news – they make news (see Schudson, 1991: 151). His point in drawing this distinction is that research that demonstrates the values and ideologies intrinsic to news production does not expose journalistic dishonesty but rather highlights how journalists unavoidably make meaning through their discursive activities. From this perspective, the normative professional ideals of Anglo–American journalism – the commitment to absolute objectivity, neutrality and unprejudiced witness – are revealed as a philosophical impossibility.

However, war is a context where questions of journalistic fakery do retain significance. Authorities curb media autonomy through exceptional censorial powers and coerce and recruit journalists into acts of deception to confuse and demoralise their enemies. Journalists often struggle to determine where their professional obligations end and their patriotic duties begin. Although such factors are evident in peacetime, it is during war that they acquire acute intensity.

Evans describes the pressures of 'propaganda' and 'professionalism' that journalists confront at times of war (2004: 35). Journalists have most professional discretion in conflicts that have no direct implications for their nation of origin. Conversely, the graver the threat to national security, the more journalists will be expected to subordinate their independence to the propaganda needs of the nation. It follows, therefore, that the greatest tensions between professionalism and propaganda in war reporting tend to occur in those conflicts where serious national interests are at stake but not matters of national survival. The Spanish Civil War was precisely such a conflict for British and North American journalists. Furthermore, it was a war where 'the competitive ecstasy of hate' (ibid.) was

particularly polarised and visceral and the propagandistic pressure, as a consequence, intensive. As Hans von Kaltenborn, correspondent for CBS, reflected:

> Not once while I was in Spain did I hear an impartial or dispassionate
> analysis of the Civil War. There was always bitterness, prejudice and
> hatred. Calm analysis was impossible for any Spaniard. While atrocities
> were bad enough, each side emphasized and exaggerated those committed
> by their opponents. In all my experiences with large and small conflicts I
> have never felt the curse of war more keenly than while reporting the
> Spanish Civil War. (1950: 199–200)

Absolute propaganda and total professionalism are of course polarities on a
continuum with many gradations. For this reason, I extend the dichotomy to dis-
tinguish between journalists who acted as 'propagandists', 'partisans', 'sympathisers' and 'agnostics' in the Spanish war.

Propagandists

'Propagandist' is a term with plenty of negative connotations. As in previous
chapters, my usage here is intended in a descriptive sense to identify those correspondents who were members or agents of a combatant force. On the
Republican side, the distinction between correspondents and combatants sometimes became blurred. Louis Fischer (*The Nation*) and Jim Lardner (*New York
Herald Tribune*) joined the International Brigades. Tom Wintringham, who was
a key figure in the creation of the Brigades, originally entered Spain as military
correspondent for the *Daily Worker*. Arthur Koestler later admitted that his connections with the Comintern gave him military authority in the Republic
(Koestler, 1966: 6). Several people who came to Spain to fight later turned their
hands to journalism. For example, Keith Scott-Watson resigned from the Tom
Mann Centuria, the first organised group of British volunteers to fight in defence
of the Republic, to assist Sefton Delmer at the *Daily Express* (Scott-Watson,
1937: 189). He fled Spain under threat of detention for desertion (Delmer, 1961:
305) but later reported from Bilbao and Barcelona as correspondent for the
London *Star* and the *Daily Herald* (Scott-Watson, 1939: 244; Buchanan, 2007:
23, 25). Sam Lesser, another of the first British volunteers in Spain, later assisted
with shortwave foreign radio broadcasts from Barcelona following his injury in
battle. This led to his recruitment as the Barcelona correspondent for the *Daily
Worker*, for whom he wrote under the byline 'Sam Russell'.

Many of these correspondents were Communist Party members and they
structured their news reporting in accordance with the requests, dictates and
imperatives of the Party. Claud Cockburn of the *Daily Worker* was a particularly
influential and controversial figure in this respect. His reputation as an able propagandist was acknowledged even in Nationalist circles (McCullagh, 1937: 108)
and he had no qualms about confecting stories for the military and political
advantage of the Communists. As he put it to Virginia Cowles, 'I am not interested in watching revolutions; my job is *making* them' (Cowles, 1941: 32).

Cecil Gerahty of the *Daily Mail*

An ardent Francoist, Gerahty travelled extensively across Nationalist territory. He helped publicise false evidence about a planned Communist revolution, was part of a *Mail* campaign about BBC political coverage of Spain and was involved in attempts to defame the journalists who reported the aftermath of Guernica.

There is some irony in this statement, as some of his most influential work was in legitimising the suppression of the POUM and the Anarchists in Barcelona through the articles he published in the *Daily Worker* under his pseudonym 'Frank Pitcairn' (Orwell, 1938: 215–42). Among the specious allegations he peddled was a claim that the revolt in Catalonia had been orchestrated directly by Hitler and Mussolini (see, for example, 'Pitcairn lifts Barcelona veil: Trotskyist rising as signal', the *Daily Worker*, 11 May 1937). On another occasion, he conspired with Otto Katz of the Communist Agence Espagne news agency in writing an entirely fictional account of an anti-Franco rebellion in Tetuán to persuade the French government to continue to allow the covert trafficking of military supplies to the Republic.

Because of the centralised and militarised structure of Nationalist forces, there were no US and UK correspondents who were, in strictly technical terms, members or agents of the insurgency. However, there were journalists and news organisations that colluded so closely with the Nationalists that it is legitimate to classify them in these terms. For example, at the beginning of the war the *Daily Mail* acted as though it was de facto the London press bureau for Franco and its correspondents were granted considerable privileges by the Nationalists as a consequence. One of the paper's special correspondents, Cecil Gerahty, travelled extensively around Nationalist Spain and was invited by General Queipo de Llano to make a shortwave propaganda broadcast on behalf of the Nationalists. He also played a key role in publicising documents that were said to prove that radical insurrections were being planned at the time the army revolted (1937: 40–1; 214–19). History has exposed these forgeries but, as Southworth notes in his forensic dissection of the documents' provenance and credibility, Gerahty's willingness to publicise their contents reveals his eagerness 'to find a justification for Franco's revolt (Southworth, 1999: 12). Ironically, Gerahty also participated in orchestrated attacks on the BBC by the *Daily Mail*, accusing it of a pro-left bias and citing news talks on Spain as evidence ('Listeners' Attack on BBC', *Daily Mail*, 14 January 1937).

Partisans

Distinguishing between journalists as 'propagandists' and 'partisans' may seem like hair-splitting. However, I use the term 'partisan' to identify those journalists who were passionately committed to one side but had an associative rather than formal relationship with a cause or a party.

An example of such a correspondent on the Nationalist side was Francis McCullagh who represented a number of small newspapers dispersed across the British colonies. Although his book contains a litany of complaints about the frustration and inconveniences of reporting with the Nationalists, it also offers homage to the validity and morality of Franco's rebellion and ends with 'with the cry: *Viva España! Viva el General Franco! Viva el Ejército Salvador. Arriba España!*' (1937: 323). In a similar vein, Theo Rogers, Spanish correspondent for the English language *Philippines Free Press*, concluded his book with:

I have come out unequivocally for the side of General Franco . . . when all the wrongs and rights are weighed in an impartial scale, there can be but one decision. You must take sides. It is impossible to remain a straddler. (1937: 203–4)

In contrast to obscure figures like McCullagh and Rogers, some of the most iconic figures of twentieth-century journalism can be classified as Republican partisans with Robert Capa, Ernest Hemingway, George Steer, Martha Gellhorn, Herbert Matthews among them. Although all were open about their sympathies some were less forthcoming about the extent of the actual support they provided. For example, George Steer of *The Times* did not hide his respect for the Basque people but recent research by Tom Buchanan has uncovered significant new evidence about the extent of his involvement in promoting the Basque cause through his influential political contacts in Britain. Buchanan concludes:

It is now clear that Steer worked assiduously behind the scenes in support of the Basques, in collaboration with the Basque government. While it would be an exaggeration to suggest that Steer choreographed the British response to the Basque crisis, there is no doubt that his private briefings influenced political opinion just as his newspaper dispatches influenced public opinion. (2007: 39)[4]

Like 'propagandists', 'partisans' were not inclined to pay obeisance to conventional professional expectations of neutrality and even-handedness in their journalistic practice. Indeed, it was believed that observance of what Martha Gellhorn memorably dismissed as ' "all that objectivity shit" ' only served to muddy the realities of the war and give succour to the enemy (Moorehead, 2003: 150). Instead, partisans cast themselves as impassioned witnesses, identifying with a moral rather than professional responsibility to communicate the horrors and significance of events in Spain (see Romeiser, 1982). As the *Paris Soir* correspondent, Louis Delaprée put it, a few weeks before his death, 'All the images of Madrid suffering martyrdom, which I shall try to put before your eyes – and which most of the time challenge description – I have seen them. I can be believed. I demand to be believed' (1937: 21).

Delaprée's remarks help to draw attention to another difference between 'partisans' and 'propagandists'. With the latter, the emphasis was often upon the plausibility of an account, rather than its fidelity. Partisans, in contrast, retained concerns about truth through their work, asserting that this was attained through trusting their judgements, observations and emotions, rather than adhering to the strategic rituals of 'objective journalism' and its reification of arid facts and accredited second-hand opinion. Sebba notes in her description of Martha Gellhorn's personal view of her political and professional obligations in the war that 'Martha believed passionately in being partisan: *as long as you describe accurately what you have seen*, why should there be a need to put the case for the other side too' (1994: 103 (*emphasis added*)).

Having said this, there were also occasions when commitment to the cause led these correspondents to tailor their news gathering for political purposes. For example, Caroline Moorehead claims that Gellhorn, Hemingway and Matthews consciously avoided reporting Republican persecutions, torture and execution for fear of the political damage it would cause (2003: 150). But here again there is a point of distinction with propagandists as these constituted sins of omission rather than commission and are explicable in terms of the journalists' emotional connection with the war. As Knightley observes:

> The failure of correspondents to report the imperfect face of the Republic does not seem to be due, except in the case of confessed propagandists, to any policy of duplicity, but to their preoccupation with the effect the war was having on them personally. (1975: 215)

Sympathisers

I use the term 'sympathisers' to categorise those journalists who identified with particular antagonists but whose ardour was more measured and conditional than the partisans. Most of the journalists who developed experiential affinities would be grouped under this category.

The different strength of their affiliation is significant because it had implications for the balance they struck between their professional practices and political sympathies. With partisans, the two were indivisible; with sympathisers there was an intention to retain some distance between them. For example, Virginia Cowles maintained a sense of obligation 'to give both sides a fair hearing' (Sebba, 1994: 103) despite her personal dislike of the Nationalists. Lawrence Fernsworth, Barcelona correspondent of *The Times* and *The New York Times*, was highly sympathetic to the Republic but felt obliged to report the elimination of the 'enemies of the people' in Barcelona at the start of the war:

> I knew the facts would be harmful to the Republican cause for which, as an American, I felt a deep sympathy believing that in its essence the struggle was one for the rights of man. But it was the truth and had to be told. As a reporter I have never shirked at telling the truth regardless of whom it might please or displease. (1939: 46)

An illustration of the different pressures and priorities sympathisers felt in comparison with propagandists and partisans is offered in Vincent Sheean's account of his experiences reporting the war for the *Chicago Tribune* (1939: 78–80). In April 1938, he was travelling with Joseph North, correspondent for the Communist newspaper the *Daily Worker*, to the front near the river Ebro. After a candid high-level military briefing, he realised that the Nationalists' great Aragon objective was just about to achieve its primary objective of cutting the Republic into two. Although personally distressed at this event, he describes his frenetic activities to be the first to break the story internationally as an example of the 'fever' of his 'occupational disease' (ibid.: 79). North, by comparison, felt no compunction to rush to the phone lines because his paper would never publish a story with such negative implications for the Republic.[5]

Agnostics

The final category of foreign journalists in Spain, the 'agnostics', were those correspondents who did not connect to any significant extent with the politics of the conflict but focused instead on its intrinsic value as a news story. This is a position where concerns about professionalism were dominant. Few of the journalists' accounts published in book form during and after the war could be said to typify this stance. The closest example I have found is Alan Dick's description of his experiences reporting the war for the *Daily Telegraph* from the Basque region of Nationalist Spain. Although in his concluding remarks he claimed 'to feel deeply for the people of Spain' and for 'their courage as they faced the mechanised might of Nazi-ism and Fascism' (1943: 153) his account has a descriptive, even anodyne, quality as he recounts his working conditions and professional relationships and says next to nothing about the political issues at stake (see also MacColl, 1956). Dick concedes:

> I have written lightly, perhaps frivolously, of my experiences during part of the Spanish Civil War. That is not because I did not appreciate the momentous issues involved in that fratricidal struggle . . . The reason is that I do not feel qualified to discuss the deeper meaning of the Spanish Civil War after a visit of only a few months, and then only to one side. I have attempted to give an objective running commentary on my own experiences. (ibid.)

Most news agency correspondents would be appropriately defined as 'agnostics' as their responsibility for providing spot and breaking news for diverse client news organisations required them to adopt an informational rather than analytical role and to demonstrate a greater 'will to facticity' than other correspondents (Allan, 2003: 73). Their values were concisely summarised by Frances Davis in her description of their arrival in the Nationalist zone in late 1936:

> The string men who cover cheaply from the border are left behind, and the freelances and the colour feature men. In their place are the wire service men who beat every story into routine coverage and waste the least time and motion and words in telling it. (1940: 128–9)

Vice or virtue?

Differentiating between the types of foreign correspondents in Spain clarifies the contrapuntal relationship between professionalism and propaganda in the war and the extent to which orientations to these two trends differed across the international press corps. The relationship between the professional and political activities of journalists also raises ethical questions and there may be a tempta-tion to characterise the continuum from 'propagandists' to 'agnostics' as a path from vice to virtue. Such a view is problematic for several reasons.

First, there is some question as to whether the interpretative agency and eval-uative engagement of many of the correspondents actually violated objectivity norms in the first place. Foreign correspondents have always been permitted more freedom and autonomy than home correspondents and are expected to fulfil a role of 'independent experts, free to make judgements, less as dependent and supervisable employees' (Schudson 2001: 164). In other words, political engagement was, at least to some extent, part of their brief.

Second, although some theorists wish to retain 'objectivity' as an ideal for journalistic endeavour (see, for example, Lichtenberg, 2000), many studies have shown that the routine professional strategies by which this is pursued – factic-ity, neutrality, balancing – produce a highly structured discourse that tends to privilege accredited sources of knowledge and permits journalists to abdicate personal responsibility for their work (see, for example, Gitlin, 1980; Tuchman, 1972). Indeed, it has been argued that formulaic observance of these professional principles can obscure, confuse and relativise important political issues. For example, Rosen claims that 'journalism shows us that often balance is a flight from truth rather than an avenue into truth' (1993: 49).

To give an illustration of this point from the Spanish Civil War, strict obser-vance of professional norms would have required that any report of the aerial attack on Guernica should give equal prominence to Nationalist counterclaims that the destruction was wrought by retreating 'Red' forces, even though these were false. Such coverage would be 'balanced' but could it claim greater integrity and accuracy than the unequivocal testimony of George Steer, Noel Monks and the other correspondents who witnessed the immediate aftermath of the raid and did not baulk at apportioning blame? As Herbert Matthews noted bitterly about the editorial policy of *The New York Times*:

> The publisher laid down a mechanical, theoretically impartial, plan of operation – print both sides, equal prominence, equal length, equal treat-ment. This often meant equality for the bad with the good – the official handouts hundreds of miles from the front lines with the eye-witness stories, the tricky with the honest, the wrong with the right. I say that not only I, but the truth suffered. (1972: 39)

Third, in the case of the Spanish Civil War, the middle ground between the warring factions was itself a highly politicised position. Dispassionate reporting that uncritically juxtaposed the claims and counterclaims of the antagonists invited a political equivalence that buttressed the non-intervention policies of the North European and American governments. Furthermore, it was evident to most journalists on the ground that this policy offered significant advantages to Franco (see Moradiellos, 1999) and this appreciation angered many correspon-dents. Certainly the British government were very keen to see 'balance' in cover-age and, in the case of the BBC, steps were taken to engineer it (see Chapter 5).

Concluding remarks

This chapter has examined the experiences, attitudes and perceptions of the considerable numbers of British and American correspondents who covered the Spanish Civil War directly. The analysis shows that the international news net in the war was more extensive and effectively organised in Republican-held territories and that, taken overall, the political sympathies of the Anglo-US news corps inclined more towards the Republican cause than the Nationalists. These often reflected pre-existing political viewpoints ('elective affinities') but, in many cases, these sympathies were forged through correspondents' experiences in Spain ('experiential affinities'). One thing that most pro-Republican journalists shared was an antagonism towards the more revolutionary factions and ambitions of the Republic.

Foreign correspondents interpreted their professional roles and responsibilities in a variety of ways. Some embraced partisanship whereas others tried to separate their professional activities from their opinions. But even this professional response of balancing the competing perspectives had significant political implications in the war as it buttressed the case for non-intervention.

It does not necessarily follow from this that Anglo-US news coverage showed a pro-Republican bias. The contributions of these foreign correspondents can only be considered a preliminary level of mediation – as in journalism, no copy is sacrosanct and is always ultimately subject to editorial selection and amendment. Furthermore, a significant amount of British reporting concerning the Spanish Civil War was not conducted at the scene but back in the UK and USA, as numerous other journalists and senior editors mused over where their nation's responsibilities and best interests really lay. Any appraisal of the overall political disposition of British and American news media demands a more extensive analysis that incorporates an investigation of actual trends in media output. All these matters are addressed in the chapters that follow.

Even so, the trends uncovered in this chapter raise critical questions about the performance of the international news corps in covering one the biggest news stories in what has been labelled a 'golden era' of foreign reporting. Without question, the Spanish Civil War generated some magnificent coverage, written by some iconic figures, but there were also structural failings. News organisations did not appreciate the gravity of the Spanish situation before war broke out and, during the first crucial months, often relied heavily on inexperienced correspondents. Draconian censorship practices in the Nationalist sectors impeded journalists' presence and performance across the conflict. And, although considerable editorial resources were in place by mid 1937, these levels were not sustained as a large proportion of the international news corps moved on to the next international crisis.

Notes

1. The retreat of Republican forces from Catalonia to France in early 1939 saw a brief reprise in border-based reporting (see Chapter 6).
2. Frederick Voigt, diplomatic correspondent of the *Manchester Guardian* wrote in a letter to the paper's editor that Delmer 'has the mentality of a fascist gangster' (Voigt to William Crozier, 31 March 1937, MGA, 217/224).
3. There were exceptions to this rule. Denzil Batchelor (1961) and Theo Rogers (1937) experienced both sides of the conflict and came out in support of Franco. H. Edward Knoblaugh of Associated Press and Ernest de Caux of *The Times* reported the war solely from Republican territory and were highly critical of what they saw as the extremism and brutality of the Republican regime. It is clear, however, are that all of these correspondents had strong political predispositions towards the Nationalist cause (see, for example, Phillip Knightley's comments on aspects of Knoblaugh's book which he believed 'epitomised the very worst of the pro-Franco atrocity propaganda' (1975: 198) and Southworth's observations about de Caux's pro-monarchism (1977: 332)).
4. In light of this new evidence it might seem that Phillip Knightley's criticisms of Steer, discussed in Chapter 1, were not as devastating as they could have been, as he was unaware of the extent of Steer's partisanship. However, although Buchanan describes Steer as 'disingenuous' for hiding the extent of his advocacy, he concludes, 'There is no question that Steer was one of those journalists who reported the war in the Basque country (in the telling words of Noel Monks) "factually and, as far as was possible, objectively"' (2007: 39). Most importantly, Buchanan raises no questions about the accuracy or integrity of Steer's specific report on the destruction of Guernica.
5. These differences are also exposed in an anecdote by Joseph North about a major road accident he witnessed when travelling with Ernest Hemingway and Herbert Matthews in 1938. As Hemingway rushed to offer medical assistance, Matthews started to interview the injured and dying. North remarks with some disgust, 'After all, he was first and foremost, "a *Times* man" and deadlines to even the most humane of *Times* men were more urgent than life and death' (1958: 142).

4

'The Aliveness of Speaking Faces' – Women Correspondents in the Spanish Civil War

'Me, I am going to Spain with the boys. I don't know who the boys are, but I am going with them.' (Martha Gellhorn, 1937, quoted in Moorehead, 2003: 10)

This chapter extends the analysis of journalists in Spain to examine the role, experiences and distinctive contributions made by women correspondents in the reporting of the war. This might seem a strange aspect to elaborate upon as women were a small minority in the international press corps that covered the war and none commanded much status within their organisations. Women correspondents represented just ten percent of the total number of British and North American journalists I have identified as having reported from Spain during the war.

It could be argued that it is this atypicality which makes these journalists such interesting cases for consideration but this is hardly a convincing justification. A more compelling reason is the historical neglect of the significance of gender in news production, which has led to an underestimation of the important contribution of female news professionals. For example, war reporting is sometimes characterised as a male preserve. As Dafna Lemish says, 'It is mostly men who perpetrate the violence, organise a violent response, and present media stories about it' (2005: 275). Although it is difficult to dispute the general legitimacy of this observation, there is a need to be wary of overgeneralisation. One can readily think of many contemporary exceptions to the proposition that war stories are always male stories. For example, in the UK, there is the influential presence of female journalists like Orla Guerin, Maggie O'Kane and Kate Adie. Furthermore, there is a historical lineage to female war correspondence that can be traced back to the 1840s (Sebba, 1994).

An important aspect of the recognition that 'the media politics of gender deserve more attention than they have received to date' (Carter et al., 1998: 3) is the development of a historically informed perspective that retains and, where necessary, recovers appreciation of the past contributions, achievements and trials of women working in these male-dominated environments. Central to this project is the need to examine the extent to which these pioneering women introduced different values and perspectives from their male counterparts and the reasons for these differences.

Table 4.1 Women Correspondents in Spain and the sectors in which they worked

Republican sector only	Isabel de Palencia (*Daily Herald*)
	Paula Leclerc (*Daily Telegraph*)
	Fifi Roberts (*News Chronicle*)
	Jose Shercliff (*Daily Herald*)
	Dorothy Parker (*New Masses*)
	Lorna Woods (*Manchester Guardian*)
	Josephine Herbst (*New York Times*)
	Helen Seldes (*New York Times*)
	Martha Gellhorn (*Collier's*)
	Barbro 'Bang' Alving (*Dagens Nyheter*)
	Martha Huysmans (*Peuple*)
	Gerda Taro (*Ce Soir, Vu, Life*)
	Hilde Marchant (*Daily Express*)
	Elizabeth Wilkinson (*Daily Worker*)
	Anna Strong (various Communist newspapers)
	Charlotte Haldane (*Daily Worker* and *Daily Mirror*)
	Kitty Bowler (*Manchester Guardian* and *Toronto Star*)
	Gerda Grepp (the Norwegian press)
Republican then Nationalist sector	Virginia Cowles (*Sunday Times* and *New York Times*)
Nationalist then Republican sector	Eleanor Packard (*United Press Bureau*)
Nationalist sector only	Frances Davis (*Daily Mail* and *Chicago Daily News*)
	Sheila Grant Duff (*Chicago Daily News*)
Spanish–French Borders	Nancy Cunard (*Manchester Guardian*)

There is also a specific reason why the contribution of women journalists in Spain warrants particular consideration. In this chapter I identify a 'high-profile/low status' paradox in female reporting, by which I mean that accounts written by women were often given considerable prominence in national newspapers, despite the lack of seniority of their authors. This shows that female voices mattered in Spanish coverage but what did they contribute?

Women journalists in Spain

Table 4.1 lists those women I have firmly identified as having visited Spain or its immediate environs and provided editorial copy for international news organisations during the war. This list should not be seen definitive for two reasons. It is biased towards English language news organisations, which reflects the wider focus of this book. Furthermore, the list probably excludes the names of other women who worked for Anglo-American news organisations during the war.[1] But if the list is not comprehensive, it can be said to include those women whose reporting had most public impact during the conflict.

Table 4.1 shows that most of these female correspondents reported from Republican-held territories. To some extent, this differential distribution mirrored the general numerical imbalance in the international news net which, in turn, reflected the different attitudes the combatants had towards foreign journalists and their work (see Chapters 2 and 3). As discussed, Republican news management was framed by a political rather than military culture, reflecting a clear perception of the need to communicate with international audiences. Within this context, a further gender-specific factor worked to marginalise the presence of female correspondents in Nationalist territories. Most of the women worked for left-wing or left-of-centre newspapers many of which were banned or restricted by the Nationalists.

However, these structural factors only provide a partial explanation as to why most female reporters covered the war from the Republican side. In particular, they don't address the political agency of these women and how this affected their working practices. To gain such insight, there is a need to look more closely at the personal and professional lives of these correspondents.

Personal histories, professional choices

Most of these female correspondents came from privileged backgrounds and were highly educated. Nancy Cunard was the only child of an English baronet and was educated in private schools across Europe. Martha Gellhorn and Kitty Bowler came from wealthy professional families and both attended the women's university Bryn Mawr College based in Philadelphia. Gerda Taro was born into 'a bookish family' in Germany and studied in a commercial school in the Weimar Republic prior to its downfall (Kershaw, 2002: 24). Virginia Cowles was able to pursue a journalistic career in Europe as a result of a large personal inheritance (Sebba, 1994: 94) and Sheila Grant Duff studied at Oxford University and was the daughter of a lieutenant colonel and a baronet's daughter. Such advantages in wealth, class and cultural capital no doubt helped compensate for the barriers of gender discrimination to some extent as, at that time, journalism – even the elite realms of foreign correspondence – was deemed an occupation of low status (see Cox, 1999).[2]

What these women shared was an antipathy to class and gender conventions and a strong affinity with progressive and left-wing politics. Some had sought to channel their political energies through journalistic activities prior to the outbreak of war in Spain whereas others became involved in reporting the conflict through more circuitous and serendipitous routes. Virginia Cowles started her career on a small journal called *Entre Nous* in 1931. Two years later she started working as a freelancer for the Hearst Press and then began travelling around Europe filing reports on a pay-for-publication basis. Prior to going to Spain, she had visited Italy and Libya and interviewed Mussolini (Sebba, 1994: 94–5). Martha Gellhorn abandoned her university studies early to pursue a career as a writer and journalist. In the early 1930s, she travelled Europe as an aspiring foreign correspondent, filing reports for a variety of magazines and newspapers in the US. Sheila Grant Duff graduated from Oxford University in 1934 and became an apprentice of the renowned foreign correspondent, Edgar Mowrer of the *Chicago Daily News*, who was, at that stage, based in Paris.

Other women correspondents had more tenuous connections with journalism before the war. During the 1920s, Nancy Cunard had been involved in a wide range of cultural and artistic activities in Europe. In the late 1920s, she founded Hours Press and became immersed in a range of progressive political causes, in particular the American civil rights movement (Chisholm, 1979: 200–44). She visited Spain on several occasions during the war and was a key figure behind the publication of the pamphlet 'Authors Take Sides on the Spanish War', which invited leading literary figures to state their political allegiances in the conflict. Her journalistic involvement only came at the end of the conflict when, covering her own personal expenses, she reported on the internment and mistreatment of Republican refugees on the Franco-Spanish border in January and February 1939 for the *Manchester Guardian*. Her correspondence with the paper's editor reveals her professional uncertainty and inexperience: 'Now, I really would feel relieved to know if the articles I have sent are suitable. Give me some criticism, some suggestion – are they too long or too much about refugees?' (letter from Cunard to W. P. Crozier, 3 February 1939, MGA, B/C290A/27).

Regardless of their journalistic experience, female correspondents had little status within their news organisations. Apart from Hilde Marchant, who was a staff correspondent at the *Daily Express*, all the women were employed on a freelance basis and most secured their commissions after they had arrived in Spain. For example, Frances Davis was an aspiring freelance journalist based in Paris, who rushed to Spain at the start of the war having given little prior thought as to who the combatants were or what were the issues at stake. Her recruitment as a special correspondent for the *Daily Mail* came about accidentally. In the earliest days of the war, she teamed up with a group of male correspondents that included the *Daily Mail*'s correspondent, Harold Cardozo. The journalists made daily forays over the Franco-Spanish border into the war zone by car and, when it was not possible for the group to return to their French base, Davis took responsibility for couriering the copy over the border. After one lengthy solo trip returning Cardozo's copy, she had to remonstrate with the *Mail*'s London desk to get them to take the story. Her tenaciousness created an impression and she was offered a job by the paper's editor:

> I put the telephone receiver back and I grin from ear to ear. If there were someone near me I would hug him. It's awful to keep such glory and excitement to myself. I am a newspaper reporter. I work for the London *Daily Mail*. I will carry credentials. I am not excess baggage in a car. I'm not a free-lance doing mail columns. I'm Davis of the *Daily Mail*. (1940: 101)

Unlike Davis, Martha Gellhorn was initially drawn to Spain for political reasons but she too gained her commission with *Collier's* magazine after her arrival and almost by accident. As she later recollected:

I went to Spain with no intention of writing anything about it . . . And then somebody said, 'Why don't you write about life in Madrid?' So I just wrote a piece about daily life in Madrid where shells used to hit our hotel every-day – things like that. And sent it off to a friend of mine who worked on *Collier's* and the next thing I saw I was on the masthead as a war correspondent. (*Great Lives*, BBC Radio 4, 16 January 2007)

It is a measure of their junior status that none of the women was recruited to provide daily news. This was often the source of some frustration as deadlines would have provided discipline, status and opportunities in their reporting (see, for example, Herbst, 1991: 139–40; Davis, 1940: 84; and Cowles, 1941: 21). Instead, the role of the women correspondent was to provide 'colour stories' – reportage that offered some human interest and provided a personal context for the hard news stories about political manoeuvrings and military conflicts in the Iberian peninsula (Davis, 1940: 103).

As discussed in the previous chapter, reportage abounded in foreign coverage of Spain and was not an exclusively female preserve (see also Chapter 6). Nevertheless, female reportage had a distinctive quality. Rather than describing the drama and horrors of open combat, their reports focused more frequently upon the impact of the war on ordinary people and their everyday lives. Virginia Cowles said she was 'much more interested in the human side – the forces that urged people to such a test of endurance' (1941: 55). Martha Gellhorn wrote about 'the ordinary people caught up in the war' ('Martha Gellhorn: On the Record', BBC Four, 24 May 2004). Both Josephine Herbst and Hilde Marchant were separately encouraged by their editors to provide a 'women's angle' on the effect the war was having on daily life (Sebba, 1994: 91 and 148). According to Angela Jackson, these concerns represented more than just a difference of emphasis:

Women's writing on Spain frequently allowed space for the personal, and empathy, in many cases, overrode detachment. This should not be dismissed as a mere trick for propaganda purposes, aiming to obscure objectivity by an appeal to the emotions. It was, in many cases, a reflection of a different agenda. (2002: 132)

It is also striking how consistently this empathetic approach translated into active sympathy, even advocacy, for the Republic. In some cases and in common with many of their male colleagues, these developed as a direct result of their experiences in Spain (see, for example, the experiences of Virginia Cowles and Frances Davis discussed in the previous chapter) but most of these women arrived with their allegiances clearly established. Sheila Grant Duff felt a 'passionate commitment to the cause of Spanish freedom' (1982: 151) and, in 1937, was sent in to Nationalist territory to discover the fate of the journalist Arthur Koestler, who was then under sentence of death. On this occasion, Duff's lack of status and experience was seen by her senior colleagues as advantageous as she would be unknown to Nationalist authorities who were antagonistic towards the

(Reprinted with the permission of the estate of Frances Davis Cohen.)

Frances Davis (the *Daily Mail* and *Chicago News*) at the international border near Irun, speaking with French border guards, August 1936

During the early stages of the war, foreign correspondents frequently commuted to France to telephone their dispatches. Throughout the war censors on both sides sought to obstruct such practices and closely monitored international news coverage to identify transgressions.

(© Bettman/Corbis)

Virginia Cowles (*The Sunday Times* and *The New York Times*) and Martha Gellhorn (*Collier's* magazine), London, 1946

Although a freelancer, Cowles (on the left) was one of the few foreign correspondents to report first from the Republican side before entering Nationalist territory. Gellhorn did not originally intend to report on the war but, after her arrival in Spain, she obtained a commission from *Collier's* magazine.

Chicago Daily News. She was so successful in slipping under the radar and into the confidences of the Nationalists that she was invited to witness the summary execution of Republican prisoners. She immediately appreciated the conflict this created:

> For a journalist it would be a sensational *coup*; for a spy it would really be seeing what Franco's men were at; for a human being it would be to stand and watch people whom I regarded as friends and allies being put to death in cold blood. I knew I would not be able to live with it. I did not go. (Duff, 1976: 81–2)

Martha Gellhorn's affinity for the Republic endured throughout her life and was unaffected by the vicissitudes of historical revisionism. She claimed never to have read a book on the war because, however factually accurate they were, they could not capture "'the emotion, the commitment, the feeling that we were all in it together, the certainty that we were right'" (quoted in Knightley, 1975: 103).

A united Republic

The almost total unanimity of support for the Republic among women correspondents contrasts with the more diverse distribution of allegiances among their male colleagues (see Chapter 3). Furthermore, it had a distinctive quality. As discussed in the previous chapter, many male correspondents in Spain also arrived with or developed pro-Republican sympathies. However, male endorsements often contained conditions and qualifications that displayed approval for certain elements of the Republic and disapproval of others. Such conditions and distinctions are signally absent from the opinions expressed by the women correspondents of their time in Spain. Rather, they seemed to connect with a broader and undifferentiated conception of the Republic and its values.[3] As Josephine Herbst put it, 'I have never had much heart for party polemics, and it was not for factionalism I had come to Spain' (1991: 135). But why did these women often identify so unconditionally with the Republic?

One of the indisputably revolutionary elements of the Popular Front was its commitment to gender equality and female emancipation (see, for example, Nash, 1995; Ackelsberg, 2005). These ideals contrasted starkly with the chauvinistic codes of traditional Spain defended by the Nationalists, which sequestered the lives of women (see Knickerbocker, 1936: 44; de la Mora, 1939: 53–123). This is not to suggest that women correspondents were disengaged from the wider political issues at stake in the Spanish war – they were as aware of the anti-Fascist implications of the conflict as their male colleagues – but rather that the gender politics of the conflict added a further point of connection and identification with the Republic.

A further question is why women's reportage focused so much upon the inner lives and lived experiences of the 'ordinary' citizens of the Republic. One way of explaining this is to invoke those strands of feminist theory that identify deep-seated psychological gender differences, such as Carol Gilligan's (1982) proposition that men are governed by rationalistic concerns about rules and justice whereas women are naturally orientated to an ethics of caring, which privileges emotions, relationships and empathy. However, there is a strong essentialist logic in such explanations that has been criticised by many contemporary feminist theorists (see, for example, Lister, 2003; Oakley, 1998). Furthermore, it deflects attention from the material reasons that compelled these women to focus on the politics of the everyday in their writing. As noted, most female correspondents were freelancers with tenuous contractual arrangements. This lack of status restricted their news-gathering opportunities and many voiced their frustrations at being denied the access, accreditation, transportation and communication facilities provided for their senior male colleagues. However, without the pressures of daily deadlines, these women had more opportunity to integrate with local people and absorb the local culture. There was some inevitability, therefore, that these everyday observations and interactions became a central subject of their work. In Josephine Herbst's words:

> I had been assured at the press bureau that I would get to go places, but for days I was suspended, wondering, Where? In a situation like that it becomes second nature to hide one's ineptitude. You can't admit that you aren't bustling about, knowing exactly what it all means. If I had been a regular correspondent, I would have been obliged to show something for each day. But I was on a special kind of assignment, which meant I would write about other subjects than those covered by the news accounts . . . I did a lot of walking around, looking hard at faces. There was almost nothing to buy except oranges and shoelaces, and all this seemed wonderful to me. The place had been stripped of senseless commodities, and what had been left was the aliveness of speaking faces. (1991: 139–40)

Male mentors

Many women correspondents formed close professional and sometimes personal relationships with male colleagues. Lorna Wood, Helen Seldes and Eleanor Packard were all married to senior male journalists and came to Spain because of their partners' deployment to the region.[4] Kitty Bowler entered into a relationship with Tom Wintringham, who initially came to Madrid as a military correspondent for the *Daily Worker* and had a key role in the creation of the International Brigades. Gerda Taro had been the partner, colleague and agent of Robert Capa before the war and collaborated with him in photojournalistic work in Spain until her death in July 1937.

The most famous journalistic liaison forged in the Spanish war was between Martha Gellhorn and Ernest Hemingway. They became lovers soon after Gellhorn's arrival in Madrid in March 1937 and this generated some resentment among the other international journalists gathered in the Hotel Florida in

The death of Gerda Taro

89   **Woman Photographer Crushed by Loyalist Tank**

Probably the first woman photographer ever killed in action, pretty Gerda Taro covering the Spanish Civil War for the Paris "Ce Soir," was crushed by a Loyalist tank during the great battle of Brunete on July 26, 1937. The Loyalists had taken Brunete, lost it, taken it again, and then lost it. Gerda Taro had left Brunete once in the retreat, and then decided to join the Loyalist rear guard in the city. For almost an hour she had crouched with a remaining battalion under Rebel bombardment. Finally she hopped on the running board of a press car. Suddenly, as part of a Loyalist counter attack, a tank, cruising blind, careened into view. With an unexpected swerve the creeping, shell-spitting monster bumped the daring young woman from her perch and crushed her beneath the revolving lugs! She died the following morning in the Escorial Hospital her husband-photographer, Robert Capa, at her side.

To know the HORRORS OF WAR is to want PEACE

This is one of a series of 240 True Stories of Modern Warfare. Save to get them all. Copyright 1938, GUM, INC., Phila., Pa.

(From the author's own collection.)

Gerda Taro was a photojournalist who had a close personal and professional relationship with Robert Capa. Her death in the Republican retreat from Brunete in 1937 was the subject of much media comment – one measure of which was its inclusion as a subject in the 1938 American 'HORRORS OF WAR' gum card series.

Madrid because it delivered Gellhorn greater opportunities in terms of transport and access to influential sources (see Moorehead, 2003: 142; Herbst, 1991: 138). Gellhorn herself admitted to an element of pragmatism in her relationship with Hemingway. As she dryly commented, 'I was just about the only blonde in the country. It was much better to belong to someone' ('Martha Gellhorn: On the Record', BBC Four, 24 May 2004).

The cynicism of this remark needs to be placed in the context of the subsequent, acrimonious breakdown of her relationship with Hemingway and it is not my intention to suggest that it typifies a calculating motivation on the part of these women correspondents to cultivate male contacts purely out of professional self-interest. Rather, these relationships demonstrate that, for all the pioneering feminist spirit of many of these women and despite the principles of gender equality at the heart of the Republic, the professional environment they were working in was highly patriarchal and their status and opportunities were restricted and facilitated by their male contacts, both in the field and 'up line' in the editorial departments of their news organisations.

Valuing women's perspectives

The significance of editors in the allocation of these women's roles and the use of their copy links to a final question regarding the function of women correspondents in the war. Why were news organisations so interested in obtaining female perspectives on the war? Despite the low professional status of these women, newspapers often used their contributions prominently and frequently emphasised the gender of the author (see, for example, Frances Davis, 'A girl looks at a battle', Daily Mail, 6 August 1936; José Shercliff: '"I was Taken for a Spy!" How a Woman Reporter Sent the News From Spain', Daily Herald, 14 August 1936). Nancy Cunard's dispatches in 1939 on the plight of Republican refugees at the Franco-Spanish border and their internment by the French authorities dominated the Manchester Guardian's international coverage for several days. As previously noted, Hilde Marchant and Josephine Herbst were instructed by their editors to provide a woman's perspective on the war.

A range of factors explains this 'low status/high profile' paradox. The first relates to the intense competitiveness and circulation wars of the newspaper industry in the late 1930s, particularly in the UK. Specifically, this was manifested in the strenuous attempts by newspapers to dramatise and personalise their coverage of foreign affairs to attract and retain readers (Gannon, 1971: 3). The inclusion of women's perspectives was often used strategically to vitalise foreign coverage. More generally, the 1930s saw an intensifying of the 'feminization of news' that had began with the Northcliffe revolution at the start of the twentieth century (Tusan, 2005: 243). This 'New Journalism' was based on a recognition of 'women consumers as an important audience on their own terms' (Carter et al., 1998: 1) and involved the inclusion of 'softer' news stories – items and features related to lifestyle, human interest and celebrity issues. Here again, the inclusion of feminine perspectives on the personal, emotional and domestic consequences of international events was seen to assist in connecting with these lucrative female markets.

Broader cultural trends also framed the editorial appetite for the kind of empathetic reportage of everyday events these women correspondents provided. The 1930s saw the emergence of the mass observation studies,[5] the documentary film movement[6] and new photojournalist publications such as *Life* and *Picture Post* that in their separate ways shared an interest in delineating the details and dramas of ordinary lives.

A final reason why women's views of the Spanish Civil War were valued related to the nature of the war itself. Across Europe, and in the UK in particular, political and public opinion in the 1930s 'was overshadowed and, to a great extent, determined by an obsessional and, in retrospect, exaggerated fear of air attack' (Morris, 1991: 48). This so-called 'air fear' assumed that significant advances in aircraft and bombing technology meant that nations would be defeated by devastating and irresistible aerial assaults on civilian populations. In 1932 the British Prime Minister Stanley Baldwin delivered the apocalyptic warning to the House of Commons: 'The bomber will always get through. The only defence is in offence, which means that you have to kill more women and children more quickly than the enemy if you want to save yourselves' (Hansard, 5C/270, 10 November 1932, 632). This conviction was a central pillar of Britain's subsequent policy of appeasement towards the German and Italian dictatorships. As the Spanish Civil War represented the first total war on European soil, in which 'the shadow of the bomber' removed distinctions between frontline and home front, and combatants and civilians, it was inevitable that there would be immense public and media interest in the impact these assaults had on citizens' lives and morale (Bailer, 1980).

Concluding remarks

This chapter has examined the important and distinctive contribution that women correspondents made to the coverage of the Spanish Civil War in the international news media. This is not the first study to identify a distinct emphasis and quality to female war reporting and foreign correspondence through history (see, for example, Sorel, 1999). Indeed, such differences are still identified today. In 1999, Victoria Brittain, deputy foreign news editor of *The Guardian*, asserted:

> Men's response to fear is usually bravado, and in war some male journalists do the same: they become obsessed with weapons and start identifying with the military, in the hope of feeling stronger themselves. Women's response is to identify with the people whose lives are shattered. (McLaughlin, 2002: 169)

The legitimacy of such distinctions is not accepted by all. For example, McLaughlin argues that 'it is certainly wrong to suggest that there is a strict gender difference in style between men and women reporter' (ibid.: 170). The basis of his objection is that there are plenty of examples in war coverage that do not conform to the pattern – cases where men provide compassionate reportage about the human and emotional costs of military conflict and examples where women provide dramatic and significant hard-news scoops. With reference to Spain, one can certainly find such exceptions. Nevertheless, the tendency for male correspondents to focus on dramatic military events and high-altitude political manoeuvrings in their coverage of the Spanish Civil War and for female correspondents to concentrate on the war's impact on ordinary lives behind the lines is so obvious that it cannot be ignored. However, I share McLaughlin's concern about the suspicion of essentialism in many accounts that identify absolute gender differences in war reporting and indeed journalism in general. This is not just because it does a disservice to the 'good guys' on the international news beat but because these distinctions can also inadvertently demean and patronise women's contributions. As Ann Oakley notes, the logic of such reasoning:

> is likely to be the construction of 'difference' feminism where women are described as owning distinctive ways of thinking, knowing and feeling, and the danger is that these new moral characterisations will play into the hands of those who use gender as a means of discriminating against women. (1998: 725)

It is not necessary to resort to essentialism to explain why these gender distinctions occurred in Spain. Although highly educated, these women lacked status within their occupational field and were often reliant on the sponsorship and support of male colleagues and editors. This restricted their news-gathering opportunities both in terms of access to senior political figures and physical mobility. Thus, their interest in reporting the impact of the war on everyday lives was, to some extent, a case of making a virtue of necessity. Certainly, when some of these women were provided with the opportunities to visit the front, they exhibited an equivalent appetite to that of their male colleagues for observing and reporting battles. They also matched them for bravery and, occasionally, recklessness. In July 1937, this resulted in tragedy when the photojournalist Gerda Taro was crushed to death by a tank during the military retreat of Republican forces from Brunete.

Despite the subordinate status of women journalists, news organisations valued and encouraged the production of a female perspective of the war. In part this represented intensification in the general feminisation of news during this period, but it also revealed specific public and political interest in the experiences of citizens in coping with the traumas of total war. In this respect, these micronarratives about everyday experience – which can be seen as symptomatic of the exclusion of women correspondents from wider public affairs – had a subtle but profound impact upon international power politics and military planning. By the late 1930s, the 'air fear' that had shaped the foreign policy of European democracies through the mid 1930s started to lose credibility. A key reason for this was the eyewitness testimony provided by journalists in Spain, many of them women, which showed that civilian morale was stiffened by rather than destroyed by air attack and that the devastating impact of incendiaries and bombs could be mitigated by effective air-raid precautions.[7] By late 1938, press and political discourses in the UK had shifted decisively towards the development of air-raid precautions to help defend civilian populations (Morris, 1992: 65). Thus, by identifying resilience and stoicism amidst the trauma and suffering, female reportage helped fortify the political and public will of democratic nations as they prepared to confront the terrible trials in prospect. It is a striking illustration of how the politics of the personal are not only of intrinsic importance but can also have major, if unforeseen, macro-political consequences.

Notes

1. For example, in his account of his traumatic incarceration by Nationalist forces in 1937, Arthur Koestler describes meeting a woman who acted in a dual capacity as both a Nationalist press officer and a correspondent for the Hearst Press in the USA (Koestler, 1937: 284–8). Unfortunately, I have yet to identify her.
2. Hilde Marchant was an exception and came from a working-class background.
3. Angela Jackson notes that this distaste for factionalism was common amongst many other women activists who were involved in offering practical and political support to the Republic (2002: 85).
4. Their partners were, respectively, Joseph Swire of Reuters, George Seldes, a radical freelance journalist who submitted copy to the *New York Post*, and Reynolds Packard of the *New York Times*.
5. The first mass observation study commissioned by the British government examined public attitudes to the abdication crisis but soon expanded into a broad anthropological investigation of the everyday lives of British citizens (Hubble, 2005).
6. The British Documentary Movement, founded by the Scottish film-maker John Grierson and sponsored by the British governmental agencies, was also at its most influential during the late 1930s. This movement was defined by its commitment to social realism in film and conveying the experiences of real places and real people.
7. See, for example, an article by Charlotte Haldane published in the *Daily Mirror* (8 March 1938: 14) relating her observations on the effects of the bombing of civilians in Madrid, and the most effective way of defending against its worst consequences. She concludes: 'Mothers who want to protect their babies in the next war must be prepared to fight for such protection now'.

5

Rear-Guard Reactions – Governmental and Commercial Influence on Spanish Civil War Reporting in Britain

Foreign news in any national context is always viewed through the prisms of local interest and local interests – that is, judgements as to whether distant events are relevant to domestic audiences, and, if they are, which definitions dominate and in whose interests.

In the context of a rapid destabilisation of collective security in Europe, there was never any doubt that the outbreak of war in Spain would be a big news story in Britain, particularly when it became clear that other major powers were intervening militarily and politically. However, questions as to the nation's moral responsibilities and strategic interests remained contested throughout the war. This chapter examines how powerful material and ideological interests within Britain, operating both within and outside news organisations, attempted to control the tone, orientation and extent of British news coverage.

The Spanish Civil War divided opinion within the public and political classes in complex and unprecedented ways and a comprehensive analysis of all the activists and propaganda activities mobilised by the war within Britain would require far lengthier discussion than is possible here. Consequently, this chapter focuses on what I judge to be the most significant sources of domestic influence on the editorial priorities and policies of the British news media during the conflict. These were, respectively, the British government, media proprietors and the senior editorial figures within news organisations who commissioned and processed news from their correspondents in Spain.

Official news management and Spain

The government is always a key 'leadership arena' in the reporting of public policy, particularly in the realm of foreign policy (Seymour-Ure, 1987). As Schlesinger notes, 'Official sources may not always have to be believed, but they do have to be taken seriously' (1990: 81). There were also specific reasons why the British executive assumed paramount significance as a source of information and opinion for the British media during the Spanish Civil War. The dominance of ministerial and other official sources was not disrupted significantly by the cross-tidal pull of party political debate. It took a considerable period of time for party political opposition to government to coalesce and mobilise. Most

Conservative MPs were inclined to support Franco, at least at the beginning of the war, and the Labour Party leadership, although highly sympathetic to the Republican cause, continued to endorse the official government policy of non-intervention in the conflict until late 1937, in part because it felt that the cauterisation of the war would work in the best interests of the Republic and in part because of its political antipathy towards the Communist Party of Great Britain (see Fleay and Sanders, 1985; Buchanan, 1997: 78–83). Additionally, the National government, controlled by the Conservative party, had an unassailable political dominance. In the 1935 general election, Labour recovered some of ground lost in its devastating electoral defeat of 1931 but could only muster a parliamentary presence of 154 MPs and the Liberal Party remained in political free fall, winning merely twenty-one seats in 1935, seventeen fewer than in 1931.

Furthermore, the start of the Spanish Civil War coincided with a major expansion in official communication and promotional activities in Britain, particularly in the realm of foreign policy. After the First World War, there had been a significant retrenchment in the propaganda activities of the British state, in part because the levels of expenditure on these activities in wartime were deemed unnecessary in peacetime and in part because of a broader 'quest for normalcy' in the immediate aftermath of a war that was supposed to end all wars (Taylor, 1999: 72). By the mid 1930s, however, the situation had changed dramatically. Totalitarian regimes in Europe and beyond had embraced new propaganda techniques and mass communication technologies to consolidate their power bases domestically and extend their influence internationally. Many influential figures within the British establishment began to assert that Britain had to develop a strategic and competitive response to these challenges.

The News Department of the Foreign Office – which, as will be shown, was a key source of influence on British news coverage of Spain – also played a pivotal role in the reconstruction of the promotional infrastructure of the British state, for two reasons. First, the Department had been the only survivor of the decommissioning process at the end of the First World War, even though it had had to survive on frugal resources provided by the Treasury for many years (ibid.). Second, international diplomacy and commerce were the realms where there was most pressing need for more extensive and effective state propaganda, both internationally and domestically (Stenton, 1980). In January 1936, Sir Reginald 'Rex' Leeper, head of the News Department, outlined plans for a campaign 'for the education of the public' on foreign affairs using the press, the BBC, the League of Nations Union 'and perhaps the churches'. He wrote:

> We are approaching a stage in international relations where the people of this country will have to be brought face to face with realities in a way that has not happened since the last war. We have to rearm our people not only materially, but morally. The easy-going post-war period came to an end openly and dramatically when Italy attacked Abyssinia . . . The word 'propaganda' has many evil associations from the last war and I will therefore substitute the cleaner word 'education' for what I have in mind . . . We

have allowed Germany to get ahead in this respect and with all Germany's advantages of secrecy and dictatorship we shall never catch up unaided. We must therefore concentrate not only on our rearmament, but on bringing other nations to our side and by instilling in them such confidence in our leadership and determination that they too will rearm and abandon an attitude of defeatism vis à vis Germany. But if we are to inspire them with this confidence, education must begin at home. We must be swift, bold and persistent. It is insufficient to make a few public speeches for the News Department of the Foreign Office to make points with the press. I suggest the whole programme must be conceived on wider and bolder lines if it is to bear fruit and to bear fruit quickly. (27 January 1936, The National Archives (TNA), FO 395/541, Paper p332/332/150: 74–5)

Leeper's recommendations were roundly endorsed by Sir Robert Vansittart, then Permanent Under-Secretary at the Foreign Office, who, in a covering note, also acknowledged the urgent need to steel public opinion 'against the impending tests' (ibid.: 73).

The dominance of the Foreign Office News Department during the early phases of Britain's re-engagement lent a distinctive quality to the strategies that emerged. In promoting the values and virtues of an 'open' political system, there was an aversion to the brashness, aggression and instrumentalism that typified the propaganda of the 'closed' totalitarian systems. Emphasis was placed instead on 'cultural propaganda' designed to foster awareness and appreciation of British institutions and values, rather than to deprecate competitors or enemies. The creation of the British Council in 1934 exemplified this approach, with its role in the promotion of international knowledge of the United Kingdom and closer cultural relations with other nations. These values also infused the news management strategies developed by the Foreign Office, which sought to encourage factual and measured debate of international matters rather than impassioned and partisan commentary. Furthermore, it was envisaged this 'propaganda with facts' approach would be sustained even in the event a major conflict since 'an account of what we are doing ourselves would be more effective than abuse of an enemy' (Rex Leeper, 13 November 1935, quoted in Willcox, 1983: 107).[1]

A measure of the News Department's significance at this stage was Leeper's appointment as chair of a subcommittee for the Committee of Imperial Defence charged with outlining plans for the creation of a Ministry of Information.[2] The report tabled by Leeper's subcommittee in July 1936 recommended a Ministry of Information should only be created in the event of war and its introduction should be phased (TNA, FO 395/538, Paper 2826/74/150: 92). Within the committee's initial conception, any future ministry would co-ordinate but not control the communication activities of the different departments and the News Department in particular would retain a significant degree of autonomy. However, this vision changed with the appointment of Sir Stephen Tallents as director general designate of the shadow ministry, who had worked previously as head of public relations at the BBC. Building on the reservations of some of the initial subcommittee members, Tallents argued that the News Department would need to be subsumed within a single, centralised ministry because it lacked the capacity and experience to deal with domestic propaganda. He also recommended a more forceful approach to media censorship and news management than that favoured by the News Department. This antagonised Leeper who resigned from the subcommittee in 1938, objecting to Tallents' failure to conceive a role for the British Council in the planning process (Willcox, 1983: 105).

This internal wrangling over the future form of the shadow ministry linked with other major divisions within official circles and eventually led to the complete dismantling of the News Department's role. On the day of Leeper's resignation, the government announced the creation of a further committee to examine the development of international publicity. The committee was headed by Sir Robert Vansittart who, in January 1938, had been 'promoted' to the role of chief diplomatic adviser.[3] Leeper was also involved centrally in its work. In May 1938, Vansittart submitted a lengthy report to the Prime Minister recommending the retention of the Foreign Office's role in international publicity, a continued adherence to the principles of cultural propaganda and fact-first 'publicity' and the immediate commitment of £500,000 further expenditure on publicity activities (Willcox, 1983: 106–7). Vansittart also suggested that Leeper be promoted to Assistant Under-Secretary at the Foreign Office, in recognition of his growing responsibilities. These requests were not well received by Chamberlain and several of his senior officials. A copy of an eighteen-page critique written by an unidentifiable Treasury Official in June 1938 and held in The National Archives Office at Kew contains additional hand-written comments by Sir Warren Fisher, Permanent Under-Secretary at the Treasury. On the first page, Fisher dismissed Vansittart's plans as 'very amateurish' (original emphasis) and, in confirming his opposition to Leeper's promotion, stated, 'Mr Leeper is already overpaid, tho I wd [sic] be prepared to pay him more as a pension' (TNA, PREM, 1/272: 2, 15, original emphasis).

The *ad hominem* nature of these remarks reveals the bitter divisions within the British government over the formation and communication of foreign policy and, in particular, how best to deal with Italy and Germany. The author of the Treasury's response concluded:

> I do not believe that in the long run it will be possible to combine the policy of appeasement with a forward policy in propaganda. Armaments may be infinitely more expensive than propaganda, but they, at least, have the virtue of being dumb, and do not cause the same ill-will. From the point of view of appeasement, the propaganda race seems to me to be the most serious danger. (ibid.: 17)

This observation is particularly significant as Vansittart and Leeper were the most vehement opponents within the British establishment to Chamberlain's conciliatory stance towards Hitler and Mussolini and the Prime Minister had become incensed at their use of the press via the Foreign Office News Department 'to sabotage the government's zeal for appeasement' (Cockett, 1990: 79). In this context, it was unsurprising that Chamberlain and his allies in the Treasury and the Cabinet Office refused to condone any strengthening of their opponents' position or broadening of their responsibilities. In the event, Leeper and Vansittart were dismissed a few months later and the News Department was silenced over the Munich Agreement that ceded control of the disputed Sudetenland regions of Czechoslovakia to Germany.

From this point, the Prime Minister asserted a tight command of the communication of foreign policy via the British media, managing to suppress critical commentary of appeasement by utilising close personal contacts with senior editors and proprietors and exploiting the effectiveness of the parliamentary lobby system developed by George Steward, his press relations officer in the Cabinet Office (Adamthwaite, 1983). In Richard Cockett's opinion, the 'increasingly singular and partisan conduct of foreign affairs run by Chamberlain from Downing Street' meant this was a period where the boundaries between the public interest of the nation and the political self-interest of the Prime Minister became blurred insidiously (Cockett, 1990: 82; see also Cockett, 1989: 5–16).

Managing Spain

Appreciation of these general trends and tensions in official communication and publicity strategies during the late 1930s not only provides context to an examination of British government news management in the Spanish Civil War but also reveals how, in many respects, the government's policy on this matter confounded these wider patterns. In political terms, the Foreign Office News Department may have been a major location for official resistance to the policy of appeasement but this opposition never materialised to any significant extent with regard to Spain. When war broke out in July 1936 – an event that took the Foreign Office as much by surprise as it did the international media (see Peters, 1986: 228) – the Prime Minister, Stanley Baldwin, instructed Anthony Eden, the Foreign Secretary, that 'on no account' must Britain be brought 'into the fight on the side of the Russians' (Edwards, 1979: 18). Eden later resigned in February 1938 in protest at Chamberlain's decision to enter into negotiations with Mussolini, despite Italy's flagrant interventions in Spain, and became a key figure in Conservative Party opposition to appeasement (see Rose, 1982). Nevertheless, he shared Baldwin's views at the outset that British interests were best served by remaining neutral over the conflict and, in seeking to dissuade France from providing arms to the Republic, played a central role in the development of the international agreement on non-intervention. Vansittart and Leeper concurred as well and, whilst it is true that Eden's position modified as evidence gathered of Italian and German duplicity over non-intervention, his preferred strategy for standing firm against the dictators was to bolster rather than abandon non-intervention through the introduction of effective frontier and sea patrols and the prohibition of the despatch of foreign volunteers.

There were several reasons why the anti-appeasers within the Foreign Office did not see Spain as a cause for resisting the wider thrust of government foreign policy. In 1936, appeasement was an emerging rather than established policy and the full extent of Italy and Germany's aggressive intentions had not yet become clear. There had been a general breakdown in the cordiality of relations between the Spanish and British governments prior to the war and British ministers and diplomats had a propensity to identify more closely with the social and military elites behind the rebellion. But the principal reason lay in the Foreign Office's fear of Communism (see Little, 1988). According to Jill Edwards:

> While Fascism and Communism were regarded in the Foreign Office as the 'mumps and measles' of world society, the former was believed to be an urgent but short-term problem; the latter a longer-term one, which in consequence was never quite out of view, and especially in regard towards France and Spain. (Edwards, 1979: 3)

One implication of this political cohesion was that there was none of the conflicts and counter-briefings that were so apparent in official communication in the lead-up to the Munich crisis (see Adamthwaite, 1983: 289). The British government spoke with one voice over Spain and, in contrast to the wider picture where appeasers generally opposed any increase in official propaganda and anti-appeasers advocated it, all sides sought to avoid, even suppress, public debate about the war. For example, in March 1937, Eden complained to the Cabinet that 'the difficulties of the present situation were being very much increased with the attitude of the Press and Parliament' and reminded Cabinet members:

> that the British Broadcasting Corporation published daily bulletins in regard to Spain, as well as weekly talks, and that these had a widespread effect resulting in pressure being put by constituents on Members of Parliament. If the British Broadcasting Corporation could be induced to drop their nightly statements it was suggested that it would have a quietening effect. (TNA, FO 395/546, Paper p1473/20/150: 220)

In response, Leeper undertook to speak to the BBC's Director of Programmes 'about these talks on Spain, but I am doubtful how far I can succeed' (ibid.: 219). Such recalcitrance was rooted in the official policy of non-intervention and the sustained concern of the British government to isolate the conflict symbolically, materially and politically. Furthermore, the Foreign Office News Department was the primary mechanism by which this policy was implemented as the acute intra-governmental conflict that led to its marginalisation occurred after the most intense period of media and public interest in the Spanish war had passed.

Foreign Office news management operated principally through two means – the routine, off-the-record briefings of senior diplomatic correspondents and the high-level consultations with senior editors, managers and proprietors of the major news organisations. Both of these aspects are explored in the sections that follow.

Diplomatic correspondents and the Foreign Office

I trust it will cause no offence if I say that by many in our service the journalist is regarded as a potential enemy rather than a willing collaborator. With few exceptions he is undoubtedly the latter, but he is very quick to guess when he is regarded as the former. Tactful handling of the press is surely as much a part of diplomacy as tactful handling of foreign governments. I doubt how far this is appreciated by some of our missions. (Rex Leeper, 31 July 1937, TNA, FO 395/ 553, Paper p3228/56/150: 273–4)

The News Department's cultivation of close links with a select group of diplomatic correspondents was one manifestation of Rex Leeper's belief that the British government needed to think on 'wider and bolder lines' in its communication strategies. These regular briefings, in which Leeper often spoke with surprising candour about Foreign Office concerns, proved highly effective in influencing press opinion during this period and marked a departure from the suspicious stance traditionally adopted by the Foreign Office towards journalists. As Cockett notes, '[Leeper] realised that, with a certain degree of flattery, openness and coercion, the diplomatic correspondents could be welded into a cohesive body who would always put the Foreign Office view in the press' (1990: 74).

Most journalists in Leeper's cadre represented 'up-market' newspapers, revealing the Foreign Office's principal concern with elite opinion formation, both domestically and internationally (Adamthwaite, 1983: 282). Ministers and officials recognised that British news was closely monitored by other governments and the Foreign Office was keen to avoid situations where negative, inaccurate or provocative media analysis could exacerbate international tensions. The BBC was of particular concern on this score as the principle of public broadcasting, in which a state-funded media corporation retained significant autonomy from government control, was still a novel conception in the 1930s and one that was imperfectly understood overseas, especially in the Fascist states where the BBC was seen as the official mouthpiece of the British government (Haworth, 1981: 48).

Despite these political sensitivities, Leeper's lobby was not a significant element in official management of the editorial content of the BBC for two reasons. First, these arrangements were intended to shape rather than respond to the news agenda through the strategic and selective release of factual information and unattributed comment. But the BBC was not a major news-gathering organisation during this period and its news service was heavily dependent on news agency material (Scannell and Cardiff, 1991: 105). This news-processing function was, of course, important and required the Foreign Office News Department to remain in 'almost daily' contact with the BBC on the material used. Nevertheless, Leeper acknowledged this was largely an ex post facto process, very different from the agenda-building function of the diplomatic lobby:

News comes into the BBC from agencies up to the last minute and we have to rely on the judgement of the BBC staff as to what is broadcast by them.

When they are in doubt they telephone to us and we advise them, but very often they may have no doubts where they ought to have them. The Foreign Office cannot under existing arrangements do more to check the news bulletins than is being done at present. (Foreign Office minute, 13 March 1937, TNA, FO 395/546, Paper p3261/1/150: 22)

Second, for all its emerging independence of spirit, the BBC remained formally accountable to government and, as is shown later, there were strong institutional mechanisms in place by which government ministers and officials could directly exert influence on editorial content at the highest levels. It is also true that consultations and representations of this kind occurred with the proprietors and senior editors of privately owned newspapers but the government had to tread more cautiously in these dealings and their effectiveness depended, ultimately, on the co-operation and biddability of particular proprietors and editors. One benefit of Leeper's diplomatic lobby was that it allowed Foreign Office influence to extend more widely, encompassing newspapers less sympathetically predisposed towards the government and its foreign policy.[4]

An example of this is offered by the case of Frederick Voigt, who worked as Diplomatic Correspondent for the *Manchester Guardian* during the war and was one of the most influential figures in Leeper's lobby. By the late 1930s, the *Manchester Guardian* had an international status that belied its regional origins and was admired for the quality of its international news coverage and analysis (see, for example Orwell, 1938: 85). Under the guidance of its editor, William Crozier, the paper was staunchly critical of the Fascist regimes in Europe (see Ayerst, 1971: 507–28) and supported the Republic in its resistance to Franco's rebellion. It was also opposed the British government's policy on Spain. As Crozier explained in a letter to Voigt about the paper's stance on non-intervention:

> No, we are not against non-intervention, but we have the right, and exercise it, of attacking the Government when its non-intervention policy works out, as in my opinion it does, as intervention against the Spanish government.
>
> I will not go into the whole question of what, or how much, the Spanish government stands for, nor what sort of regime will follow it if it wins the war. My view is that the victory of Franco will mean a detestable government for the Spanish people, a bad one for the international ideas in which I believe, and a dangerous one for this country. (letter from Crozier to Voigt, 12 Feb 1937, MGA: 217/103a)

Frederick Voigt was the Berlin correspondent for the *Manchester Guardian* between 1920 and 1933 but moved to Paris after threats were made against him for his critical coverage of the rise of the Nazis. He returned to London in 1934 and was appointed diplomatic correspondent for the paper, a post specifically created for him by Crozier. However, if Voigt's anti-Fascist credentials were as impeccable as his editor's, his opinions on the Spanish Civil War diverged to a considerable degree. He professed to pro-Republican sympathies but his support was more qualified and conditional in tone than that of his colleagues.

One major theme is his correspondence with Crozier during the early stages of the civil war was the military impotence of Britain and its inability to impose its will by force. He wrote in December 1936:

> Had the Spanish Civil War broken out in, say 1910 or 1912, we should have said to Italy or Germany 'hands off!' Had it been postponed to 1937 or 1938 we should also be able to say 'hands off!' Now we cannot – it is too dangerous, all the more so as we still have Italy as well as Germany as a potential foe. . . . To keep the gangsters from our doorsteps should be the essence of our foreign policy, once we have made sure that they cannot break through the doors . . . Until our defences are much stronger, we shall have no freedom of manoeuvre and must lie low. (letter from Voigt to Crozier, 14 December 1936, MGA: 216/376h–j)

In the same letter, Voigt also questioned the democratic credentials of the Republican government, commenting:

> The M.G. [Manchester Guardian] has, in its leaders, shown a bias in favour of Republican Spain – rightly, in my opinion, and realistically, though I would personally have been less inclined to refer to Republican Spain as 'democratic', for there can be no democracy in civil war and a Government victory doesn't necessarily mean that democracy will prevail. (letter from Voigt to Crozier, 14 December 1936, MGA: 216/376c)

He elaborated this point in later correspondence with Crozier:

> I must say the Government seems to me like a sort of Committee of Defence, though an efficient one. I doubt whether its writ runs outside Madrid or Valencia. Even in Madrid, where its military authority must be considerable, its civil authority seems to be very weak . . . The government are not the one that was returned in the last elections. They hardly represent the Spanish people. But, of course, in civil war there can be no representative government, no democracy. (letter from Voigt to Crozier, 31 December 1936, MGA: 216/409a–b)

Voigt's scepticism derived from two sources – his concerns about Republican atrocities and his hostility towards the Soviet Union and its influence in Spain ('Germany under the blackest despotism would be nearer to us than Russia under the most enlightened rule' (letter from Voigt to Crozier, 14 December 1936, MGA: 216/376d).) The issue of Republican 'terror' became something of a personal fixation that he returned to time and again in his correspondence. He estimated that 10,000 executions had been conducted in Madrid alone by the end of 1936 and claimed, 'The terror in Madrid is appalling – it isn't just a little revolutionary ebullition in times of stress and civil war' (letter from Voigt to Crozier, 31 December 1936, MGA: 216/409a–b). He raised this estimate to 50,000 four days later and, in February 1937, wrote:

> The Spaniards, I mean those who are taking part, are more and more leaving the foreigners to fight and are themselves committing atrocities

behind the lines or getting into the various committees that spring up everywhere à la Russe. Many decent Spaniards in Loyalist territory are praying for Franco to come. I have no doubt that if Franco had suffered defeat exactly the same state of affairs would prevail in his territory – as far as atrocities are concerned there is little to choose between the two factions (though the atrocities differ somewhat in character, for the Spanish government has tried to stop them while the Rebel government has not, as far as I can discover) . . . It does seem to me that the main lesson we should try to impart is horror and disgust over this and every civil war. (letter from Voigt to Crozier, 11 March 1937, MGA, 217/99d–e)

For all these reasons, Voigt supported the British government policy of non-intervention, initially with reluctance – describing it as 'the least of the evils we have to choose from' (ibid.) – but later with greater, and misguided, optimism – 'NON INTERVENTION IS NOW WORKING IN FAVOUR OF THE LOYALISTS AND EUROPEAN PEACE' (telegram from Voigt to Crozier, 31 March 1937, MGA, 217/225).

Voigt's views were not popular with his colleagues at the paper. His most vocal critic was Robert Dell, the paper's Geneva correspondent, who felt that Voigt's articles about the war were compromising the paper's editorial stance. In November 1936, he complained to Gordon Phillips, who was acting as editor of the paper following Crozier's absence through illness:

The mischief about Voigt's articles is that they are continually quoted in the foreign press as the opinions of the M.G. and are believed to be quotations from leaders. As they are often quite opposed to the policy of the paper, people think the M.G. is wobbling. (letter from Dell to Phillips, 4 November 1937, MGA: 216/310b)

Dell reiterated his concerns two months later, claiming that an unedited piece written by Voigt had been sent directly to the French news agency Havas and was reported as an example of a shift in the *Manchester Guardian*'s stance. (The implication taken from the report was that the paper approved of plans to cede control of Spanish Morocco to Germany in the event of a Republican victory.) Gordon Phillips expressed alarm at this news, in particular to discover the possibility that Havas was using Voigt's material when it had not been 'passed by Manchester' (letter from Phillips to Dell, 17 January 1937, MGA: 217/34).

It is not just the discordance of Voigt's views with the mainstream of opinion at the *Manchester Guardian* that is striking but also how closely they accorded with Foreign Office thinking over Spain. Dell was convinced that Voigt had become unduly influenced by his Foreign Office contacts and was too readily disposed to accept Foreign Office views (see also Cockett, 1989: 21). He wrote to Phillips saying, 'He has become a die-hard Tory Imperialist and accepts everything that Vansittart and Leeper say as gospel truth . . . It is a great pity that he does not use his own judgement' (letter from Dell to Phillips, 4 November 1936,

MGA, 216/310b). Phillips agreed, commenting, 'Voigt is surprisingly ready to act as a mouthpiece for the Foreign Office' (letter from Phillips to Dell, 9 November 1936, MGA, 216/311a).

The convergence between Voigt's opinions and the lines advanced by the Foreign Office over Spain does not, on its own, prove his complicity. The similarity in their opinions could have been coincidental. Certainly, Voigt was no political naif – he wrote widely on international affairs (see Voigt, 1938, 1949a, 1949b) and his reputation as an experienced, thoughtful and erudite public commentator extended beyond his death in 1957 (see, for example, Gannon, 1971: 80–8; Haworth, 1981: 53). However, there are several indications that suggest there was some justification in Dell and Phillips' suspicions.

First, it is clear that Voigt held his Foreign Office contacts in high esteem. In November 1936 he wrote to Phillips saying, 'Of the British, French and German Foreign Offices, I find the British by far the most informative and least propagandist' (25 November 1936, MGA, 216/399c). A measure of his trust in the veracity of Foreign Office information was the confidence with which he pontificated about the situation in Spain, despite having no personal experience of the war during its initial stages. For example, his assessments of the scale of Republican 'terror' in Madrid and the miserable lives of its citizens could only have been derived from Foreign Office evidence, accounts and interpretations, as he did not visit the city himself until June 1937 (and then only briefly). Furthermore, there was no discussion in his correspondence about the political orientations of the Foreign Office and the impact this might have had on the information and interpretations provided.

Second, he never complained about the restrictions placed upon him, he took great care to maintain his departmental links and was anxious to avoid the publication of any information that could compromise this relationship. The extent of his (over-) sensitivity on this matter was revealed in a testy memo he sent to Gordon Phillips, in which he claimed that a recent leader column in the paper had drawn on 'strictly confidential' information he had passed on about the possibility of a British blockade of Spanish ports:

> Perhaps the leader writer got the information from another source. But in that case it would have been better to send me word asking whether any harm could be done by publishing it. The code in these matters is very rigid here – a single indiscretion may be enough to close all sources for ever to any 'diplomatic correspondent'. I wonder whether it would not be better if messages marked 'confidential' by myself (and Friday's was marked 'strictly confidential') were seen only by the editor or acting editor . . . I trust that Eden's attention will not be called to this morning's leader. If he asks 'how did the M.G. get to know?', I shall be in a nice mess . . . I daresay everything will be alright but I must say that if the F.O. take me to task this afternoon, they will be entirely justified. I am sorry to bother you with this matter, but I feel that it is of the utmost importance. (11 January 1937, MGA: 217/28b–c)

In response, Phillips reassured him that the information about the blockade plans had been reported extensively in other national newspapers over the previous few days but agreed that 'great care should be taken when information is divulged on a purely confidential basis – at least, that is, until the facts have been assumed or disclosed elsewhere' (12 January 1937, MGA: 217/32).[5]

The third indication of the extent to which Voigt's autonomy had been compromised concerns events related to the trip he made to Spain in mid 1937, to witness the war first-hand. Initially, Voigt planned to visit Republican and Nationalist territories and to travel extensively in both zones. Crozier convinced him that it was unlikely that Franco's press controllers would grant permission to a representative of the paper and, even if they did, he would be at grave personal risk from Gestapo agents. Despite this, Crozier had high hopes for Voigt's visit to Republican Spain and drew up a detailed list of 'subjects under which [he] might group [his] material' (13 April 1937, MGA, 217/266a–b).[6] Voigt arrived in Madrid in June 1937 and he established contact with several of the main foreign correspondents based in the city. Despite the wide-ranging agenda proposed by Crozier, he focused considerable effort on pursuing the Red Terror angle and, on one occasion, tried to persuade the journalist Martha Gellhorn to smuggle what he claimed was an innocuous dispatch out of Spain. What he was actually giving her was a graphic account of atrocities that he had not personally witnessed. Ernest Hemingway was so outraged by Voigt's actions he had to be restrained from assaulting him (Moorehead, 2003: 149).

However, it was only on his return from Madrid that the full extent of his obsession with this subject became apparent. On 1 July 1937, Mark Patrick, a Member of Parliament, wrote to Lord Cranborne, Eden's deputy at the Foreign Office recording the details of a conversation Voigt had recently had with Harold Nicolson, then a National Labour Party MP. Voigt, he said, was 'obsessed with the stories of massacre in the earlier stages of the war, and his first object was to find out what he could of the truth' (letter from Patrick to Lord Cranborne, 1 July 1937, TNA, FO 371/21296, Paper w12905/1/41: 318). As part of his investigations, Voigt claimed to have gained access to the Madrid police files by posing as a representative of an English insurance company seeking information on the death of some clients. He claimed that every execution in the Madrid area had been recorded individually on a pink card and, as he did not have time to conduct a full count of all the cards, he measured the length of a thousand cards and used this to estimate the total number of cards in the police files. On this basis, Voigt calculated there were 32,000 records of executions in the metropolitan area of Madrid alone. From this he projected 'that a total of forty-five thousand victims for the whole Madrid area would be a conservative estimate' and that, across the Republican sector as a whole, 'the total number of victims must have run into hundreds of thousands' (ibid.: 319–20).

Historians still dispute the full scale of the Red Terror in Republican Spain but most would agree that Voigt's figures considerably overestimated its extent.[7] Nevertheless, this should have been a sensational journalistic coup, assuming the veracity of his claims to have accessed official records. The international media had been full of atrocity stories for months and those opposed to the Republic in particular would have seized on 'independent' evidence of this kind. But the story did not gain any prominence anywhere and no record survives in the Guardian Archives of him having discussed his findings with Crozier. Voigt alluded to the statistics in the latter part of an article he wrote on his return from Spain but made no mention of how he had acquired the numbers ('THE DESTINY OF SPAIN: A Conflict That is Destroying a Civilization', the *Manchester Guardian*, 1 July 1937: 11). He also claimed that he had decided to provide the information to his parliamentary contacts 'because he knew that the Manchester Guardian would not print his story' (letter from Patrick to Lord Cranborne, ibid.). This was a serious allegation of unprofessionalism against his colleagues and one that begs the question as to why he sought the information in the first place. It could have been an intelligence-gathering exercise intended for official sources in Britain as, within a year, he was acting as an agent for the shadowy 'Z Organisation', an informal spy ring set up by Sir Robert Vansittart to gather intelligence on Nazi Germany (Read and Fischer, 1984: 84).

Certainly, the claims generated considerable interest in Foreign Office circles. John Cairncross,[8] private secretary to Lord Hankey, the head of Intelligence Services, described the information as 'highly important, filling in and completing certain gaps in our own reports. For the first time we have a fairly reliable estimate of the number of non-combatants killed in Madrid' (TNA, FO 371/21296, Paper w12905/1/41: 316). Anthony Eden agreed, describing the figures as 'most interesting'. Another Foreign Office official recommended these 'grim figures' should remain for internal use only and that the Department's response to a recently tabled parliamentary question on the subject 'should answer in general terms . . . to avoid controversial cross-questions' (ibid.: 317).

High level representations

Voigt's activities demonstrate how effectively Leeper's diplomatic lobby system could influence the perceptions and practices of senior journalists and, thereby, infiltrate the editorial content of their parent organisations. The rules governing non-attribution of information meant that much Foreign Office information could neither be ignored nor contested because its origins were obscured. As Gordon Phillips reflected, during his term as acting editor at the *Manchester Guardian*:

> The pity is that we cannot say point blank that these are these views and assertions are the result of close contact with the Foreign Office. Naturally, professional students of foreign affairs are well aware of that point by this time, but one also has to bear in mind, and perhaps should bear in mind more insistently, the attitude of the ordinary newspaper reader who is still unsteeped in the subtleties of our diplomatic correspondent. (letter from Phillips to Dell, 9 November 1936, MGA, 216/311a)

But indirect, tactical manoeuvring of this kind was not the sum of the government's news management over Spain. Ministers and officials also exerted influence more directly by making frequent representations to news proprietors, managers and editors. The government's preferred approach in this respect 'was based on persuasion rather than compulsion' (Adamthwaite, 1983: 282).

As noted, the BBC was a particular concern and the Foreign Office was in frequent contact with senior managers at the Corporation over matters related to its news and current affairs coverage throughout the 1930s. Although ministers and officials frequently paid lip service to the principles of BBC independence, in practice they were often vexed by what they perceived as unnecessarily contentious and controversial coverage. Their most acute concerns in this respect were the BBC news talks programmes in which selected politicians, journalists and academics were invited to contribute comments on topical issues.

On many occasions, the government made retrospective complaints about the content of particular talks. For example, in 1933 the Foreign Office was incensed when the respected journalist Vernon Bartlett suggested that Germany was justified in feeling aggrieved at its post-war settlement. Leeper claimed this commentary contravened the BBC Charter and, although Bartlett received public support for his comments, he was removed from the BBC roster for several years as a consequence (Haworth, 1981: 48). On other occasions, the government moved to prevent programmes from being broadcast. In 1935, the BBC proposed a series of talks by British politicians that would include Oswald Mosley, the leader of the British Union of Fascists, and Harry Pollit, General Secretary of the Communist Party of Great Britain. Officials quickly communicated their displeasure, particularly at the prospect of Pollit's presence, and both news talks were eventually abandoned after a directive from the Board of Governors (ibid.: 49).

The early stages of the Spanish Civil War coincided with the period when tensions between the BBC and the government were at their most acute during the inter-war period. By early 1937, however, senior managers at the BBC and the Foreign Office News Department started negotiations intended to facilitate greater mutual understanding and to create a situation where the BBC could participate fully 'in the ventilation of questions affecting foreign affairs' whilst remaining mindful that 'His Majesty's Government are not thereby embarrassed in the conduct of their affairs' (letter from Cecil Graves, BBC Director of Programmes, to Leeper, 26 April 1937, TNA FO 395/547, Paper p2120/20/150: 279). The Corporation's coverage of the Spanish Civil War was a prominent consideration in these negotiations. In May 1937, Leeper had a meeting with the BBC's Director of Programmes and Director of Talks in which, according to his account, '[t]hey tried to tie me down to what could or could not be said about Spain or what they wanted me to say about other countries' (ibid.: 276).

> I gave them my own view of the proper function of the BBC as regards foreign affairs. My criticism of the press and of the BBC was that they never led the public into real channels of thought, but allowed themselves to be led by the sensation-mongers . . . What seemed to me to be required,

I told them, was that the BBC should deal with the subjects that really mattered to this country and should thereby try to get the public thinking on sensible lines. I suggested therefore a meeting in the Sec of State's room with Sir R. Vansittart, Mr Graves and Sir R. Maconachie for the BBC at which a general discussion might take place on the major objectives of British foreign policy which would explain to the BBC on what subjects they should try to fasten public attention during the next 6 months. The press unfortunately worked on a day to day programme, whereas the BBC should have a long term programme in mind. (ibid.)

The specific triggers for this meeting were Foreign Office objections to two news talks broadcast in early 1937. One of the talks outlined the Nazis' perspective on international relations and the second extolled the successes of Communism in Russia. Leeper and Vansittart pilloried both talks, respectively condemning them as 'pernicious stuff' and 'quite intolerable' (TNA FO 395/546, Paper p1223/20/150: 213 and 218) and Vansittart requested an urgent meeting with Sir John Reith, the Director General of the BBC, to discuss their wider implications.

A comparison of Vansittart's and Reith's separate accounts of this meeting, held on 9 March 1937, provides a valuable insight into the government's specific editorial interventions over BBC coverage of Spain (see ibid.: 218–19; and BBC Written Records R34/440). The initial part of the meeting concerned the two disputed programmes and both accounts concur closely as to the substance of this discussion. Reith summarised Vansittart's wishes regarding future broadcasts in a secret memorandum to Cecil Graves, the BBC's Controller of Programmes:

> What he would like is for us to keep off Communism and Nazi-ism and Fascism for the next year or two, and if, for any reason, we were unable or unwilling to do so, he asked that there might be good liaison with his people in order that the ground might be properly prepared and such talks as were given not be open to misunderstanding and, above all, not be liable to cause trouble to the Foreign Office in the delicate state of affairs existing and likely to continue to exist. (memorandum from Reith to Cecil Graves, 9 March 1937 BBC Written Records Archive R34/440)

Vansittart's record of the meeting concludes on this point, with an expression of his satisfaction that:

> [Reith] was in complete agreement about the need for close collaboration between us . . . He was most friendly and helpful and suggested that the purpose I had in view might be achieved by even closer contact between Mr Leeper on the one hand and Mr Graves and Sir Richard Maconachie on the other. (NA, FO 371/546)

Reith's account, however, details an additional discussion concerning the BBC's news coverage of the Spanish Civil War. It is worth relating Reith's record of this part of the conversation in full:

With regard to Spanish news, [Vansittart] says there is now little doubt that Franco will be in Madrid and in due course in control of Spain. He says Franco feels that the B.B.C. and The Times are against him and therefore the Government must be against him too. He says this is deplorable, since it will send Franco more into the arms of Italy and Germany than ever. The Foreign Office are very anxious to prevent the establishment of a new Fascist state in Spain, which would, of course, put France in a nice position, and the British Government is the only power that can prevent this from happening. He quite honestly feels that our Spanish news will make a considerable difference to the future in this respect.

He would be very grateful if we could at least put out no more [Republican] government news, irrespective of the amount that comes in, than Insurgent news. It is quite obvious, in fact, that he would be glad if we became sufficiently obviously pro-Insurgent to convince Franco that we and therefore the Government are not anti-Franco. He would, in addition be very pleased if we could see our way to dropping the term 'insurgent', which apparently is resented on that side, adopting perhaps 'Nationalists'.

You will want to have a talk with me about this when you consider the matter. I think we can without inconvenience do what he wants with regards to Spanish news, but I don't think we can adopt the new term. We might, however, drop the old one. (memorandum from Reith to Cecil Graves, 9 March 1937, BBC Written Records Archive R34/440)

This is definitive evidence of the degree to which the British government engaged in special pleading on Franco's behalf, even to the extent of proposing that the BBC should bias coverage intentionally in the Nationalist's favour. It also shows the readiness with which British officials were prepared to write off the Republic's chances, even though the war still had two years to run at this stage. Furthermore, it demonstrates how willingly the government invoked issues of national security as justification for these requests, an argument that proved very potent a year later in securing the supplication of the British news media in their reporting of the Munich Agreement and appeasement more generally. Reith's response is also revealing in that it demonstrates a considerable pliability to Vansittart's requests, even though he expressed reservations about the adoption of the term 'Nationalist', presumably due to concerns about audience comprehension.

It might be assumed that the BBC was a special case in terms of government influence for, apart from the political, financial and regulatory connections between the BBC and the state, the Corporation's management during this period was renowned for its 'old-guard rectitude', 'staid respectability' and 'unimaginative trustworthiness' (Haworth, 1981: 51–2). However, high-level representations were also made to other media organisations about Spanish coverage. For example, in September 1936, Sir George Mounsey, an Assistant Under-Secretary at the Foreign Office, received news was from the British Consul in Palma that a Reuter's correspondent had been alerted to Italian contraventions of the non-intervention agreement and was seeking to publicise their details. One of Mounsey's officials commented:

If this is done, we can well imagine the renewed flood of criticism and counter-accusations which will at once be let loose in our own and the continental press . . . I assume that we wish breaches of the agreement, if they must be, to be considered by the Madison Committee and in a reasonably calm atmosphere. Publication of these details will have the opposite effect and I submit that we should reply accordingly at once [to the Vice Consul in Palma] and, in case Reuters have by now received anything, speak to their Head Office. (memorandum from W. Roberts to Sir George Mounsey, 9 September 1936, TNA FO 371/2053, Paper w10854/62/41: 39)

Mounsey immediately consulted Vansittart and responded by saying:

The line we wish to maintain is that while Reuters or other press agents are of course at liberty to publish what information they please, we are for our part anxious to let the past, in which no government has a clean slate, be ignored, in the hope that the [non-intervention] agreement which has been confirmed by the meeting of the Committee today may have a chance of being carried out in a friendly and harmonious atmosphere . . . Perhaps [the] News Department would speak to Reuters in the same sense. (letter from Sir George Mounsey to W. Roberts, ibid.)

Leeper duly contacted a senior editorial representative at Reuters the following day outlining the official position.

Government sources persisted in the pursuit of this 'line', even when the credibility of non-intervention was under severe pressure. For example, in March 1938, *The Evening News* ran a story based on a British United Press agency report of a speech by Mussolini that was being interpreted as a warning to France not to intervene in Spain ('FRANCE WARNED BY MUSSOLINI: "KEEP OUT OF SPAIN OR – "', *The Evening News*, 23 March 1938). Sir Alexander Cadogan at the Foreign Office immediately wrote to Sir Horace Wilson at Downing Street:

I send you herewith a cutting from this evening's 'Evening News' . . . I think you will agree that if Mussolini in fact expressed himself as reported by the British United Press, these headlines are a monstrous perversion of the truth. The paper 'Il Tevere', from which a quotation was also made, is well known to be a scurrilous rag with no circulation and little influence: it often expresses itself in terms contrary to the policy of the Fascist Government.

I was wondering if in the circumstances the Prime Minister would like some representations made to the Editor or Proprietor of the 'Evening News'? I can hardly imagine that such mischief-making is likely to appeal to Mr. Chamberlain at a moment when it is above all in our interests to come to some arrangements with the Italian Government. (letter from Cadogan to Wilson, 24 March 1938, TNA, FO 395/562, Paper p1407/4/150: 114–15)

Wilson agreed that representations should be made to *The Evening News* but voiced his suspicion that the questionable interpretation 'was another instance of mischief arising from the activities of the "British (!) United Press" ' (ibid.) – an accusation that proved groundless on further investigation. As a News Department official reported:

> I spoke on this matter to Mr Gayton of 'The Evening News', who will inform his editor of our representations. The trouble arises from irresponsible sub-editing and I do not think that, on this occasion, the British United Press can be really blamed. (ibid.: 113)

These examples not only show that ministers and officials sought to intervene in the editorial activities of news organisations operating in the free market but also their confidence that these representations would be acted upon promptly and fully by these editors and proprietors. This begs the question as to why officials felt they had could depend on their discretion on such a divisive and contentious foreign policy matter.

Owners and editors

The compliance of several proprietors and editors over Spain contrasts with the tensions and conflicts that punctuated their relations with the government on other occasions during the inter-war periods. The British establishment viewed press barons like Lord Beaverbrook and Lord Rothermere with considerable suspicion and no little fear, recognising that their political interests and interventions did not always align with those of the government or Conservative Party leadership. The most notorious occasion occurred in 1930–31 when Rothermere and Beaverbrook used their papers to challenge Stanley Baldwin's leadership of the Conservative Party in their battle to secure free trade in the British Empire which was protected by external tariffs. Their actions led to Baldwin's famous admonition that they exercised 'power without responsibility – the prerogative of the harlot through the ages' (speech given by Baldwin, 18 March 1931, see Curran and Seaton, 2003: 38).

To understand why conflict of this kind was not prominent in 'free media' relations over Spain, there is a need to examine the broader political economy of these sectors in the late 1930s and the manner in which it shaped the specific motives and concerns of proprietors and senior editors on this topic. Tables 5.1 and 5.2 provide a summary of several key political, economic and organisational features of the main daily morning newspapers in Britain during the Spanish Civil War period (note that the *Manchester Guardian* has also been included because of its influential international status during this period).

The circulation figures demonstrate the vast audiences several of these newspapers commanded. Newspaper readership in Britain increased exponentially during the 1930s, to the extent that, by the end of the decade, seventy per cent of the adult population regularly read a daily paper (Bingham, 2004). This phenomenal level of market penetration was the result of an intense circulation war that began in the early 1930s and continued, albeit at a lower level of intensity, up until the start of the Second World War. Capitalisation costs escalated, as popular newspapers, in particular, expanded and revolutionised their formats to provide more lifestyle, celebrity and sports coverage and conducted expensive promotional campaigns, in which readers were offered a variety of free goods and services in return for their subscriptions (see Curran and Seaton, 2003: 57). Some were more successful than others in maintaining profitability as, by 1937, eighteen per cent of national and local newspapers in Britain were operating at a loss (Koss, 1990: 997). That same year, *The Morning Post*, a high-Tory paper established in 1772, merged with the *Daily Telegraph* due to a steep decline in its circulation.

Revenue yields from advertising also increased in significance – specifically, because technological innovations in photography and printing permitted the development of new forms of display advertising in the press and, more generally, because consumer spending on luxury, lifestyle and leisure products grew throughout the decade, marking the formative manifestation of contemporary consumer society (Constantine, 1983). The impact of advertising revenue affected the sector differently. For the elite newspapers, it provided a buttress against the need for slavish pursuit of mass circulation as advertisers valued the elite composition of their readership. For the popular press, however, it accelerated the competition for readers, as commercial interests sought to gain access to mass working-class markets (Curran and Seaton, 2003: 63).

The changing business structure of the press had two implications for the editorial content of the national press. First, many newspapers started to downgrade coverage of political and foreign affairs, in recognition that 'human interest' stories were a better guarantor of increased circulation than 'public interest' ones. This process was most evident in the popular press. For example, the *Daily Mirror* nearly doubled its circulation between 1930 and 1939 and, over the same period, halved its coverage of political, social and economic issues (ibid.). This de-emphasising of politics and foreign affairs also occurred, albeit to a lesser extent, in the elite press (Koss, 1990: 998). Second, commercial demands, particularly in the popular press sector, tended to discourage editors from dwelling on the gravity of the international situation, as circulations and advertising revenues were likely to suffer from pessimistic prognoses (Williams, 1998: 127).

These increasing economic pressures provide one explanation as to why some proprietors were receptive to the government's requests regarding their coverage of the Spanish Civil War, as their commercial self-interest in maintaining a climate conducive to consumer confidence chimed with the government's political reasons for seeking to cool public debate about Spain (Cudlipp, 1980: 283). However, this Panglossian propensity was not universal – commercial inhibition of the coverage of foreign affairs was less acutely felt in the 'up-market' press (which adds a further explanation as to why so much government news management was targeted at this sector) and there was at least one popular title that sought to guide their readers on foreign affairs. The *News Chronicle* supported

Table 5.1 British 'popular' daily press (1936–39)

Paper	Principal proprietorial figures	Party–political orientation of paper	Strength of party affiliation	General position on international affairs	Editor(s)	Editorial autonomy	Circulation figures in 1937
Daily Mail	Harold Harmsworth (Lord Rothermere)	Conservative	Variable – anti-Baldwin, pro-Chamberlain	Anti-Communist, anti-Russian, pro-Fascist, pro-German, pro-rearmament, pro-appeasement	A. L. Cranfield (1936–38) R. J. Prew (1939–44)	Very limited	1,580,000
Daily Express	William Maxwell Aitken (Lord Beaverbrook)	Conservative	Variable – anti-Baldwin, anti-Churchill, pro-Chamberlain	'Splendid isolationism' – anti-Fascist, anti-Communist, cultivation of Empire, pro-appeasement	Arthur Christiansen (1933–56)	Very limited	2,329,000
News Chronicle	The Cadbury Family Trust	Liberal	Moderate – Liberal inclined, sympathetic to aspects of Labour policy	Anti-Fascist, anti-Communist and anti-Stalinist but sympathetic to aspects of the Soviet system, anti-appeasement, pro-League of Nations and	Gerald Barry (1936–47)	Moderate	1,324,000

Daily Herald	51 per cent of shares owned by J.S. Elias (Odhams Press), 49 per cent owned by trustees of the Labour Party and the TUC	Labour	Moderate to strong – connected and committed to the Labour Party; however, the paper often diverged from official policy	Anti-Fascist, anti-Communist and anti-Stalinist but sympathetic to aspects of the Soviet system, anti-appeasement pro-League of Nations and collective security; did not advocate rearmament	W. H. Stevenson (1931–37) Francis Williams (1937–40)	Weak to moderate	Over 2 million
Daily Mirror	No individual shareholding was sufficient to be deemed a controlling interest	Conservative	Weak – pro-Baldwin, anti-Chamberlain, pro-Eden, pro-Churchill	Anti-Fascist, anti-appeasement, pro-rearmament	Cecil Thomas (1934–49)	High	1,367,000
Daily Sketch	William Berry (Lord Camrose) and Gomer Berry (Lord Kemsley) (1928–36) Gomer Berry (Lord Kemsley) (1937–)	Conservative	Strong – pro-Baldwin, pro-Chamberlain, anti-Churchill	Anti-Communist, pro-appeasement	A. F. W. Sinclair (1936–1939)	Very limited	850,000

Table 5.2 British 'class' daily press (1936–39)

Paper	Principal proprietorial figures	Party-political orientation of paper	Strength of party affiliation	General position on international affairs	Editor(s)	Editorial autonomy	Circulation figures
Manchester Guardian	The Scott Trust	Liberal	Anti-Chamberlain	Anti-Fascist, anti-appeasement, pro-rearmament	W. Crozier (1932–44)	High	56,000
The Times	John Jacob Astor (90 per cent shareholding) John Walter IV (10 per cent shareholding)	Conservative	Strong – pro-Chamberlain	Cultivation of Empire, pro-appeasement, anti-Communist	Geoffrey Dawson (1912–19, 1923–41)	High	192,000 (1937)
Daily Telegraph	William Ewert Berry (Lord Camrose)	Conservative	Mixed – generally pro-Chamberlain but more sympathetic to the Eden/ Churchill line on Germany	Anti-Fascist, anti-Communist, anti-appeasement	Arthur E. Watson (1924–1950)	Low to moderate	489,568 (1936) 565,262 (1937) 662,730 (1938) 763,557 (1939)
Morning Post*	William Ewert Berry (Lord Camrose) (1937)	Conservative	Mixed – critical of Baldwin and Chamberlain but did not endorse alternatives	Anti-Fascist, anti-Communist, anti-appeasement, cultivation of Empire, pro-rearmament	H. A. Gwynne (1911–37)	High	132,000 (1930)

*merged with the Daily Telegraph in October 1937

the Republican government of Spain actively and highlighted the use of concentration camps in Germany, even though, as its senior editorial figures later testified, these policies sometimes resulted in a ' "loss of popularity and sale" ' (quoted in Koss, 1990: 993). Such an exception shows that economic compulsion was not the only factor that affected the editorial dispositions of particular papers during this period. Two other dimensions in particular need to be considered – the party-political relations of the press and the structures of their internal editorial decision-making.

By the late 1930s, the political affiliations of the British press were volunteered rather than commanded, as direct party-political control of national newspapers had effectively ended (Negrine, 1989: 57). Only the *Daily Herald* had a significant amount of party-political share ownership but, even here, the political interests of the Labour leadership often had to defer to the commercial interests of a paper seeking readerships beyond the party demographic (Gannon, 1971: 42–3). In the 1935 general election seven out of the ten national titles declared for Stanley Baldwin and his Conservative-led National Party. On face value, this could be seen to offer a further explanation for many papers' quiescence to the government agenda on Spain. But this would be to overstate the strength of the papers' party affiliations, and their general willingness to defer to the government's line on international affairs. The columns in Tables 5.1 and 5.2 on 'Strength of party affiliation' and 'General position on international affairs' represent a summation of each paper's political disposition around the time of the Spanish Civil War, and is derived from authoritative analyses of the press during this period (see Gannon, 1971; Koss, 1990; Cockett, 1989; Curran and Seaton, 2003). The results show that the national press occupied a diversity of political stances, many of which contradicted government policy. For example, much has been written about the failure of the British press to challenge Chamberlain's pursuit of appeasement to any concerted extent (see, for example, Adamthwaite, 1983; Cockett, 1989; Williams, 1998) but, while many were cowed into silence, only a minority endorsed the policy actively (the *Daily Mail*, the *Daily Express*, the *Daily Sketch* and *The Times*). Even the *Daily Telegraph* was often critical of the government's policy towards Germany, despite its traditional location in the Tory Party mainstream and approval of most other facets of government policy. There were also differences between the pro-appeasement papers. For example, the *Daily Mail*'s endorsement was a logical outcome of its fascist cheerleading throughout the 1930s, whereas the support of the *Daily Express* was rooted in its enthusiasm for 'splendid isolationism', in which Britain cultivated its imperial interests and ties with the United States and avoided becoming embroiled in the ideological divisions on the European mainland. Opinions were also divided inconsistently over the case for re-armament – endorsed by some papers in the pro-appeasement camp but criticised by others that also opposed appeasement (the *Daily Herald* and the *News Chronicle* for example).

Intra-party affiliations were at least as important as party affiliations in the ways newspapers negotiated their political positions, particularly on international affairs. Factional divisions within the Conservative Party were significant here as they destabilised the opportunities for consensus among the pro-Tory titles. Both the *Mail* and the *Express* supported Chamberlain but were hostile to his predecessor as a result of the long-standing personal enmities of their proprietors. More significantly, the emergence of an anti-appeasement lobby within the Conservative Party in late 1938, led by Churchill and Eden, provided a focus for, and expression of, individual papers' political stance on dealing with the Fascist powers.

These divisions within the government and dominant political party of the period over appeasement provide a further explanation for the nature of the political responses of many sections of the national press to the conflict in Spain. Contemporary media research has demonstrated that one tends to find the greatest constriction in media opinion and comment when there is greatest consensus among political and economic elites (see, for example, Schlesinger, 1989). The Spanish Civil War divided British society in many profound ways but the government's policy of non-intervention did not divide the British establishment to any significant extent. Even the main opposition party, which expressed its support for the Republic at the outset of the war, only belatedly translated this into opposition to non-intervention. In the context of this tacit but powerful political consensus, it is not surprising that many proprietors and editors, particularly those with pro-Conservative proclivities, were receptive to official representations that they should assist in cooling and containing the conflict through 'responsible' reporting practices.

The final decision-making over each paper's editorial policy varied according to its financial and organisational structure. Tunstall highlights two major patterns of editorship that prevailed in Britain until the 1960s. The first was that of an 'editor-manager' whose responsibility was to defer to editorial policies determined by the dominant owner or controlling interest. The second was the 'sovereign editor' who had considerable autonomy from proprietorial diktat (1996: 95). These distinctions are, of course, ideal types and should be thought of as extremes on a continuum in which the freedom of an editor to determine editorial policy ranges from the comprehensive to the highly restricted (see 'Editorial autonomy' in Tables 5.1 and 5.2). At the *Daily Mail*, the *Daily Express* and the *Daily Sketch*, the editors were kept on a tight rein by their proprietors. As Arthur Christiansen, editor at the *Daily Express* during the 1930s, conceded, ' "The policies were Lord Beaverbrook's job, the presentation mine" ' (Gannon, 1971: 36). However, if press barons still wielded considerable and instrumental influence in the 1930s, it was also a period occupied by 'editorial luminaries' who 'were self-consciously their own men' and who 'effectively established their hegemonies by discountenancing their hegemonies from above and by manifesting an ambivalent attitude towards their reading publics' (Koss, 1990: 1011). Examples of these included Geoffrey Dawson at *The Times*, Howell Arthur Gwynne at the *Morning Post*, William Crozier at the *Manchester Guardian* and Gerald Barry at the *News Chronicle*. In all of these cases, the political freedoms enjoyed by the editors were assisted by the diffuse patterns of ownership at their papers.[9]

In the case of the *Manchester Guardian*, this editorial autonomy resulted in an environment in which a variety of political opinions among its correspondents could be tolerated and accommodated. Gordon Phillips commented, during his stint as acting editor at the paper, 'There are times when you are all apt to seem to me, a rather wayward team' (letter from Phillips to Robert Dell, 9 November 1936, MGA, 216/311a). However, editorial sovereignty was not always a guarantee of political freedom or plurality – something which is most clearly demonstrated by an examination of the internal editorial politics of *The Times* during this period.

Tough Times

The Times' Geoffrey Dawson might be considered the doyen of British sovereign editors during this period for, throughout his tenure, he consistently resisted proprietorial interventions in the content of a paper that still commanded considerable international prestige and influence. He was first appointed in 1912 but resigned in 1919 in protest at the increased intrusiveness of the paper's new owner, Lord Northcliffe, in editorial matters. Following Northcliffe's death, Dawson was reappointed in 1923 and remained in post until his retirement in 1941. One reason for his longevity was that the new proprietors were less inclined to intervene than their predecessor but, on the occasions they did, Dawson remained defiant. For example, in 1938, John Walter, one of the co-proprietors, challenged a *Times*' leader item that supported the surrendering the Sudetenland to Germany. Dawson's response effectively disregarded Walter's objections, citing his 'own experience' of international affairs as justification (Koss, 1990: 1011).

Despite this independence, historical assessments have identified three major deficiencies in Dawson's editorship. First, *The Times* lost much of its vitality and ambition under his supervision, particularly in relation to its coverage of foreign affairs. As the paper's official history notes:

> The difference in the policy of *The Times* towards Germany from 1908 to 1914, and in the years from 1928 to 1939, is simply stated: in the former period the paper habitually led public opinion, in the latter it habitually followed it. (*History of* The Times, vol. IV, 1952: 817–18; see also Driberg, 1956: 227)

Second, a core aspect of this conservatism was loss of political independence. Dawson's resistance to proprietorial intervention found no equivalent expression in his dealings with government. He had always been a close confidant of senior government figures but these connections strengthened as international tensions grew. In his role as editor, he became one of the major apologists for appeasement and, in his political lobbying, he became one of its minor architects. He was a key figure in the 'Cliveden Set',[10] and 'identified not so much with the Conservative interest as with the ministerial mind' (Koss, 1990: 1008).

Third, his editorship was intolerant of dissenting voices – indeed, it could be argued he pursued his own political agenda as fervently as any press baron. In

1929 he abolished the position of Foreign Editor, following the death of Dr Harold Williams, which enabled him to assert greater direct control of this key element of the paper's coverage (Wrench, 1955: 818).

Dawson and his Foreign News Editor, Ralph Deakin, were perturbed by the complaints from pro-Nationalist sources that *The Times* was hostile to their cause and they expended considerable efforts to anticipate and allay such criticism. For example, the ultimate purpose of Deakin's investigation of the reasons for the unaccountable delays in telegrams from the Nationalist sector, discussed in Chapter 2, was to secure more news from Franco's side. Deakin wrote to Holburn, their principal correspondent on the Nationalist side:

> The authorities serving General Franco still complain that we publish too little from their side. *We want more*, but it is apparently not to be had, and every message transmitted limps into London a worthless and emaciated apology for news. (letter from Deakin to Holburn, 5 March 1937, Deakin Papers, TNL Archive, original emphasis)

Despite the apparent intractability of these difficulties, Deakin promised to 'remain as cheerful as we can, and go on trying' and, in a letter to Dawson, recommended that the paper should engineer equivalence through concerted editorial strategy:

> The Night Staff might be well advised to give a rather better show to Holburn's material. It is, of course, partly a question of space, but if the attitude is that, 'There is only so much space, and Madrid and Valencia must take precedence, and there is nothing left for Salamanca', it would be futile to leave Holburn in Spain. With a little statecraft we may yet achieve a good service from him. (This is not to suggest that the paper should be victimised in order to cover the censor's delinquencies.) All that matters is that the Night Staff should be instructed that The Times' policy requires that the service from the two belligerent sides should be as nicely balanced as possible. (letter from Deakin to Dawson, 7 March 1937, Deakin Papers, TNL Archive)[11]

However, before the strategy could be implemented, the paper's relationship with the Nationalists was plunged into crisis, following the publication of George Steer's eyewitness account of the aerial destruction of Guernica by German aviators under Nationalist command (see Chapter 2). One element in the Nationalists' response to the international outcry over the incident was to impugn the integrity of both Steer and *The Times*, an issue that was also picked up in high-level representations made by the German government. Dawson was deeply shocked by the escalating ramifications of the controversy and, in an infamous letter to the paper's Berlin correspondent, revealed his fixation with not offending German sensibilities:

> '[I]t would interest me to know precisely what it is in *The Times* that has produced this antagonism in Germany. I do my utmost, night after night,

to keep out of the paper anything that might hurt their sensibilities. I can really think of nothing that has been printed now for many months past which they could possibly take exception to as unfair comment. No doubt they were annoyed by Steer's first story of the bombing of Guernica, but its essential accuracy has never been disputed, and there has not been any attempt here to rub it in or harp upon it.' (quoted in Rankin, 2003: 147)[12]

Part of this process of not 'harp[ing] upon' the attack was the paper's publication of an alternative account of the reasons for the destruction of Guernica, written by Holburn, in which consideration is given to the Nationalist claims that the town was burnt by retreating Republican forces ('THE RUINS OF GUERNICA: A RIVAL VIEW', *The Times*, 5 May 1937, p. 16). Steer was incensed by the report which he believed 'was mostly a rewrite of a document published for the whole foreign and "nationalist" press at Vitoria' (Southworth, 1977: 82).[13] He never worked for the paper again and, in 1939, sued an author who claimed he only had the status of an occasional freelance at *The Times* at the time he filed his report on the Guernica attack and was sacked as a consequence of the report. When organising his defence, Steer found the paper was frustratingly evasive in confirming his actual status and reasons for leaving. In the opinion of Steer's biographer:

> The real reason for the chilliness was that Steer's messages, however 'useful', had embarrassed *The Times*. Respectable opinion – and no one could be more respectable than Geoffrey Dawson, Editor of *The Times* – supported the British government's policy of non-intervention, but at the end of the day would rather have had Franco's side win. (Rankin, 2003: 146)

Steer was not alone in being ostracised by *The Times*' editors for his political views over the conflict. Lawrence Fernsworth worked as the main Barcelona correspondent for the early stages of the war. He had arrived in Andorra in 1929 on a sabbatical from his journalistic career to research local customs. Following the proclamation of the Spanish Republic in 1931, he moved to Barcelona and provided coverage for a range of newspapers, including *The Times* and *The New York Times*. When the military rebellion occurred in July 1936, he was the first journalist to supply an eyewitness account of the revolution and resistance in the Catalonian capital, returning through 'a gauntlet of ambushes and barricades' to telephone his article to *The Times* from Perpignan:

> I was so happy about it that I forgot to feel tired. And *The Times* was happy to get that first instalment. It *was* the first story to come out of revolutionary Spain, to tell what was happening inside Barcelona, that blast furnace of passions and hates. (Fernsworth, 1939: 44, original emphasis)

A clear measure of the value *The Times* editors placed on Fernsworth's Barcelona service was their decision to place him on a £50 monthly retainer from the 1 Jan 1937 (up until that point he had been paid solely on space rates). Deakin wrote to Fernsworth:

> We have greatly appreciated the work you have done since your appoint-
> ment as Correspondent of *The Times*, and have done our best to publish
> adequately the material you have transmitted to this office. It seems evident
> that the Spanish trouble will continue for a considerable time, even for a
> term of years, and we hope, therefore, that you will continue the service.
> (letter from Deakin to Fernsworth, 10 January 1937, Fernsworth
> Managerial File, TNL Archive)

This arrangement was suspended in mid 1937 when Fernsworth took six months' home leave in the US to get married but it was resumed on his return to Barcelona in 1 January 1938. However, the arrangement was terminated soon afterwards. On 11 April 1938, Deakin notified Fernsworth that his retainer would cease and that he would only receive space rates from 1 June onwards. This decision was partly motivated by a wish to reduce the paper's editorial costs in Spain. Ernest de Caux, the paper's main correspondent in Republican Spain (see Chapter 3) had, by this stage, moved from Madrid to Barcelona, thus creat-ing duplication in the paper's Catalan service. But a further significant factor was Deakin's deepening antagonism towards Fernworth's personal views on the war.

Fernsworth freely acknowledged his Republican sympathies but maintained that these never obstructed him from reporting the conflict openly and without prejudice (Fernsworth, 1939: 46). In de Caux's opinion, however, these affinities had intensified to the point where they were compromising his reliability. He wrote to Deakin saying, 'Fernsworth, I fear, from a sympathiser has become a partisan. I cannot talk the situation over with him without it becoming a discus-sion' (letter from de Caux to Deakin, 4 May 1938, de Caux Files, TNL Archive). Deakin concurred and, in a memorandum to the paper's deputy editor later that month, recommended Fernsworth's retainer be rescinded as he had 'become too dangerously partisan' (memorandum from Deakin to Barrington-Ward, 25 May 1938, Fernsworth's Managerial File, TNL Archive).

There is no doubt that Fernsworth became disillusioned with the paper's edi-torial line on Spain, which he felt used the smokescreen of neutrality to advance a pro-Nationalist agenda. In February 1939, with his connexions with the paper terminated, he challenged Deakin directly, criticising several *Times*' leaders that had questioned the integrity of Republican refugee accounts of Nationalist atroc-ities in Catalonia. Deakin dismissed the accusations with froideur, writing to de Caux, 'Fernsworth suggested that *The Times* needed an open-minded corre-spondent to move about among the refugees. We certainly do not feel the need of his additional help' (letter from Deakin to de Caux, 13 February 1939, Deakin Papers, TNL Archive).

It is clear that Fernsworth's passionate engagement did not fit well within an organisational culture that valued coolness and detachment in their correspon-dents.[14] As de Caux commented, 'He is so very temperamental! Let us hope

(Reprinted with the permission of the family of Frederick Voigt.)

Frederick Voigt, diplomatic correspondent of the *Manchester Guardian*, London, 1937

Voigt was a key figure in the lobby of diplomatic correspondents organised by Sir Reginald ('Rex') Leeper of the News Department of the Foreign Office. Although a highly respected journalist, his actions and opinions over Spain raise questions about his political independence from Foreign Office influence.

(Reproduced with the permission of Santa Clara University.)

Lawrence Fernsworth, Barcelona correspondent for *The Times* and *The New York Times*, Barcelona, 1937

Fernsworth left *The Times* in 1938 partly as a consequence of disagreements over the paper's editorial policy on Spain.

that matrimony will make him more sensible' (letter from de Caux to Deakin, 21 July 1938, de Caux Papers, TNL Archive). But Fernsworth was not alone in being emotionally affected by his experiences. De Caux also expressed trenchant opinions in emotive terms in his correspondence with Deakin, particularly during the early phases of the war, in which he attributed responsibility for the misery and privations of life in Madrid to the violence, extremism and incompetence of the Republican authorities.[15] These assessments received neither censure nor comment from Deakin and, on this basis, it is difficult to avoid the conclusion that Fernsworth's cardinal sin for the senior editors at *The Times* was not in holding strong views about Spain but in holding the wrong views.

Concluding remarks

This chapter has examined the influence of the British government, media proprietors and news editors on British news coverage of the Spanish Civil War. It has been shown that these sources sought to cool and constrain media debate on the conflict for separate but compatible reasons. On the one hand, the British government's barely concealed political and ideological antipathy to the Republic intertwined with general concerns about inflaming international tensions and antagonising the Fascist regimes in Germany and Italy. On the other hand, several senior figures within the media sector recognised that their commercial self-interests were best served by ensuring that the equilibrium of the British economy was not unsettled by an escalating public debate about wider political prospects and ideological principles.

However, it is one thing to identify how a cabal of official and commercial interests sought to dictate the terms of media representation, it is another to assume that they were successful in achieving their objectives. Certainly, there were significant countervailing forces that challenged this control, both within news organisations and in society more generally. We have seen in the previous chapter how many journalists who visited Spain developed committed and critical views on British policy on the war. And, whilst it is true that newsrooms are autocracies not democracies, we need to be wary of assuming that senior editorial control always and inevitably closed down dissenting opinion from within.

George Gerbner once remarked that '[e]very decision to communicate something is, at the same time, a decision to suppress everything else. What comes out is a result of competitive pressures breaking through structured inhibitions' (Gerbner, 1969: 205). Any final reckoning of whether 'competitive pressures' or 'structured inhibitions' ultimately prevailed in British news reporting of the Spanish Civil War needs to be based on careful analysis of the texts themselves. It is to this matter that the discussion now turns.

Notes

1. Joseph Goebbels, the Nazi Minister of Propaganda, conceded the effectiveness of Britain's 'propaganda with facts' approach during the Second World War (Chapman, 2005: 188).
2. Other members of the committee included Sir Maurice Hankey, the Secretary to the Cabinet; Sir Warren Fisher, Permanent Under Secretary at the Treasury and Head of the Civil Service; and Sir John Reith, Director General of the BBC (Stenton, 1980: 48).
3. Although defined as a promotion, it was effectively a demotion as it denied Vansittart access to the daily work of the Foreign Office.
4. For example, the *News Chronicle* was very critical of British government policy in Spain throughout the war. In September 1936, the British Consular General in Barcelona complained to the Foreign Office about the paper's publication of a letter from the poet Stephen Spender, in which he criticised the level of support offered by the Consulate to British expatriates. The News Department was requested to communicate official objections to Spender's criticisms via the paper's diplomatic correspondent. As a result, the *News Chronicle* published a short diary report on 21 September that praised the efficiency of staff at the Consulate and obscured the official origins of the corrective. It began, 'Some impressions of Barcelona in these days came to me from an English business, just returned' (TNA, FO 371/20538 Paper w11209/62/41: 241–2)
5. Voigt was also one of the first to complain about the silencing of the News Department from mid 1938 onwards. In a submission to the Foreign Office, co-authored with Gordon Lennox of the *Daily Telegraph* and C. Tower of the *Yorkshire Post*, he wrote, 'Unfortunately of late it has been increasingly apparent that the News Department was no longer in the same advantageous position, whether through lack of information or lack of authorisation to talk freely it is not for us to say' (2 August 1938, TNA, FO 371/562, Paper p2404/4/150: 241–2).
6. The subjects he suggested were:
   1. the history of the International Brigade
   2. the regional character of the Civil War
   3. regional separatism in general
   4. the position of the church and the reasons for anticlericalism
   5. German and Italian intervention
   6. local attitudes towards foreigners
   7. the military direction of the war on both sides
   8. tensions and factionalism within the Republic
   9. the life of everyday people
   10. munitions supplies on both sides
   11. the financial side of the war and Franco's financial support
   12. the position and importance of Spanish Morocco
   13. the future prospects in the event of a government victory or nationalist victory
7. Anthony Beevor estimates the total number of dead for all Republican zones, for the entire war, was 38,000. Nearly half of these people were killed in Madrid and Catalonia during the first months of the war (8,815 and 8,352, respectively). By comparison, Nationalist killings during the war and its aftermath are projected in the region of 200,000 (see Beevor, 2007: 97 and 105). Ruiz (2007) estimates there were at least 37,843 executions in the Republic and a maximum of 150,000 executions in Nationalist Spain (including 50,000 after the war).

8. Cairncross was later exposed as the fifth member of the Cambridge spy ring that infiltrated the British security services during the war and passed secrets to the Soviet Union.

9. In contrast, the political freedom enjoyed by Cecil Thomas at the *Daily Mirror* was largely an unintentional outcome of Rothermere's decision to divest his controlling interest in the early 1930s, which meant that, by the end of the decade, no share owner held a controlling interest. Although the paper's circulation increased dramatically in the late 1930s, its political status did not approach the level that it acquired in the aftermath of the Second World War.

10. The 'Cliveden Set' was coined to describe a group of prominent right-wing public figures who sought to exert influence over British foreign policy. The name came from Cliveden House, the family home of Waldorf and Nancy Astor, where the group were reputed to meet.

11. Reuters shared similar concerns about achieving parity in coverage. In a memorandum sent on 9 February 1937, the Day News Editor noted:

> I agree with you that we have not had so many reports of arrivals in Spain of Russian, Frenchmen etc for the Govt as we have had of Italians and Germans for Franco. The fact that we have not had such reports has been one of my major worries as Day News Editor and has not been for want of trying . . . We have been very careful to emphasise the material help the Russians have been giving the Govt in aeroplanes, tanks and so on . . . Only the other day we sat tight on a message saying that there had actually been fighting between Spaniards and Germans in Seville. I personally have done my utmost to get as much of both sides as I could. The trouble has been that on both sides there seems to have been an effort to keep the curtain down. (The Reuters Archive)

12. This letter has sometimes been taken as evidence that Dawson suppressed news that did not fit his editorial line. The prominence given to Steer's initial report on Guernica provides an obvious challenge to such a suggestion – according the Buchanan (2007), there was never any question that the story would be spiked. Furthermore, staff testimonies from the time refute that Dawson directly censored news (see, McLachlan, 1971; and Wrench, 1955: 360–2). In the main, Dawson's editorial influence was exerted through the recruitment, retention and promotion of staff he deemed politically and socially compatible.

13. In Southworth's judgement Steer's accusation was unfounded as Holburn had visited the town personally and, in the details of his article, provided evidence that supported Steer's original claims. However, Southworth also notices some logical inconsistencies in Holburn's article (in particular his contradictory observations that 'it would be difficult to establish how the fire started' and that Guernica did not show 'signs of fire'). Southworth concludes this was caused by 'bad editing' back in London which mistakenly replaced a reference to the town of Durango with that of Guernica (Southworth, 1977: 83).

14. For example, Deakin was delighted to hear of Kim Philby's stoicism when injured in an artillery attack that killed three other journalists on New Year's Eve 1937.

15. For example he wrote to Deakin in December 1936:

> This class destruction is the most efficient branch of the revolution. It is systematic and relentless and those that carry it out defy the government

apparently without consequences. I am afraid that I have written more than I intended. It just wells out. There are many details that one cannot tell yet. It seems the government machine will break down altogether, but it manages to get along, as you have described in your leaders, on pretence. (letter from de Caux to Deakin, 19 December 1936, de Caux Papers, TNL Archive)

6

Ominous and Indifferent? British Press Coverage of the Spanish Civil War

In England, the ominous grey paper, with its
indifferent headline, its news from our own
correspondent away from the fighting
> Geoffrey Grigson, 'The Non-Interveners', 1937 (quoted in Skelton, 1964: 164)

From the moment it began, the Spanish Civil War was big news in Britain. To give some idea of the scale of media interest, *The Times* and the *Manchester Guardian* published 11,150 items between 15 July 1938 and 15 April 1939 that mainly or exclusively focused on the conflict and its ramifications. From mid July to the end of 1936, these papers averaged, respectively, nine and eight items per day on the war and, although this kind of intense media attention was not sustained for the entire duration of the conflict, the war frequently returned to the forefront of the British media agenda over the ensuing two years and three months.

Coverage also extended across a wide range of media outlets. The prevalence of local, regional and national newspapers in Britain has been noted and, in 1938, it amounted to 175 daily and 1566 weekly titles (see PEP, 1938: 47). Broadcasting was still a public service monopoly during this period but the news division of the BBC was expanding its role and influence. Other media forms also contributed significantly to the informational diet of British citizens – in particular, cinema newsreels, photo-journals, weekly current affairs magazines and political journals.

The challenge in analysing British news reporting is not just about coping with the amount of coverage but also doing justice to the complexity of media responses. Treating the British 'media' as an undifferentiated composite obscures some important distinctions and dimensions. For this reason, the discussion of media representations of the war has been divided over two chapters. This chapter focuses solely on the coverage given to the war in the British national daily press and the next examines its treatment in newsreels, news photography and national weekly papers. The prioritisation implicit in this ordering is warranted because the national daily press constituted the primary news arena in Britain at this time. Daily national newspapers commanded the largest audiences and, because of the regularity and rapidity of their publication, were the most significant sources in the reporting and interpretation of breaking news about the conflict. For example, the British press published news of the attack on Guernica within twenty-four hours of the dispatch of the first accounts from Bilbao but it was ten days before it was covered by newsreel report (Aldgate, 1979: 158–9). Furthermore, national newspapers were both significant news gatherers in their own right and the primary recipients of news agency material.

The analysis concentrates on press coverage produced over three sample periods: (a) 16 July–15 August 1936; (b) 16 April–15 May 1937; and (c) 16 January–15 February 1939.[1] This sampling was necessitated by the sheer volume of coverage and these periods were selected because they coincided with pivotal political and military moments in the conflict and because, in loose terms, they covered the start of the war, its midpoint and its conclusion.[2]

Daily national press coverage in Britain

The editorial stances of the British national press in the Spanish Civil War have been the subject of some comment in general histories of the war. These accounts are typically restricted to categorising whether news organisations were pro-Nationalist or pro-Republican although, in some cases, passing references are made to the strength of any support. A comparison of several examples is set out in Table 6.1.

Shorthand summaries of this kind are of only limited value for several reasons. First, there is a surprising level of disagreement as to the political orientations of particular papers. For example, a literal interpretation of Antony Beevor's statement that '[t]he Republic was supported by the *News Chronicle* and the *Manchester Guardian*. *The Times* and the *Telegraph* remained more or less neutral, while the rest supported the nationalists' (2007: 262) consigns the *Daily Worker* and the *Daily Herald* to the Franco camp, alongside the *Daily Mail*, *Morning Post*, *Daily Sketch*, *Daily Express* and *Daily Mirror*. This categorisation of the left-wing *Daily Worker* and *Daily Herald* is patently the unintended consequence of a mistaken generalisation but Beevor's classification of the dispositions of the *Daily Mirror* and the *Daily Express* as pro-Nationalist does not accord with those of other historians. For example, Hugh Thomas claims both papers were 'generally Republican' (2003: 344).

Second, categorisations of this kind invite the presumption that the affiliations of the press remained stable throughout the conflict. However, as shall be shown, this was not the case. To give a preliminary example, the earliest editorials in the *Daily Mirror* were infused with moral equivalence and the conviction that Britain should not become embroiled in a war that it believed was driven by mutual extremism and intolerance (see, for example, 'This country has no intention of intervening in this diabolical war between the Reds and the Blacks in Spain', 'KEEP OUT OF IT', the *Daily Mirror*, 24 August 1936: 11). By April 1938, however, the paper's leader writers were reviling the Nationalists as 'baby

Table 6.1 Republican and Nationalist affiliations attributed to the British press

	Fryth, 1986	Buchanan, 1997	Beevor, 2007	Thomas, 2003
The Times	Pro-Nationalist (weak)	Supportive of non-intervention	'More or less neutral' (p. 272)	'Tried to be impartial' (p. 334)
Manchester Guardian	Pro-Republican	Pro-Republican (strong)	Pro-Republican	Pro-Republican (moderate)
Daily Telegraph	Pro-Nationalist	Supportive of non-intervention	'More or less neutral' (p. 272)	'Tried to be impartial' (p. 334)
Morning Post	Pro-Nationalist (strong)	Pro-Nationalist (strong)	Pro-Nationalist	Pro-Nationalist
Daily Mail	Pro-Nationalist (strong)	Pro-Nationalist (strong)	Pro-Nationalist	Pro-Nationalist
Daily Express	Pro-Nationalist (weak)	Pro-Nationalist (weak)	Pro-Nationalist	Pro-Republican (moderate)
Daily Mirror	No reference	No reference	Pro-Nationalist	Pro-Republican (moderate)
News Chronicle	Pro-Republican	Pro-Republican (strong)	Pro-Republican	Pro-Republican (moderate)
Daily Worker	Pro-Republican	No reference	Unclear	No reference
Daily Herald	Pro-Republican (weak)	Pro-Republican (weak)	Unclear	Pro-Republican (moderate)
Daily Sketch	Pro-Nationalist (strong)	No reference	Pro-Nationalist	No reference

bombers' and ridiculing the 'futile palaver' of the international Non-Intervention Committee ('NON-INTERVENTIONIST!', the *Daily Mirror*, 1 April 1938: 13). Such changes in editorial opinion may explain the lack of agreement noted in the existing categorisations of press affiliations but they also highlight the need to attend to the volatility and contingency of media opinion.

Third, any claims about the 'neutrality' or 'impartiality' of particular titles have to be dealt with sceptically. This is more than an objection to the philosophical tenability of such claims. As discussed in Chapter 3, non-alignment in the war effectively reinforced the British government's policy of non-intervention in the war, which had a crucial, arguably determining, impact on its outcome. Far from being neutral or impartial, therefore, it was a deeply politicised stance to adopt.

Finally, there are problems in restricting the categorisation of media opinion to evaluative issues. For example, to define a paper as 'pro-Republican' begs the further question of which version (and faction) of the Republican cause was being endorsed. Was it the radical vision of the Republic's resistance as heralding a social revolution against both capitalism and fascism or was it the version that defined the war as the defence of an elected government against totalitarian oppression? To answer questions of this kind requires consideration of the *interpretative* dimensions of the coverage – which issues, voices and perspectives were prioritised and which were marginalised (see Deacon and Golding, 1994: 19). Put simply, what was the war seen to be about?

The discussion that follows examines the interpretative and evaluative dimensions of press coverage and their inter-relationship. It begins with an examination of the extent and temporal distribution of civil war coverage in the British national daily press.

Levels of coverage

When news of the rebellion broke internationally in July 1936, a significant rump of British press opinion assumed that the conflict would be resolved quickly. Headlines wrote of 'routs', 'collapses' and 'decisive battles' although there was less agreement as to who was winning. The *Daily Mail*, for example, published several confident predictions about the imminent collapse of the Republic (for example, 'MADRID'S FALL "CERTAIN THIS WEEK"', 24 July 1936: 12; 'MADRID CUT OFF BY ANTI-REDS: Waiting to Strike', 31 July 1936: 10, 'ROUT OF SPANISH RED ARMY', 1 August 1936: 10; 'Spain's Reds Leaders Get Ready to Flee', 11 August 1936: 9). In contrast, liberal and left-wing newspapers anticipated the swift suppression of the revolt, following Madrid and Barcelona's successful resistance to the coup (for example, 'SPANISH REBELS FACE DEFEAT', the *News Chronicle*, 30 July 1937: 1; 'EYEWITNESS STORY OF BARCELONA: How Workers' Power Smashed Fascism: MARCHING ON TO TRIUMPH', the *Daily Worker*, 22 July 1936: 1; 'WORKERS' ARMY BREAKS FASCIST SIEGE OF MADRID: Rebels Flee in Disorder As Mountainside is Stormed', the *Daily Herald*, 25 July 1936: 1).

The fog of war is never thicker than during the initial disorientating days of combat and these mistaken and contradictory assumptions are easily explained by the combination of poor information and political predispositions. Nevertheless, these responses suggest that many news organisations were psychologically unprepared for a long war and there were several subsequent occasions when journalists seriously misjudged the likely duration of the fighting. For example, in November 1936 many confidently predicted the downfall of Madrid and, in some cases, reported erroneously that Nationalist forces had captured the city (see, for example, Matthews, 1972: 22; Aldgate, 1979: 134). When the Basque region fell to the Nationalists the following year, many other journalists adjudged that the game was more or less up for the Republic.

These examples raise questions about the extent to which the British media sustained their interest in what turned out to be a protracted war of attrition. Figure 6.1 compares the monthly distribution of Spanish Civil War items published in *The Times* and the *Manchester Guardian* from mid July 1936 to April

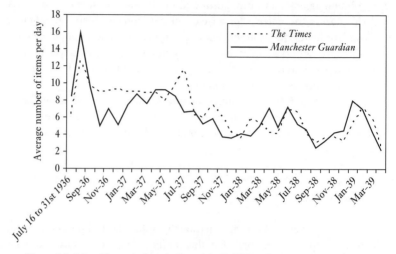

Figure 6.1 Monthly variations in Spanish Civil War Coverage in *The Times* and
Manchester Guardian (15 July 1936–15 April 1939)

1939. The total coverage of these titles was calculated because of their international prestige during the 1930s, particularly in relation to their foreign coverage. Of all daily papers in Britain, these were the most likely to give extensive and
sustained coverage to events in Spain. (Note that, although the *Manchester
Guardian* was a regional paper during this period, it has been included here and
in the general review of press opinion that follows because it was de facto of
national status and had a considerable international reputation.)

The results show that nearly half of all coverage in both papers occurred
during the first year of the war (forty-seven per cent in both cases) and, although
the war retained news value to the end, there was a clear reduction in coverage
from mid 1937 onwards.[3]

The analysis of national press coverage during the three sample periods
identified 4763 news items, leader columns, commentaries and letters that
mainly or solely focused on the Spanish Civil War. (Note that, as with *The Times*
and the *Manchester Guardian* count, items that referred to the war incidentally
were *not* included in the analysis.) Table 6.2 shows the distribution of these items
by newspaper and sample period and confirms a general reduction in coverage
towards the end of the war, with forty-one per cent of all items appearing between
16 July and 15 August, thirty-one per cent between 16 April and 15 May 1937
and twenty-eight per cent between 16 January and 15 February 1939. Only two
titles confounded this trend – the *News Chronicle* increased its coverage between
1936 and 1939, whereas the *Daily Mirror*'s reporting levels remained more or less
constant.

These changes demonstrate the impact of several processes discussed in
Chapter 3, in particular the displacement effects of other major international
events, the sense among newsmakers that Spain was becoming an old news

Table 6.2 Total number of Spanish Civil War related items – 1936, 1937 and 1939

	16 July–15 August 1936	16 April–15 May 1937	16 Jan–15 Feb 1939
The Times	233	210	185
Daily Telegraph	353	200	196
News Chronicle	144	155	161
Daily Express	207	116	121
Daily Mail	262	173	128
Daily Mirror	41	34	36
Daily Herald	180	152	105
Daily Worker	225	201	172
Manchester Guardian	315	241	217

story and the subsequent redeployment of many senior correspondents from Spain that gathered pace from mid 1937 onwards. These totals also show that the war was not the main preserve of the 'class' press. Most popular newspapers dedicated considerable attention towards it and there was no greater attrition rate in their reporting. The only exception was the *Daily Mirror* whose coverage of the war was four times less than that of the *Daily Express* (the paper with the second least number of items on the war). These unusually low levels of coverage were a clear product of the paper's distinct editorial strategy at this time (see Chapter 5) which had slashed foreign, political and economic coverage in the slavish pursuit of circulation (Curran and Seaton, 2003: 67; Thomas, 2004).

Ninety per cent of the articles on Spain were news items – that is, they had a factual orientation and provided new or developing information about military, political and/or human-interest matters concerning Spain. Feature items and commentaries accounted for only one per cent of items, readers' letters four per cent and newspaper leader columns – the spaces sanctioned for the manifest assertion of editorial judgements and concerns – five per cent. Of course, the significance of the latter is not, essentially, a quantitative matter for, no matter how infrequently they appear, editorials provide invaluable insights into both the general politics of a newspaper and its internal political dynamics, particularly in relation to proprietorial influence (Deacon and Wring, 2002: 200). Nevertheless, these general distributions demonstrate that 'news' about the war dominated 'views' about it, something that contrasts with contemporary trends in the British press, where columnists and opinions abound.

This does not mean, however, that British press coverage was anodyne or lacked engagement with the issues at stake in Spain. As shall be shown, even when reporters adopted a veneer of neutrality in the tone and manner of their presentation, the issues they highlighted and the labels they applied revealed highly political views of the war. Moreover, there were many instances in news reporting where the boundaries between sacral fact and free comment were knowingly blurred, particularly in the more overtly partisan sections of the popular press.

This tendency was also evident in the extensive reportage of the war – the 'I coverage' described by the *Daily Express* journalist, Noel Monks, in which the personal experiences of the correspondents themselves became copy (Monks, 1955: 95). One in ten news items were found to contain some reference to the correspondents' own observations and opinions and this personal testimony was often the fulcrum of the item. Sometimes the presence of the perpendicular pronoun was used to sell a story by stressing the journalist's unique proximity to dramatic developments and major figures (for example, 'GENERAL FRANCO INSISTS THAT HE WILL WIN. I have just come from Tetuan where I had a sensational interview with General Francisco Franco', the *News Chronicle*, 29 July 1936: 1; 'DAILY EXPRESS REPORTER IS RUNNING BLOCKADE', the *Daily Express*, 23 April 1937: 1; 'SHIPS SHELLED: Daily Express Reporter Aboard Tells of Navy's Rescue Dash', the *Daily Express*, 24 April 1937: 1). On other occasions, journalists' personal accounts offered eyewitness testimony to attest to the veracity of events and sometimes to appraise the claims and counterclaims that followed in their wake (for example, 'At 2am to-day when I visited the town the whole of it was a horrible sight, flaming from end to end', in 'THE TRAGEDY OF GUERNICA: TOWN DESTROYED IN AIR ATTACK, EYEWITNESS'S ACCOUNT', *The Times*, 28 April 1937: 17).

But there were many times when 'I coverage' extended freely into overt politicising and moralising about the war, the tone of which expressed and reinforced the broader editorial line of the paper in which it appeared (for example, 'VICTORY OF CITIZEN ARMY – THE FACTS FROM SPAIN. Barcelona is a proud city today. Rising out of the ashes of its night of fire is a belief that it has made history and that Spain has once more given something to humanity', the *News Chronicle*, 11 August 1936: 1; 'WHAT I SAW IN BARCELONA. DAILY EXPRESS REPORTER IN RED FLAG CITY . . . It is vitally important that the truth should be known. For in Barcelona, and throughout the home-rule region of Catalonia, of which it is the capital, the Reds are triumphant', the *Daily Express*, 3 August 1936: 1).

A significant minority of the news reporting about the war was openly credited to news agencies – fifteen per cent of all news items. The agencies most commonly used were, in rank order:

- Reuters   481 items
- British United Press   198 items
- Associated Press   50 items
- Exchange   48 items
- The Spanish Press Agency   18 items
- Central News   13 items
- Havas   5 items[4]

Where was the news? Locating the Civil War

> These separate campaigns seem to me to be a little tiresome . . . It is the
> queerest war that I have known.
> (letter from William Crozier to Frederick Voigt, 9 April 1937,
> MGA, 217/257)

These general figures about the scale and nature of press coverage give some
indication of the considerable but changing news value of events in Spain. This
section examines the geographic distribution of news coverage, both in terms of
the areas that were reported upon and the locations from which reports were dispatched. Taken together, these provide insights into the comprehensiveness of
the British news net in the war and the impact that various news management
and censorship activities had on the distribution of news coverage.

Figures 6.2 to 6.4 identify the areas of Spain that received most coverage
during the three sample periods. In July and August 1936, most attention focused
on events in Madrid and Barcelona but there were considerable amounts of
reporting of activity in the Basque region and Spanish Morocco, the region in
which Franco and many of his key military resources were located during the
initial days of the rebellion.

By April–May 1937, the spatial emphasis of coverage had shifted and con-
stricted. In part, these can be explained by major military developments around
this time. In the preceding months, the Nationalist threat to Madrid had been
alleviated by Republican successes in the battles of Jarama (6–28 February 1937)
and Guadalajara (8–22/23 March 1937). But, at the end of March 1937, a major
Nationalist offensive was launched in the Basque region. That this stimulated an
increase in press coverage in this sector is not surprising but what is noticeable
is the extent to which it dominated coverage during this period. Events in the
Basque region accounted for fifty-six per cent of the coverage during this second
sample month. Particularly remarkable is the comparatively low levels of coverage of Barcelona, despite the outbreak of a 'civil war within the civil war' in its
streets (Beevor, 2007: 294), as the Republican government moved to suppress the
activities of the Confederación Nacional de Trabajo (CNT) – the Anarchist-
Syndicalist trade union – the Federación Anarquista Ibérica (FAI) – the
Anarchist federation in Spain – and the Partido Obrero de Unificación Marxista
(POUM) – the anti-Stalinist Communist party.

In January and February 1939, coverage clustered in a similar way in
Catalonia, again tracing the progress of a successful military offensive by
Franco's forces. Barcelona came under sustained attack through January and fell
to the Nationalists on twenty-sixth of that month. The insurgents then pressed
the retreating Republicans to the Pyrenees, forcing the French government to
open its borders. The significance of the Pyrenean borders in figure 6.3 reveals
the extent of British press interest in recording the plight of the retreating
refugees and Republican soldiers and many of these reports emphasised a generosity and sympathy in the French response that bore no relation to the enforced

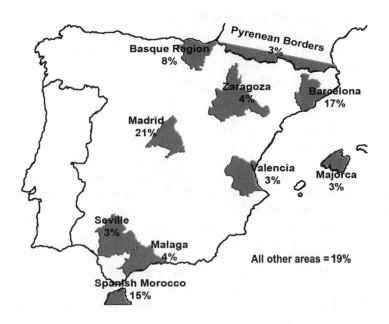

Figure 6.2 The principal regions covered in British press items (16 July–15 August 1936)[5]

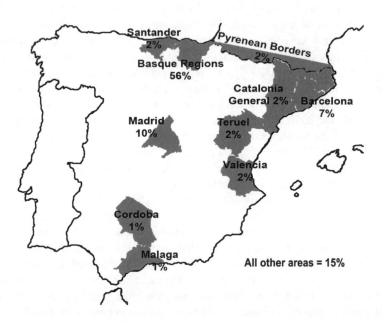

Figure 6.3 The principal regions covered in British press items (16 April–15 May 1937)

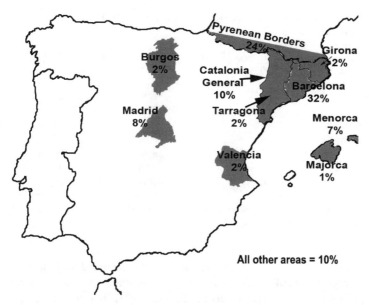

Figure 6.4 The principal regions covered in British press items (16 April–15 May 1937)

detention in concentration camps with inadequate shelter, food and healthcare that actually awaited the retreating Republicans (see, for example, 'REFUGEES SEE LAND OF PEACE BEFORE THEM', the *Daily Express*, 30 January 1939: 20; 'Sufferings of the Refugees', *The Times*, 31 January 1939: 12; 'EXITS TO SAFETY' the *Daily Mail*, 7 February 1939; 'THE TREK ACROSS THE FRONTIER INTO HOSPITABLE FRANCE', the *News Chronicle*, 8 February 1939; 'THE FLIGHT FROM SPAIN: HEAVY FEET . . . HEAVY HEARTS', *Mirror*, 9 February 1939: 17).[6]

Two general points can be deduced from the spatial distribution of Spanish coverage across the three sample periods. First, it shows that British press attention focused mainly on military rather than political developments within Spain, as the centres of political authority on both sides commanded only a limited presence – that is, Valencia and Barcelona for the Republic (in 1937) and Salamanca and Burgos for the Nationalists (in 1937 and 1939). This gravitation to where the weapons were created weaknesses in other parts of the Spanish news net and it is clear that one practical reason why the Barcelona uprisings received so little coverage in 1937 was because the main editorial resources of the British media were focused elsewhere.[7] However, as will be shown, this was not the only reason.

Second, far more coverage was given to events from within Republican territory, whether disputed or undisputed, and, once areas became controlled by the Nationalists, they tended to disappear from view. For example, General Queipo de Llano's seizure of Seville in July 1936 generated some initial media comment but press interest in the area had ended by April and May 1937. In July and

Table 6.3 The filing locations of Spanish Civil War news in the British national press
(1936–1939)

	16 July–15 August *1936*	*16 April–15 May* *1937*	*16 Jan–15 Feb* *1939*
Republican	41 %	47 %	23 %
Nationalist	5 %	10 %	7 %
French Borders	15 %	20 %	28 %
UK locations	6 %	6 %	3 %
Other French Location	14 %	8 %	25 %
Other Nation	20 %	9 %	13 %
	(1025)	(645)	(605)

Note: the filing locations were only indicated in forty-eight per cent of the Spanish Civil War items analysed.
Figures may not add up to 100 due to rounding.

August 1936, Malaga was in Republican hands and accounted for four per cent of all coverage. International concerns were expressed about the fate of its inhabitants when it fell to Nationalist forces in February 1937[8] but, from mid April to early May 1937, its presence had become negligible. More generally, the maps from all three periods attest to a conspicuous absence of coverage of events in the uncontested heartlands of Nationalist Spain.

Far more reports were dispatched from Republican Spain as well (see Table 6.3). In Chapter 2 it was shown that: (a) the Nationalists were technically disadvantaged in distributing news internationally; and (b) that their leadership was more hostile to foreign media and imposed greater restrictions on journalists. The content analysis results suggest that it was the closed military culture of the Nationalist authorities that was the main factor to inhibit international news coverage from their territories as the levels of news dispatched from Nationalist Spain did not increase greatly through 1937 and 1939, even though the insurgents' technical disadvantages alleviated significantly and progressively in each successive period.[9]

This raises questions about the impact the Nationalists' recalcitrance had upon the representation of the warring parties in the British press. A first consideration in this respect concerns the relative news presence and news access of political, civil and military sources involved in the civil war.

Who was news? News presence and news access

News presence and news access are two linked but distinct phenomena. News presence concerns the frequency with which the actions and opinions of individuals and organisations ('news sources') are the subject of editorial discussion. News access addresses the extent to which particular sources interact directly with journalists to provide information and convey their opinions. News access is often determined by matters of opportunity and availability but it can also be a

Table 6.4 The presence of sources in Spanish Civil War news reports in the British national daily press (1936, 1937 and 1939)

		Republican source Mentioned	*Nationalist source Mentioned*	*British source Mentioned*	*Other nation source Mentioned*	*(Number)*
All Titles	%	33	25	25	18	(12242)
The Times	%	35	26	23	15	(1401)
Daily Express	%	34	30	21	15	(1191)
Daily Mail	%	34	26	21	19	(1277)
Daily Telegraph	%	31	24	25	20	(2225)
Daily Mirror	%	26	18	42	14	(306)
Daily Herald	%	33	25	26	16	(1176)
Daily Worker	%	32	19	35	15	(1576)
News Chronicle	%	29	26	27	18	(1273)
Manchester Guardian	%	32	25	21	22	(1817)

Notes: All percentages are row percentages. These figures relate solely to items designated as 'news items'. Up to five sources could be coded per item. Where the number of sources exceeded five, sources were coded according to their prominence. Figures may not add up to 100 due to rounding.

measure of sources' influence and credibility, as there is an implicit process of accreditation involved in journalists' decisions about who they talk to. To give a contemporary example, terrorist organisations often command considerable news presence through their threats and actions but their news access – opportunities to justify directly their actions, explain their demands and so on – is negligible.

Comparing which sources are most frequently mentioned in coverage and which are sidelined or ignored makes news presence a straightforward matter to assess. It is less easy to use such a comparison to measure news access as there can be occasions when powerful sources exert surreptitious influence 'behind the scenes'. Nevertheless, the frequency with which sources are directly quoted in coverage does provide a telling, if imperfect, indicator of the availability and/or perceived credibility of news sources by journalists.

Table 6.4 compares the extent to which Republican, Nationalist and other sources were mentioned in different national British newspapers. Across most titles, the greater access foreign journalists had to the interior life of the Spanish Republic did not lead to a major over-representation of Republican sources. They featured more frequently than Nationalist sources in all periods but, in the main, these differences were not dramatic.[10]

Table 6.5 examines the extent to which Republican, Nationalist and other sources were quoted directly in news coverage and reveals greater discrepancies between the two sides (Only in the *Daily Mail* coverage, and to a lesser extent that of the *Daily Express*, did the warring parties achieve comparable levels of quotation.) Did this higher incidence of Republican quotation, which can be seen as indicative of their greater news access, deliver them significant definitional

Table 6.5 The quotation of new sources in Spanish Civil War news reports in the British national daily press (1936, 1937 and 1939)

		Republican source Quoted	Nationalist source Quoted	British source Quoted	Other nation source Quoted	(Number)
All Titles	%	22	9	55	14	(1261)
The Times	%	12	4	78	6	(139)
Daily Express	%	20	17	50	13	(113)
Daily Mail	%	18	17	45	20	(128)
Daily Telegraph	%	20	7	55	18	(170)
Daily Mirror	%	16	6	75	4	(51)
Daily Herald	%	32	11	47	10	(136)
Daily Worker	%	33	2	51	14	(195)
News Chronicle	%	23	8	57	12	(138)
Manchester Guardian	%	18	12	52	18	(191)

Notes: All percentages are row percentages. These figures relate solely to items designated as 'news items'. Up to five sources could be coded per item. Where the number of sources exceeded five, sources were coded according to their prominence. Figures may not add up to 100 due to rounding.

advantages in terms of their representation in the British press? Furthermore, was their greater access simply symptomatic of their greater *availability* or did it reveal a greater *affinity* on the part of the British press with their cause?

To answer these questions definitively requires the consideration of additional evidence but it is pertinent to note the considerable presence and access accorded to British sources in press coverage. Although only a small minority of news reports concerning the war originated from Britain (six per cent, see Table 6.3), British individuals and organisations accounted for over a quarter of all news sources (see Table 6.4) and were by far the most frequently quoted, both in absolute and relative terms (see Table 6.5). Twenty-two per cent of British sources were quoted on appearance, compared with only seven per cent of Republican sources and four per cent of Nationalist sources.

Citizens not directly associated with any of the combatants were the most commonly featured British sources (thirty per cent), exceeding all references to British government and official sources (twenty-seven per cent), other British politicians (fourteen per cent) and the British military (thirteen per cent). This pattern was consistent across both the up-market and the popular titles.

This emphasis on lay perspectives and experiences in general can be taken, in part, as being indicative of a common and enduring feature of all foreign news reporting, in which journalists and editors always look for local angles, aspects and applicableness to enhance the relevance of distant events to domestic audiences. For example, after the outbreak of the war, dozens of articles were published about the experiences of British citizens caught up in the fighting (for example, 'LONDON GIRLS ESCAPE IN SPAIN', the *Daily Mail*, 22 July 36:

11; 'British Nurse is Favourite of Wounded, the *Daily Mirror*, 3 August 1936: 7; 'The Reds at Ronda: British Refugee's story', *The Times*, 5 August 1936: 11; 'ENGLISH WOMAN'S DIARY OF BARCELONA TERROR', the *Daily Telegraph*, 10 August 1936: 7). In April 1937, with Franco's forces advancing through the Basque region, press attention briefly but intensively focused on the bravery of British merchant seamen as they challenged British naval advice and entered Basque ports to deliver emergency food and supplies (for example, '"POTATO" JONES RALLIES BLOCKADED SKIPPERS', the *Daily Express*, 17 April 1937: 1; '"POTATO" JONES ORDERED HOME', the *Daily Worker*, 17 April 1937: 1; '"POTATO" JONES: I'LL TRY AGAIN', the *Daily Herald*, 17 April 1937: 1; 'Where is "Potato" Jones?', the *Daily Mail*, 21 April 1937: 13; 'HOW WE GOT THROUGH BY "CORNCOB"', the *Daily Mail*, 24 April 1937: 1).

The lesser prominence of official British sources in Spanish news coverage was not necessarily indicative of their modest success in influencing the terms of media representation. Indeed, it was probably more indicative of the effectiveness of the government's political and communication strategy which, as was shown in the previous chapter, avoided declamatory interventions, discouraged attribution and generally sought to contain and cool media speculation about the possibility of any British involvement in the conflict. It is striking that most press reporting of British government actions and intentions related to Spain focused overwhelmingly on 'front region' political activity – parliamentary debates, diplomatic statements, foreign visits, public speeches and so on (for example, 'MPs SUPPORT NON-INTERVENTION', the *Daily Telegraph*, 15 April 1936: 14; 'BRITAIN SUPPORTS NEUTRALITY IN SPANISH CIVIL WAR', the *News Chronicle*, 5 August 1936: 1; 'BRITAIN INSISTS ITALY MUST AGREE, TOO', the *Daily Express*, 5 August 1936: 1). Even though selected editors and correspondents were granted high-level access to government inner circles (see Chapter 5), the insights derived from such contact rarely appeared and even when they did it was in a very codified way. For example, many national journalists were well aware of the growing tensions between Prime Minister Chamberlain and Foreign Secretary Eden in late 1937, particularly regarding British policy in Spain. But these political differences were hardly mentioned in press coverage in the months prior to Eden's resignation in February 1938.[11]

This ethnocentric emphasis in news reporting was not just about the mechanical application of local news values to distant events. It also demonstrated an affirmation of British values and character (see also Shelmerdine, 2006). Journalists clearly valued 'ordinary' British citizens for the dispassionate perspective they brought to the tumultuous events in Spain (it is significant that British sources with active allegiances and involvement were far less frequently mentioned or quoted). The relative marginality of British governmental sources, too, can be taken as a measure of definitional influence, both in its consonance with official wishes to keep a low profile and in journalists' reluctance to dig too deeply into the motivations that underpinned this recalcitrance. Certain sections of the press may have been critical of the British government in its policy on Spain, as will be shown, but accusations that this was motivated by active malevolence and malfeasance were almost exclusively reserved to the most radical left-wing publications. In the late 1930s, the ideology of *Pax Britannica* – a belief in the fundamental benevolence of British cultural and military power – still exerted a powerful grip on the British imagination, not least among media professionals (see, for example, Bartlett, 1941: 257–8). In the main, this was a subtle aspect of coverage but occasionally it became a matter of direct editorial comment. One particularly risible example appeared in the *Daily Mirror* on August 1936, in which 'our psychologist' considered, in the context of violent civil conflict in Spain and Greece, 'WILL IT EVER HAPPEN HERE?' (11 August 1936: 10) The article began:

> The ordinary, respectable citizens grabs a gun, sees red – and fires. Wives, mothers, sisters – in an ecstasy of hate – goad on their men to crazier bravery and savagery, and even join them in the heroics and beastliness. SPANIARD SHOOTS SPANIARD AND GREEK TORTURES GREEK . . . Will it ever happen here? Will Britons rain bombs on Britons and dynamite their parliament?

The discussion linked the rise in hate politics across Europe to the psychotic personalities of dictators – 'seeds that grow like weeds' – and the widespread fear and uncertainty caused by economic deprivation. However, the sanguinity of its conclusion was only exceeded by its xenophobia:

> The Briton cannot hate: not even his enemies. But he is the World's Champion Grouser – bar none.
> And the Briton's grouse is the sign-manual of his high social intelligence, of his status as an exceptionally civilised person . . .
> Because his tradition permits him to admit his fear instead of concealing it with strutting heroics;
> Because he knows how to vent his hate in harmless grousing;
> Because his instinct for handling a crisis enables him to sense the difficulties of the leaders he grouses at; and
> Because he respects the individuality of others (the queue habit is a high expression of this) he dislikes being part of a mob. HE IS POOR MATERIAL FOR THE HATING PARANOIC.

Labels and their liabilities

I now want to consider how the British press interpreted and evaluated the indigenous participants in the War. To start this appraisal, this section examines the labels applied to the warring factions. This matter is significant for two reasons. First, the semantic implications of the labels used provide telling indications of the political orientations of the press and how they altered as the war progressed. Second, they reveal a deep narrative schemata that organised much of British press reporting.

The political intricacies of the Spanish Civil War probably exceeded its geographic complexity. As noted, the Republic was a heterogeneous alliance of Stalinist and non-Stalinist Communists, Socialists, liberals, regional nationalists, Anarchists and Syndicalists, who mobilised as political parties, trade unions and less formalised collectives. The military-led rebellion, although more hierarchical and centralised, also comprised a coalition of different parties and vested interests that included, the Phalange, the Catholic Church, Carlists and Monarchists. Such diversity alone made even the task of naming the antagonists a complex matter but issues were complicated further by the polarity, passion and enmity of the conflict. Spain offered a perfect example of the big battles that can occur over little words (to borrow a phrase from Michael Billig). All sides promoted the use of general, pejorative labels to describe their enemies (most commonly 'Fascist' and 'Red') but were sensitive to the terms applied to themselves, even when they were not blatantly negative in character. As discussed in Chapter 2, the Nationalists harassed journalists who referred to them as 'Rebels' or 'Insurgents' in their copy, even though, in literal terms, these could be claimed to have a descriptive legitimacy. Indeed, so great were their sensitivities, the British Foreign Office frequently warned journalists and others as to their choice of terminology (see Chapter 5).

Tables 6.6 and 6.7 compare the principal labels used in news headlines and texts. (Note that, where more than one label was used in an item, the most prominent was coded.) The results show that the terms 'Republican' and 'Nationalist', the labels most frequently used today, only gained media currency in the latter stages of the war. Prior to that, 'Government' and 'Rebels' appeared most regularly, although the use of the former label reduced in 1937. Overtly pejorative terms, like 'Red', 'Fascist' and 'Anti-Red', were most evident at the start of the war but were hardly used by the end.

The results also show major variations in the labels applied by individual newspapers. Predictably, newspapers that strongly identified with particular sides were more likely to deploy overly positive or pejorative names. For example, ninety-four per cent of the *Daily Worker*'s items that referred to Nationalist forces described them as 'Fascists', whereas the *Daily Mail* applied a lexicon all its own to report the conflict. It was the only newspaper that made substantial use of the terms 'Patriot' and 'Anti-Red' to label Franco's forces, albeit mainly at the start of the war (in the 1936 sample period, these terms accounted, respectively, for nineteen and forty-two per cent of the main Nationalist references). It was also the paper that made freest use of the term 'Red' to label Republican sources (fifty-three per cent of its main republican references in 1936 and thirty-nine per cent in 1937). However, unlike the *Daily Worker*, the *Daily Mail* did not persist in these practices and, by 1939, had fallen in line with reporting tendencies in other papers. In this latter period, ninety-eight per cent of its main textual references to Franco's forces used the label 'Nationalist' and seventy-six per cent of its references to Government forces used 'Republican'.

Table 6.6 Labelling the Republic

	All Periods		*16 July–15 August 1936*		*16 April–15 May 1937*		*16 Jan–15 Feb 1939*	
	Headlines %	*Text* %	*Headlines* %	*Text* %	*Headlines* %	*Text* %	*Headlines* %	*Text* %
Government	21	57	31	76	13	55	17	31
Republic(an)	9	22	6	6	–	4	42	63
Basque	28	9	–	0.1	62	31	–	1
Loyalist	10	2	15	2	5	2	16	2
Red	16	5	33	9	7	4	–	0.4
Anarchist	5	1	3	0.3	10	2	–	–
Communist	2	2	6	4	–	1	–	0.3
Other	9	2	6	3	3	1	25	2
(Number of cases)	(440)	(3853)	(176)	(1584)	(200)	(1149)	(64)	(1120)

Table 6.7 Labelling the Nationalists

	All Periods		*16 July–15 August 1936*		*16 April–15 May 1937*		*16 Jan–15 Feb 1939*	
	Headlines %	*Text* %	*Headlines* %	*Text* %	*Headlines* %	*Text* %	*Headlines* %	*Text* %
Rebel	56	45	60	52	48	49	49	31
Fascist	18	19	20	27	14	11	14	15
Nationalist	8	17	–	0.2	17	15	33	43
Insurgent	12	15	13	15	15	20	2	11
Anti-Red	2	3	2	3	4	5	–	0.1
Patriot	1	1	1	1	–	0.1	–	–
Other	4	1	5	3	2	–	2	–
(Number of cases)	(474)	(3505)	(288)	(1448)	(143)	(1026)	(43)	(1031)

Notes: Percentages = the number of items which used each term as either the sole or main label for a Republican or Nationalist source, divided by the total number of items that contained any label for Republican or Nationalist sources multiplied by 100. All percentages are rounded and totals may therefore exceed 100. If more than one label was used in the text of an item, the most frequently used term was coded. If more than one label was used in a headline and sub-headline, the first used term was coded.

Despite these differences and fluctuations, there was one strong common thread in the lexical choices of the British press. All newspapers preferred labels that had a generic and collective quality, regardless of their particular political implications. Furthermore, this preference was replicated in the routine reporting of Republican and Nationalist sources. Table 6.8 compares the extent to which politicians and groups from either side were identified by their specific factional affiliation or asso-

Table 6.8 References to factions in reporting of Republican and Nationalist sources

	1936 %	1937 %	1939 %
Republic general	51	26	40
Republic faction	7	30	16
Nationalist general	41	42	44
Nationalist faction	1	2	0.1
(number of actors)	(3335)	(2093)	(2067)

ciated more generally to the Republican and Nationalist causes. The results show that the only period when the specific identification of factional affiliations exceeded general references occurred in the reporting of Republican sources in April to May 1937. Closer analysis of Republican labelling during this period reveal that the rise in factional references was mainly due to a considerable increase in the specific identification of the Basque government and other Basque nationalist sources (thirty-three per cent of all Republican references in this sample month). In contrast, specific references to the factions involved in the fratricidal conflict in Barcelona that broke out in May 1937 were far less evident. References to 'Anarchists' – the 'Confederación Nacional de Trabajo' ('CNT') or the 'Federación Anarquista Ibérica' ('FAI') – accounted for just seven and a half per cent of all Republican sources labelled; and the 'Partido Obrero de Unificacion Marxista' ('POUM'), the anti-Stalinist communist party that joined the Anarchists in confronting the government forces in Catalonia, was barely mentioned at all (less than one per cent of cases).

This dominance of general labelling can be explained in part by the political factors that shaped the mediation of the conflict. In Chapter 2, it was shown that both Republican and Nationalist propaganda prohibited references to factional and political divisions within their own ranks and stigmatised their enemies indiscriminately. In Chapter 3 it was shown that foreign correspondents in Spain had most routine contact with the dominant political authorities in each sector and those that developed political allegiances were more inclined to favour the political mainstream.[12]

Established conventions of news presentation would have added to this compression and conflation. 'News' elicits drama through the juxtaposition of clear and opposed positions. This tendency was undoubtedly evident in coverage of Spain and explains why the imbalance in the news access of Nationalist and Republican sources did not translate into major differences in their respective news presence. Most reports that originated from Republican territory required reference to a Nationalist 'other' for the purposes of narrative balance, even if this was not based on direct contact.

However, the dichotomous structure of news often oversimplifies complex situations that cannot be reduced to an 'either/or' framework. This was particularly the case in the Spanish Civil War, which was never just a simple two-way conflict, even though it was frequently presented in such terms. This point was revealed in British press coverage of the intra-Republican conflict that flared up in Barcelona in May 1937.

Barcelona May Daze

The open fighting that broke out in Barcelona in early May 1937 was the culmination of deeply rooted political tensions (see Thomas, 2003: 629–31). Catalonia had long been a focal point for both regional separatist and anarchist politics and, when the rebellion started, it took some time for an uneasy coalition government to form. This coalition included the Catalan government of Lluís Companys, the anarchist groups the CNT and FAI and POUM, the anti-Stalinist Communists. In the first few months of the war, the social revolution demanded by some elements of the Popular Front government found its fullest expression and development in Barcelona. For example, in the early months of the war the city represented a 'triumph of collectivised industry' (ibid.: 537). However, by early 1937, counter-revolutionary forces within central government had gained dominance and, with political divisions opening up within the Catalonian government, plans began to be laid for the purging of its revolutionary components.

The crisis in Barcelona, therefore, was complicated in origins and nature and had been a long time coming (see Beevor, 2007: 283–306 for a clear and concise summary). When we consider the performance of the British press in dealing with these complexities, four points stand out. First, there was little anticipatory coverage of the fighting. *The Times* and the *Manchester Guardian* published a few articles over the preceding weeks that acknowledged rising political tensions within Catalonia but these were brief and given little priority (for example, 'The Catalan Crisis', *The Times*, 29 March 1937: 10; 'Political Crisis in Catalonia: Differences with Valencia', the *Manchester Guardian*, 13 April 1937: 15). Other papers also occasionally referred to the growing divisions before the fighting broke out but they too conveyed little sense of the gravity of events.

Second, even when news of the fighting came through, it did not command considerable prominence. Only the *Daily Herald* made it front page news and even then relegated it behind its main splash about Hitler and Mussolini's refusal to stop bombing open towns ('Cease Fire Order in Barcelona', the *Daily Herald*, 5 May 1937: 1). Neither was it the subject of much direct editorial comment. The *Daily Mail* was the only paper that provided an immediate editorial assessment, in which it freely conflated Anarchists, Communists and regional nationalists as 'Reds' and concluded that the events 'illustrate the fate which awaits a people who are deluded into believing that once the Reds have obtained office law and order can be maintained' ('ANARCHISTS IN CONTROL, 5 May 1937: 10).

Third, news coverage tended to focus on the progress of the fighting and its consequences rather than the reasons behind it (see, for example, 'TELEPHONE BUILDING CAPTURED: ANARCHISTS DISLODGED', *The Times*, 6 May 1937: 16; 'How the Confused Fighting Arose: Remarkable

Story of Outbreak', the *Manchester Guardian*, 6 May 1937: 13; 'MORE SHOOT-ING IN STREETS OF BARCELONA: ANARCHIST TANKS PATROL', the *Daily Telegraph*, 6 May 1937: 13; 'Barcelona Terror Ends: 12,000 MEN QUELL ANARCHISTS', the *Daily Express*, 11 May 1937: 2; 'REIGN OF TERROR IN BARCELONA AGAIN LAST NIGHT', the *Daily Mail*, 7 May 1937: 14). Very few articles included explanations of who the combatants were and what they were fighting about and these details were provided only several days after the story broke and were often so perfunctory as to be of little explana-tory value. For example, on 10 May 1937, the *News Chronicle* ran a front page story by John Langdon-Davies which claimed to provide the 'FIRST INSIDE STORY OF BARCELONA RISING'.[13] At the end of an analysis that blamed the revolt solely on 'a frustrated putsch by the "Trotskyist" POUM', a brief additional section claimed to explain 'What's What'. However, it was merely ninety words in length and mainly focused on what the acronyms of the key polit-ical parties stood for. The only article that made any concerted attempt to clarify the political divisions and issues at stake was published on the same day in *The Times* ('CAUSES OF THE CONFLICT', 10 May 1937: 13).

Fourth, in the absence of any engagement with the complexities of the intra-Republican fighting, new dichotomies were developed to deal with this civil war within a war. The CNT, FAI, other anarchist factions and the POUM were generically categorised as 'Anarchists' and newspapers across the political spec-trum portrayed the fighting as a conflict between the forces of order and disor-der, lawfulness and lawlessness, constitutional authority and insurrection. Within this narrative structure, central government forces were always portrayed as reacting to military and political events rather than initiating them, with 'orig-inal sin' attributed to the radical forces that resisted what had been a long-planned assertion of centralised authority (see, for example, 'CATALONIA IN STATE OF WILD DISORDER: OPEN REBELLION OF ANARCHISTS: VALENCIA TROOPS RUMOURED ON THE WAY', the *Daily Telegraph*, 4 May 1937: 13; 'FOUR DICTATORS END BARCELONA REVOLT', the *Daily Herald*, 6 May 1937: 2; 'MINISTERS SHOT IN BARCELONA', the *Daily Express*, 7 May 1937: 2).

It is not difficult to identify the political reasons for the dominance of these interpretations – the combination of external pressures placed on news profes-sionals and their own political prejudices produced a powerful cognitive com-pression about the causes of the Barcelona conflict and its political significance. However, a further reason why the Barcelona May Days did not receive thorough and detailed investigation is because did not fit with the established dichotomous framework for civil war reporting.

Interpreting the war

I now want to consider the broader interpretative dimensions of coverage. Table 6.9 presents the six main themes for each of the newspapers included in the analysis.

Table 6.9 Main themes in the British national press

The Times	%	Daily Telegraph	%	Manchester Guardian	%
Battle stories	29	Battle stories	30	Battle stories	29
Non-intervention	11	Non-intervention	12	Non-intervention	17
Air attacks on civilians	7	Impact on British interests	11	Impact on British interests	6
Impact on British interests	6	Republican politics	4	Air attacks	4
Republican politics	4	Nationalist failings	4	British public opinion	4
Republican failings	3	Republican failings	4	Republican politics	3
(n=853)		(n=940)		(n=1107)	

Daily Mail	%	Daily Express	%	Daily Mirror	%
Battle stories	28	Battle stories	34	Impact on British interests	20
Republican failings	13	Non-intervention	10	Battle stories	18
Non-intervention	9	Impact on British interests	9	Non-intervention	17
Impact on British interests	8	Nationalist failings	4	British public opinion	5
Civil issues in Spain	4	Air attacks	3	Nationalist failings	5
Other international diplomacy	3	Republican politics	3	Air attacks	5
(n=720)		(n=555)		(n=158)	

News Chronicle	%	Daily Herald	%	Daily Worker	%
Battle stories	25	Battle stories	25	Non-intervention	23
Non-intervention	17	Non-intervention	15	Battle stories	21
Impact on British interests	6	Impact on British interests	8	British public opinion	13
British public opinion	6	Nationalist failings	7	Republican politics	6
Air attacks on civilians	5	Republican politics	6	Republican virtues	5
Refugees	4	British public opinion	6	Nationalist failings	4
(n=602)		(n=597)		(n=822)	

Notes: Only the top six themes found for each newspaper are presented. All percentages are rounded. Up to three themes could be coded per item.

Reflecting the finding discussed earlier about the spatial focus of coverage, 'battle stories' dominated most newspaper coverage (for example, 'TRAGIC SIEGE OF GIJON', the *News Chronicle*, 24 August 1936: 2; 'Basques' Crushing Defeat', the *Daily Mail*, 17 May 1937: 10; 'BARCELONA EXPECTED TO FALL TO-DAY', the *Daily Telegraph*, 25 January 1939: 2). Only in the *Daily Mirror* and the *Daily Worker* were reports about the fighting not the principal theme. In the case of the *Mirror*, this is probably an anomaly of its significantly lower levels of general reporting of the war. With regard to the *Daily Worker*, the marginalisation of the war frame was a product of its unashamed editorial activism over Spain. Rather than just witnessing the war, it sought to influence the outcome through mobilising its readership in the Republic's defence and repeatedly attacking British neutrality (see, for example, 'ALL INTO ACTION TO DEFEND SPANISH REPUBLIC: THEY FIGHT FOR DEMOCRACY WITH THEIR LIVES: OUR GOVERNMENT IS HELPING FASCISTS', the *Daily Worker*, 25 July 1936: 1; 'You Can Help Them By – . . .', the *Daily Worker*, 6 August 1936: 4; 'SPANISH WORKERS NEED YOUR HELP: There Must Be Meetings Everywhere: A Call To Action: CAMPAIGN GROWS', the *Daily Worker*, 8 August 1936: 8).

The fact that the Spanish Civil War was the first total war on European soil undoubtedly added to the general interest in events on the battlefield, as journalists sought to assess the impact of the new technologies and techniques of destruction (see, for example, 'GENERAL FRANCO BUIILDING UP A NEW AIR FORCE: ANTI-AIRCRAFT GUNS OF THE LATEST TYPE', the *Daily Telegraph*, 13 August 1936: 13; 'THE BOMBER versus the BATTLESHIP', the *Daily Express*, 1 May 1937: 12; 'SPANISH NOTE TO BRITAIN: "Possible Use" of GAS', the *Manchester Guardian*, 22 April 1937: 6). During the first two sample periods, the strong political prejudices and preferences of certain newspapers also often affected their interpretation of military events as, amidst ongoing uncertainty about the outcome of the war, they tended to overemphasise the victories of their favoured side and downplay, or even ignore, the scale of their defeats (see, for example, 'ANTI-REDS SWEEP ON TO BILBAO: 15-Miles Thrust in 24 Hours', the *Daily Mail*, 26 April 1937: 13; 'ITALIANS FLEE IN BILBAO BATTLE', the *Daily Herald*, 2 May 1937: 1; 'Spain's "Alcazar of the South" Falls to Madrid', the *News Chronicle*, 17 April 1937: 2). By January and February 1939, however, there was a tacit consensus in national press opinion that the outcome of the war was now decided. Only the *Daily Worker* maintained a desperate but determined optimism that verged on denial ('WHY SPAIN WILL NEVER BE CONQUERED', the *Daily Worker* 20 January 1939: 2; 'CATALONIA WILL BE THE TOMB OF THE INVADER', the *Daily Worker*, 17 January 1939: 1; 'SPAIN RE-FORMS ITS FRONTS': Thousands Rush To Fighting Line', the *Daily Worker*, 31 January 1939: 1; 'MADRID CAN BE THEIR MASTER', the *Daily Worker*, 13 February 1939: 4).

The second most prominent theme in coverage was the debate about international 'non-intervention' in the conflict. Throughout the war endless acres of newsprint were expended on charting the International Non-Intervention

Agreement: its formulation – 'BRITAIN INSISTS ITALY MUST AGREE, TOO' (the *Daily Express*, 5 August 1936: 1); its implementation – 'ADMIRAL'S CONFERENCE ON SPAIN CONTROL' (the *Daily Telegraph*, 17 April 1937: 11); its contravention – 'PROSPECTS IN SPAIN: MOTIVES OF NAZI POLICY: NO INDICATION OF WITHDRAWAL' (*The Times*, 19 January 1937: 1); and its political legitimacy – 'HOW CABINET CLIMBED DOWN TO FRANCO' (the *Daily Herald*, 22 April 1937: 2). Because of the agreement's enormous political significance for Britain, I examine British press responses to the debate in greater detail in the section that follows. More generally, the results in Table 6.9 confirm the extent to which events in Spain were viewed through a British prism. British sources commanded a considerable presence and the impact of the war on British public opinion and British material interests was a prominent concern of the British press (see, for example, 'Panic Rush As Shells Fall On Gibraltar', the *Daily Express*, 23 July 1936: 1; 'BRITISH STAFF AT RIO TINTO STILL SAFE', the *Daily Telegraph*, 15 August 1936: 11).

With regard to events in Spain, more coverage was given to political activities within Republican zones than Nationalist areas (see the greater presence of 'Republican politics' recorded in Table 6.9). In part, this can be taken as a measure of journalists' greater access to this sector but it also undoubtedly reflected the greater political volatility within the Republican leadership throughout the war. There was more variation across the press in the extent to which the respective 'virtues' and 'failings' of the opposing sides were emphasised. The thematic categories 'Republican virtues' and 'Nationalist virtues' refer to any positive references made to the political culture, the social conditions or the lived experiences of everyday citizens on the respective sides of the war – political tolerance, high morale, social cohesion and the observance of good democratic practices, for example. Republican or Nationalist 'failings' covers their antitheses – that is, factors such as political extremism, demoralisation, intolerance, social breakdown and atrocities. The *Daily Herald* and the *Daily Worker*, predictably, paid considerable attention to the virtues of the Republic and the sins of the Nationalists. However, with other papers the pattern was more variable. The *Daily Mirror* and *Daily Express* also gave more space to 'Nationalist failings', whereas *The Times* had more to report about the deficiencies of the Republic. The *Daily Telegraph*'s reporting achieved broad parity between the two and the *News Chronicle* and *Daily Herald*, although editorially sympathetic to the Republic, did not emphasise these issues as greatly as other papers.

However, the one paper that did make these matters a prominent, even a defining, issue was the *Daily Mail*. Thirteen per cent of all the themes coded for its coverage over the three sample periods focused on Republican failings. But this general distribution masks the extent to which this theme dominated the paper's coverage during the very early stages of the war. Through July and August 1936, the *Mail* published articles that became ever more extreme in their allegations of inhumane cruelty and irreligious amorality in 'Red' Spain ('27 Burned Alive By Spanish Reds', 27 July 1936: 11; '47 ANTI-REDS BUTCHERED IN CEMETRY', 4 August 1936: 10; 'RED WOMEN BUTCHER SPANISH

PRIESTS', 6 August 1936: 10; 'FAMILIES BURNED BY REDS: Refugee Tells of a Spanish "Nero"', 7 August 1936: 10; 'SPANISH PRIEST DRAGGED FROM REDS' CAR', 8 August 1936: 10; 'SPANISH MOBS ATTACK GIRLS', 10 August 1936: 10; 'REDS DROWN 447 IN WELLS', 11 August 1936: 10; 'REDS' SHOW OF SKULLS IN ROW', 12 August 1936: 10; 'PRIESTS AND MONKS TORTURED BY NUNS', 13 August 1936: 13). These kinds of stories were not unique to the *Mail* – for example the *Telegraph*, *Express* and *Mirror* published several in a similar vein ('PRIESTS BEHEADED AND NUNS STRIPPED NAKED BY MOB, the *Daily Mirror*, 24 July 1936: 3; 'COMMUNIST TERROR IN SPAIN', the *Daily Telegraph*, 1 August 1936: 11). It was the intensity of the *Mail*'s atrocity reporting that was exceptional and, during July and August 1936, it accounted for a third of all its Spanish coverage. This reporting in turn attracted a storm of criticism and repudiations from the left-wing and liberal press ('Now We Know', the *News Chronicle*, 4 August 1936: 8; 'Lord Rothermere and The "Reds"', the *News Chronicle*, 18 August 1936: 8; 'Crazy Crusade', the *Daily Herald*, 11 August 1936: 8; 'SURPRISE PROTEST IN FLEET STREET, the *Daily Worker*, 31 July 1936: 5; 'Madrid British Say "Stop Press Lies"', the *Daily Worker*, 15 August 1936: 1).

The story of the *Mail*'s initial vituperative response is often mentioned within the civil war literature and there seems to be an assumption that it remained at this pitch and tone throughout the duration of the war. However, its levels of atrocity coverage reduced significantly as the war progressed. For example, 'Republican failings' only occupied eight per cent of its coverage in April and May 1937 and, by January and February 1939, had disappeared from the paper's agenda. The qualitative change in rhetorical tone was even more dramatic. In August 1936, its editorials had vilified Republicans as 'Murderers of priests and ravishers and murderers of nuns' (3 July 1936: 8) but with the fall of Barcelona in January 1939, its leader items paid tribute to a defence that had been 'bravely upheld' ('Spain's Last Phase', 27 January 1939: 8), described the Republican leadership as 'bold and resolute' ('PEACE AT LAST', 10 February 1939: 10) and acknowledged the 'courage' of the Madridleños ('WHO RULES SPAIN?' 8 February 1939: 10). This trend was evident across the British press as a whole. In July and August 1936, coverage of 'Republican failings' accounted for six per cent of all coded themes in the entire press sample; by April– May 1937, this figure had reduced to two per cent; and, by January–February 1939, it was down to zero point three per cent.

As coverage of Republican atrocities reduced, media coverage of air attacks on civilians increased – from two per cent overall in July–August 1936 to eight per cent in April–May 1937. As discussed in Chapter 4, 'air fear' had been one of the defining concerns of the 1930s and it was unsurprising in this context that there would be journalistic interest in the effect of the bombing on civilian morale. Although both sides engaged in these attacks, eighty-three per cent of air-attack coverage related to Nationalist bombing. Moreover, over seventy per cent of these themes had an atrocity inflection – that is, they highlighted the indiscriminate and devastating nature of the attacks and/or the defencelessness of their victims (for

example, 'PLANES SPRAY DEATH AMONG DEMENTED WOMEN', the
Daily Mirror, 5 April 1937: 2, 10; 'AIR RAIDS IN BILBAO: THOUSANDS
HUDDLE IN SHELTERS', the *Daily Telegraph*, 12 May 1937: 9; 'Franco air
squadrons bomb Barcelona every two hours: TIMETABLE OF DEATH', the
Daily Express, 23 January 1939: 2). The most famous instance of this kind of
reporting followed the bombing of Guernica, when the chance proximity of four
foreign correspondents, three of whom were British, meant the story received
immediate coverage across the British press ('Germans Blamed for Bilbao
Massacre', the *Daily Express*, 28 April 1937: 1; 'Air Raid Wipes Out Basque
Town', the *Daily Mail*, 28 April 1937: 13; 'MORE SPANISH TOWNS SET ON
FIRE', the *Daily Telegraph*, 28 April 1937: 17; 'German Airmen Atrocity Shocks
World', the *Daily Herald*, 28 April 1937: 1).

In a recent study of international propaganda surrounding civilian bombing
in Spain, the revisionist historian Robert Stradling claims that the controversy
over Nationalist air attacks was one of the principal reasons why the Spanish
Civil War became such an international cause célèbre (2008: 31) but that this
outrage was based on exaggerated, even fabricated, evidence concocted by
Republican propagandists and their willing accomplices in the foreign press
corps. Stradling goes on to claim that this 'myth' remains largely unchallenged
today and reveals a systemic pro-Republican bias in historical analyses of the
war (ibid.: 5) but the results shown here demonstrate that, while it is true that
Nationalist air attacks received considerably more attention than Republican
ones, his claims about the dominance of this topic in Spanish Civil War reporting overall are overstated. Air attacks on civilians were a significant aspect of
British reporting but not a defining concern, even in the immediate aftermath
of Guernica, which was arguably the most dramatic breaking news event of the
whole war. For example, Figure 6.5 enumerates the day-by-day publication of
articles that appeared in *The Times* that made any reference to the bombing of
Guernica between 28 April and 31 May 1937. As discussed in Chapters 3
and 5, the paper's publication of George Steer's account of the raid on 28
April had caused an international sensation, some of which had attacked *The
Times'* role in publicising the attack. However, within ten days of the publication of its first report, the issue had shifted to the margins (note that more than
half of the items appearing after 8 May only made incidental references to
Guernica in the context of other discussions). This pattern was also evident in
other national newspapers as coverage of the event became crowded out by
other major scheduled and unscheduled news stories, in particular the
Hindenburg airship disaster (6 May 1937), the coronation of George VI (12
May 1937) and the ongoing London bus strike (April–May 1937).

The British press and non-intervention

In this section I examine British press coverage of the immensely controversial
policy of international non-intervention in the war and Britain's involvement in

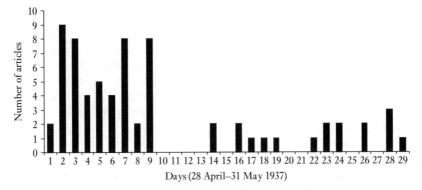

Figure 6.5 References to 'Guernica' in *The Times* 28 April–31 May 1937

its formulation and sustenance. The international agreement was conceived in haste and repented at leisure. Within days of the start of the war, compelling evidence emerged that Italy and Germany were providing arms to the Nationalists and pressure grew on the French government to open its borders and permit the free flow of arms to the Republic. The British government, however, was adamantly opposed to such a move and threatened to withdraw from mutual security agreements with France should it proceed on this path. The subsequent French proposals for an international non-intervention pact originally seemed to offer a constructive way for both diffusing the escalating international tensions and inhibiting the extension of Fascist and Communist influence in the southern Mediterranean. However, despite the establishment of an international committee on non-intervention that met regularly in London, only Britain observed the letter of the agreement. The Germans and Italians continued to pump munitions and manpower into Nationalist Spain and the Soviet Union did the same for the Republic. The French government vacillated between adhering to the agreement and tacitly condoning covert transportation of aid and arms to the Republic.

When originally mooted, the policy was welcomed by conservative and liberal opinion in Britain, although for different reasons. For the former, it was deemed to reduce the risk of a wider European war and, for the latter, it was believed that it would mainly work to the advantage of the Republic. However, Communist and other left-wing opinion quickly damned it as a form of 'malevolent neutrality' designed to ensure that Franco retained a decisive military advantage. Historical research has since shown that, whilst there was no shortage of ill will towards the Republican government in British official circles, malevolence was not the sole motivation for the British government's dogged adherence to the policy. As Tom Buchanan explains, non-intervention 'owed far more to events outside of Spain (especially the dictates of relations with Germany and Italy) than to those within it' (1997: 37). At root, the purpose of the policy was to cauterise and contain the conflict and, for all its manifest failures in Spain, the fact that events did not escalate into a European war was taken by its advocates at the time as sufficient justification for Britain's continued unilateral observance of its principles (see Padelford, 1937: 578).

Table 6.10 provides a diagrammatic summary of the stances of the British press towards non-intervention and the extent to which these altered as the war progressed. Rather than categorising press opinion merely in 'for' or 'against' terms, the classification also highlights divisions within each position that were variously advanced by different political sources during the war. 'Weak Non-Intervention' does not imply a stance that was tentatively argued but, rather, a specific position which held that Britain should do all in its jurisdiction to prevent arms and supplies entering the war zone but was not responsible for enforcing non-intervention internationally. All it could do was persuade and lead by example and, through its self-restraint, at the very least, ensure that the fires of the conflict were not stoked further. 'Strong Non-Intervention', in contrast, was a stance that asserted Britain had an international responsibility to ensure compliance to international agreements, through robust diplomatic and, if need be, military pressure. This was the position that the British Foreign Secretary, Anthony Eden, came to adopt and which was to lead to his eventual resignation in 1938 when it became clear that Chamberlain was equally convinced in his preference for the weaker variant. 'Strong Intervention' indicates the contrary proposition that Britain should intervene directly on behalf of one side in the war, whereas the 'Weak Intervention' argument asserted that Britain should allow the Republic to acquire the arms and supplies it needed for its effective defence and, at the very least, not obstruct the flow of arms and alms to the war zone.

The classification of each paper according to this typology was based on a close reading of their editorials published during each sample period, which, as noted earlier, have always been very significant indicators of the overt political orientations, concerns and sympathies of newspapers. The analysis in Table 6.10 shows that only three papers remained consistent in their editorial stance on the case for non-intervention during the three sample periods. At the start of the war, the *Daily Express* advised that 'in no circumstances whatever should this country allow itself to be drawn into the quarrel' ('The Bull Ring', 5 August 1936: 8). In January 1939, with Franco's victory virtually assured, it urged its readers to be 'glad that, as a nation, we have had no part in this senseless butchery', ('The Outcome', 17 January 1939: 8) and, the following month, claimed that '[g]reat is the part that our own Prime Minister has played in keeping this country out of the trouble' ('Don't be fooled', 10 February 1939: 10). *The Times* shared these views about the rectitude of 'weak non-intervention' and the diplomatic acuity of its principal advocate. At the start of the war, the paper asserted, 'There is no case whatever for intervention by this country' ('No Intervention', 5 August 1936: 13) and, at its denouement, eulogised Chamberlain's persistent pursuit of the policy, saying:

MR CHAMBERLAIN'S apt comparison of his own position to the younger PITT . . . is full of significance; for the mission of PITT, the

Table 6.10 Editorial stances of the national press on intervention/non-intervention

	Strong Intervention	Weak Intervention	Undecided or not stated	Weak Non-Intervention	Strong Non-Intervention
Manchester Guardian					
16 July–15 August 1936		■			
16 April–15 May 1937					■
16 Jan–15 Feb 1939			■		
Daily Herald					
16 July–15 August 1936		■			
16 April–15 May 1937					■
16 Jan–15 Feb 1939		■			
News Chronicle					
16 July–15 August 1936					■
16 April–15 May 1937					■
16 Jan–15 Feb 1939		■			
Daily Telegraph					
16 July–15 August 1936				■	
16 April–15 May 1937				■	
16 Jan–15 Feb 1939			■		
Daily Express					
16 July–15 August 1936				■	
16 April–15 May 1937				■	

Table 6.10 (Continued)

	Strong Intervention	Weak Intervention	Undecided or not stated	Weak Non-Intervention	Strong Non-Intervention
16 Jan–15 Feb 1939				■	
Daily Mail 16 July–15 August 1936		■			
16 April–15 May 1937				■	
16 Jan–15 Feb 1939				■	
Daily Worker 16 July–15 August 1936		■			
16 April–15 May 1937		■			
16 Jan–15 Feb 1939		■			
Daily Mirror 16 July–15 August 1936				■	
16 April–15 May 1937				■	
16 Jan–15 Feb 1939			■		
The Times 16 July–15 August 1936				■	
16 April–15 May 1937				■	
16 Jan–15 Feb 1939				■	

second son of an empire builder, was to devote his life to the improvement of the condition of his countrymen at home by the arts of peace. ('Mr Chamberlain's Speech', 30 January 1939: 13)

Only the *Daily Worker* consistently argued the case for intervention. In July 1936, a front-page editorial demanded the British government should:

PROVIDE THE PEOPLE'S GOVERNMENT OF SPAIN WITH THE OIL AND COAL AND FOOD SUPPLIES THEY NEED FOR THEIR WARSHIPS AND AEROPLANES. DEMAND AN END TO A FALSE NEUTRALITY THAT ONLY CONCEALS SUPPORT FOR THE FASCISTS ('ALL INTO ACTION TO DEFEND THE SPANISH REPUBLIC', 25 July 1936: 1).

It never wavered from this position throughout – see, for example, 'Restore the full right of Republican Spain to have the arms and supplies of material it needs' ('A Halt to Atrocities', 8 May 1937: 4) and 'GUNS, TANKS, PLANES & FOOD' (18 January 1939: 4). However, it is notable that the paper never campaigned for the direct involvement of British forces in the Spanish Civil War – that is, 'strong intervention' – and restricted itself to demands that the British government should not hinder the Republic from acquiring the means to effect its own defence. In the paper's analysis, the real source of salvation for the Republic was to be found in the unity and collective will of 'the working-class movement and all progressive people who hate fascism' ('Spain Calls', the *Daily Worker*, 27 July 36: 4). And no other paper advanced the case for strong intervention either.

When we consider how the majority of papers altered their position on non-intervention at different stages of the war, no consistent pattern emerges, even when they are grouped by their party-political orientation. To take the pro-Conservative press first, the *Daily Telegraph* may have been identified in some recent historical analyses of press opinion as one of the principle defenders of the policy but analysis of its leader columns suggests there was some second-thinking on its part as the war progressed. In 1936, the paper's commitment to weak non-intervention was unequivocal (for example, 'For this country, at any rate, the only policy towards the Spanish fury can be one of strict aloofness', 'SPAIN'S PERIL FROM COMMUNISM', 3 August 1936: 6). It remained broadly committed to this stance in April 1937, noting that it 'can be no part of British policy in Spain to invite a conflict, even though we have an overwhelming naval power on the spot' ('A POLICY OF STRICT NEUTRALITY', 15 April 1937: 16). However, even at this stage, its position was becoming discernibly less definitive. According to one political commentator at the time, this was due to its growing concerns about what a Nationalist victory might mean for British imperial interests in the Mediterranean and this alarm began to override its class-based antipathy to the Republic (Fenby, 1937: 253). By January 1939, these imperial concerns were ascendant and one of its editorials during this period broadly acknowledged the failure of non-intervention ('the end of the civil war will not necessarily end the European tension . . . There is a point beyond which neither France nor Britain can go to avoid challenge' ('A Stricken Field', 6 February 1939: 10).

The opinion of the remaining Conservative daily newspaper, the *Daily Mail*, took a very different trajectory. In July and August 1936, its editorials were fixated with Moscow's influence in the Republic, to such an extent that it even suggested Britain should also consider intervening on Franco's behalf, for example 'No one expects Germany and Italy to tolerate another Communist state in Europe and decent British feeling would favour the idea of joining hands with them' ('SHOULD BRITAIN INTERVENE?', 6 August 1936: 8) and 'All decent-minded Britons would welcome co-operation with Germany and Italy if they take any action to stop the murders of men and women in Spain for the satisfaction of Red blood lust' ('NOT A WORD', 15 August 1936: 10). By April–May 1937, however, it had aligned itself with the 'weak-intervention' stance and reiterated this commitment in early 1939 (see, for example, 'ERRAND OF PEACE', 14 February 1939: 14).

These movements in Conservative affiliations, however, were not as dramatic as the changes in the stances of the Liberal and Labour press opinion on non-intervention. Several papers vacillated between supporting 'weak intervention' and 'strong non-intervention' but none condoned 'weak non-intervention'. In several of its initial editorial the *Manchester Guardian* asserted the legal and constitutional right of the Republic to acquire resources for its defence – 'There is no precedent in international usage for this deliberate handicapping of a recognised, constitutional, and freely elected Government in its efforts to maintain its existence' ('THE FUTURE OF SPAIN, 12 August 1936: 8), for example. By April 1937, however, the paper had adopted a 'strong non-intervention' stance, broadly welcoming attempts to implement a new 'control scheme' designed to monitor breaches of the international agreement:

> Full of loopholes and unsatisfactory though the scheme may be, it is better that one should be enforced at all. With the 'control' scheme something at last is accomplished which can be called impartial . . . It is a step on the right road. ('The Government and Spain', 20 April 1937: 10)

By 1939, the paper had abandoned this view completely and, in a series of editorials, condemned non-intervention as 'a disgraceful policy for any British government to uphold' ('The Spanish Issue', 18 January 1939: 8) and claimed that it was 'specially odious to the British people' ('The Danger Grows', 20 January 1939: 10). Despite the bleakness and bitterness of this analysis, however, the paper's editorials during this period did not directly recommend Britain should engage in 'weak intervention' in the conflict.

At the start of the war, the *News Chronicle* firmly backed 'strong non-intervention':

> The British Government should declare with France, and all other Governments that will come in, not only their intention to be neutral, but their intention also to dispatch an international air fleet to the affected zone

to see that neutrality is observed. ('DEMOCRACY AND THE EMPIRE ARE AT STAKE', 6 August 1936: 8)

It broadly maintained this position through April and May 1937, although its patience was patently beginning to wear thin – 'For our part, we, who have not hesitated to voice our criticisms very bluntly, whole-heartedly rejoice with Mr Eden that his patience should have been rewarded at long last with this measure of success' ('Control at Last', 16 April 1937: 12). By 1939, its stance had changed completely and, in a series of editorials, it argued that the time had come for Britain to adopt a policy of 'weak intervention' (see, for example, 'Let Spain Buy Arms', 18 January 1939: 8; 'Arms for Spain!', 19 January 1939: 10; and 'Not Too Late', 27 January 1939: 10).

But the greatest volatility in editorial opinion was demonstrated by the *Daily Herald*. At the start of the war, the paper argued forcefully for 'weak intervention' in the war – 'There is an obligation on every state to permit the legal government of Spain to secure all the necessary means of defence' ('A CRIMINAL REVOLT', 30 July 1936: 8).[14] The paper also described the French government's plans for a non-intervention pact as 'an odd proposal . . . The French proposal would only penalise the constitutional forces' (3 August 1936: 8). The *Herald* persisted in this line of argumentation until the end of August 1936, when it suddenly switched to a 'strong non-intervention' stance thereby falling in line with official Labour Party policy agreed at the party's convention a few days before.

Responsible men and women cannot act instinctively and impulsively . . . The clear and obvious task then – things being as they are not as we might have wished them – is to secure the strict enforcement of the embargo by every state which has taken the pledge. ('LABOUR SPEAKS', 29 August 1936: 8)

The paper still endorsed this position in April 1937, welcoming the introduction of a new control scheme as 'the biggest and most complex mechanism of peaceful international collaboration on record' (16 April 1937: 8). However, a month later, its stance began to waver and one editorial argued that the 'best service which the British and French governments can render to non-intervention' would be to contemplate permitting the Republic to buy materials from them if Germany and Italy's flagrant contraventions of the agreement continued ('GERMANS IN SPAIN', 15 May 1937: 8). By 1939, the paper returned to its original preference for 'weak intervention', vilifying 'the ignoble part played by the democracies of the West' ('Roman Candour', 17 January 1939: 8) and calling for 'the Spanish people to be given fair play and a chance to defend themselves adequately. Only by raising the ban on arms for Spain can that be done' ('FAIR PLAY FOR SPAIN', 20 January 1939: 8).

Amidst all this passionate disagreement about the merits of non-intervention, there was one point that united all editorial commentary on the policy in the British press. All shared a presumption that Britain could act, should it wish to do so, and no editorial published during the sample periods suggested that Britain's official observance of 'weak non-intervention' might have been necessitated by the nation's military weakness. As shown in the previous chapter, many senior correspondents had been fully briefed by officials about the parlous state of Britain's armed forces in 1936–37 but this was a secret that editors and journalists preferred not to share with the general reading public.

Confidence in Britain's power also infused general coverage of British diplomatic and military actions in the war, which consistently tended to exaggerate their robustness, authoritativeness and effectiveness ('BRITISH ADMIRAL SAVED BARCELONA', the *Daily Express*, 25 July 1936: 1; 'US ARMS RUSH AS BRITAIN ACTS TO STOP WAR', the *Daily Mirror*, 6 January 1937: 1; 'Britain Sends New Warning to General Franco', the *News Chronicle*, 15 April 1937: 1; 'Eden Warns Germany and Italy', the *News Chronicle*, 7 May 1937: 2; 'HMS HOOD CLEARS FOR ACTION OFF BILBAO', the *Daily Telegraph*, 24 April 1937: 13; 'SPAIN FRONTIERS UNDER CONTROL: OBSERVERS READY TO BOARD BRITISH SHIPS', the *Daily Mail*, 20 April 1937: 14; 'BRITAIN SENDS SHIP TO SETTLE SPANISH WAR', the *Daily Mirror*, 9 February 1939: 1).

Concluding remarks

The findings discussed in this chapter show that press evaluations altered as the war progressed and many became markedly less hostile to the Republic. Nationalist sins gained prominence over Republican failings and, by the end, even those inclined to oppose the Republic became less disdainful in their terminology and demonstrated some compassion for Republican suffering and admiration for their resistance (see, for example, 'A STRICKEN FIELD', the *Daily Telegraph*, 6 February 1939: 10; and 'Sorrow for Spain', the *Daily Express*, 17 January 1939: 8).

As a way of concluding this chapter, I have summarised the editorial shifts from the start of the war to the end of the war (see Table 6.11). These categorisations are based on consideration of both the evaluative and interpretative dimensions of coverage during these periods. The classification abandons terms like 'impartiality' and 'neutrality' as explanatory categories because, as has been shown, these terms mask a privileging of the strategic interests of the British nation above and beyond any of the political and ideological issues at stake in Spain. Instead, Table 6.11 draws a tripartite distinction between 'Republican', 'Nationalist' and 'British Strategic' orientations and it also indicates whether they were staunchly held or advanced hesitantly. Because an emphasis upon 'British Strategic' interests did not preclude potential pro-Republican or Nationalist sympathies, I have entered double codings where appropriate (although in all of these cases I have indicated which was the principal stance).

The summary shows that liberal and left-wing press opinion never wavered in its support for the Republic, even though their opinions as to how its interests

Table 6.11 Press affiliations (1936 and 1939)

	July–August 1936	*Jan–Feb 1939*
The Times	British Strategic (strong) Nationalist (weak)	British Strategic (strong)
Manchester Guardian	Republican (strong)	Republican (strong)
Daily Telegraph	British Strategic (strong) Nationalist (weak)	British Strategic (strong)
Daily Express	British Strategic (strong) Nationalist (weak)	British Strategic (strong) Republican (weak)
News Chronicle	Republican (strong)	Republican (strong)
Daily Mirror	British Strategic (strong) Nationalist (weak)	Republican (strong) British Strategic (weak)
Daily Mail	Nationalist (strong)	British Strategic (strong)
Daily Worker	Republican (strong)	Republican (strong)
News Chronicle	Republican (strong)	Republican (strong)
Daily Herald	Republican (strong)	Republican (strong)

could be best served certainly did (see the previous section on non-intervention). The *Daily Telegraph* and *The Times* also never shifted from their fundamental view that Britain should avoid entanglement in the conflict at whatever cost, although the subtle anti-Republicanism evident in their initial coverage receded markedly towards the end of the war. With the remaining national papers, however, there was some major repositioning. We have already noted the major changes that occurred in the tone and concerns of *Daily Mail* editorials, which began with virulent tirades against the Republic and ended with measured discourses on how best to contain Italian expansionism in the Mediterranean. But this wasn't the only leopard that changed its spots. Both the *Daily Express* and *Daily Mirror* shifted their positions profoundly.[15]

I consider the reasons for these changes in the concluding chapter of this book but, in noting the staunch support for the Republic in some quarters and the emerging tolerance and respect in others, it is important to appreciate that it was the counter-revolutionary version of the Republic that gained approval. From the outset, the Republic's advocates promoted its democratic credentials and constitutional legitimacy and ignored the revolutionary ambitions that inspired so many citizens to take up arms in its defence, while its opponents heaped opprobrium on these radical aspects, characterising them as vindictive, irrational and destructive, while emphasising, often exaggerating, their consequences and never considering their causes. In this respect, both sides closed off any serious attempt to understand and evaluate the social revolution that infused the war during its early stages. And it is no coincidence that the most significant shifts in opinion towards the Republic occurred after central government had asserted its authority, the militias had disbanded, syndicalism and collectivisation had been abandoned and ordinary citizens had returned to their role as passive victims of a war beyond their control, rather than active agents fighting for their own political destiny.

Notes

1. My thanks to Ben Oldfield for his invaluable assistance in the quantitative coding of national press coverage.
2. The first sample month covers the start of the war – the commencement of military and political intervention by Germany, Italy and the Soviet Union and the preliminary formation of the International Non-Intervention Agreement. The second sample month encompasses the intensification of the Nationalist offensive in the Basque region and the attack on Guernica by the German Luftwaffe 'Condor Legion', the alleviation of military pressure on Madrid, the suppression of Anarchists and POUM in Barcelona and the replacement of Francisco Largo Caballero by Juan Negrín as the head of the Republican government. The third sample month covers the capture of Barcelona by Franco's forces, the flight of the Republican president Manuel Azaña from Spain and the first official recognition of the Nationalists as the government of Spain by the British and French governments.
3. Daily averages are used to permit comparisons between months of different durations.
4. It is likely that this figure underestimates the actual extent to which these sources were used. For example, only three per cent of items in The Times were attributed to news agencies (almost exclusively Reuters) but records held in the paper's archives at Wapping show that news-agency material was often incorporated within other reports and, although this provenance was often not signalled, meticulous care was taken to measure the precise amount of column space it occupied to ensure accurate remuneration to the agencies.
5. Up to three areas could be coded per item. Areas were only coded where there was a substantial reference to events in that locale (that is to say, brief namechecks were not coded). Where more than three areas were referenced in the article, the most prominently mentioned were coded.
6. The only reference made by The Times to conditions in the French camps was in an article published at the end of February 1939 which relayed a 'semi-official' note from the French government responding to criticisms about the conditions in the camps ('REFUGEE CAMPS IN FRANCE: A REPLY TO CRITICISMS', The Times, 23 February 1939: 13). The article concluded that the message laid 'justifiable stress on the remarkable fashion in which France has once thrown open her doors to unfortunates from other lands' but also concluded:

   > It must be added, without in any way detracting from the very great value of a real humanitarian effort, that even French visitors to the refugee camps have found real grounds for criticism, in the appalling conditions which still exist, as well as in the behaviour of some of the Senegalese troops and French Gardes Mobiles towards the helpless men in their power.

7. Only nine news items sent from Barcelona were published between 16 April and 2 May 1937. When the initial story of the fighting broke in the British press on 5 May 1937, all but one of the stories were sent from the French borders. This was mainly due to the temporary loss of telephonic links with Barcelona – the CNT's occupation of the Barcelona Telefonica building had been the catalyst for the fighting – but, even after their re-establishment, few stories were dispatched from Barcelona (seventeen items between 8 and 15 May 1937). Claud Cockburn, whose reports on the causes of the causes of the conflict for the Daily Worker so outraged George

Orwell (see Orwell, 1938: 215–35), was still filing reports from Madrid on the 7 May 1937. His first and most famous piece on the Barcelona May Days, that declaimed the POUM for 'their complicity as agents of a Fascist cause against the People's Front', was filed from Valencia on 10 May ('Pitcairn Lifts Barcelona Veil', the *Daily Worker*, 11 May 1937: 1). His only dispatch from Barcelona was sent on 16 May ('Republic Rounds up Hidden Arms: BARCELONA REVOLT SEQUEL: DECREE IN EFFECT TODAY', the *Daily Worker*, 17 May 1937).

8. The international press contingent also fled Malaga before it fell into Nationalist hands. Only Arthur Koestler of the *News Chronicle* remained and, because of his known Communist affiliations, he was imprisoned and sentenced to death. He was released several months later.

9. In July–August 1936 all news from Nationalist zones had to be couriered by hand to France. By April–May 1937, the Nationalists controlled the international cable heads at Vigo and Malaga. At the end of January 1939, they captured the international telephone exchange in Barcelona.

10. The greater differences in the *Daily Worker* undoubtedly reflect its highly partisan position on the conflict. With the *Daily Mirror*, the greater discrepancy is probably a factor of the exceptionally low levels of coverage of the civil war generally.

11. For example, only three articles in the *Manchester Guardian* alluded obliquely to the conflict between Chamberlain and Eden in the three months prior to Eden's resignation. The first was in an article filed from Berlin that discussed the goodwill to Chamberlain in Germany and concluded, 'The premier is at least to be congratulated upon not trying to act as a school master towards Germany and Italy, as Mr Eden is held to do' ('RESPONSE TO MR CHAMBERLAIN, BERLIN'S INTEREST', the *Manchester Guardian*, 11 November 1937: 6). The second actually denied any differences existed and claimed recent events had 'destroyed . . . the legend that there is any disharmony between Mr Chamberlain and Mr Eden' ('MR EDEN'S PRESTIGE', the *Manchester Guardian*, 3 December 1937: 6). The last reference appeared a matter of days before Eden's resignation and it fully and uncritically relayed the Foreign Secretary's statement about his 'close contact' with Chamberlain ('MR EDEN AND THE DICTATORSHIPS', the *Manchester Guardian*, 14 February 1938: 10).

12. Foreign correspondents rarely had any direct contact with Anarchist groups and viewed their actions from a distance and with some disdain (see, for example, Buckley: 1940: 275; Steer, 1938: 53). Two exceptions were the American journalists Hans von Kaltenborn (1950: 202–3) and Walter Duranty (Buchanan, 1993: 9).

13. Arthur Koestler later claimed Langdon-Davies was a member of the Communist Party at this time (Koestler, 1954: 323).

14. This stance attracted a sardonic editorial comment from the *Daily Express*, which noted that 'the socialist Daily Herald thereby achieves a United Front at last with the Communist Daily Worker' ('The Chorus of Light', 6 August 1936: 8). (This was an intentionally mischievous allusion to the continued resistance within the British Labour movement to Communist proposals that a British Popular Front needed to be formed to resist the rise of Fascism.)

15. At the start of the war, the *Express* claimed it took 'no sides on Spain' ('Get The News', 3 August 1936: 8) but published a series of articles that highlighted the lawlessness and terror abroad in Republican territory (for example, 'BARCELONA CARNAGE: BODIES PILED IN TUBE', 23 July 1936: 2; '310 Killed in Barcelona', 27 July 1936: 1; 'Mob Burn Church', 29 July 1936: 2; 'THE TERROR

IN SPAIN', 30 July 1936: 20). By early 1939, the paper still emphasised the importance of keeping Britain out of a wider war ('Peace again', 10 February 1939: 12) but ran several editorials that criticised Franco and opposed any possibility that Britain should furnish loans to aid any post-war restructuring in Spain ('Do you feel like making a gift to Mussolini? Do you wish to send a present to Hitler?', 'GIFTS ABROAD', 14 February 1939: 10; see also 'Fallen', 27 January 1939: 8). On 13 February 1939, its leader column stated that '[n]o doubt many of our readers will rejoice at the victory of Franco. But the *Daily Express* does not share their enthusiasm. We have no rejoicings at the course of events' ('One-Way Traffic', 13 February 1939: 10). The *Daily Mirror*'s coverage traced a similar trajectory although, by 1939, the paper was less convinced about the success and rectitude of Britain's non-intervention policy (for example, 'Keep out of it!', editorial, 24 August 1936: 11; 'PRIESTS BEHEADED AND NUNS STRIPPED NAKED BY MOB', 24 July 1936: 3; 'Father Forgive Them, They Know Not What They Do', 15 August 1936: 11; 'We have besought our readers to consider this question strategically, if they cannot be persuaded to consider it in mercy and pity for the desperately brave people of Spain', 'DO THEY SEE IT AT LAST?', 17 January 1939: 11; 'THE RACE TO BLACK FRANCO'S BOOTS', 18 February 1939: 14).

7

Other Avenues of Spanish News

The daily national press may have been the principal news arena in Britain in the late 1930s but it was not the only one of importance. In this chapter, I consider the representation of the Spanish Civil War in other supplementary but significant contexts – in particular, newsreel coverage, photographic news and the weekly national press. In this review, I draw on several exemplary studies that have been undertaken on these topics. Where appropriate, I also contribute additional primary and secondary analysis and, wherever possible, relate these analyses to the issues raised in the previous chapter to highlight areas of similarity and difference in civil war coverage across the various media arenas.

Real news and newsreels

By the late 1930s, newsreels represented a key information resource for the British public. Cinema attendance was burgeoning and this meant that these brief, informative bulletins about the major issues of the day had guaranteed access to considerable audiences. In 1936, there were five main newsreel companies in Britain – British Paramount News, Gaumont, British Movietone News, Pathé Gazette and Universal News.

Anthony Aldgate's book *Cinema and History: British Newsreels and the Spanish Civil War* (1979) remains the definitive work on the role of these companies in the reporting of the Spanish Civil War and the discussion that follows focuses mainly on the details he provides and analysis he develops. Aldgate's textual analysis is entirely qualitative but, in his book's appendix, the date, content and length of every British newsreel item on Spain is listed. Before examining the detail of his analysis, I begin with a statistical examination of these valuable raw data.

As the Spanish Civil War was the first European war to occur since the advent of sound, newsreels companies had an added incentive for covering the war extensively (see ibid.: 112). British Paramount News produced most coverage of the war (126 items), followed by Gaumont (76), British Movietone News (75), Pathé Gazette (64) and Universal News (39).

Figure 7.1 shows the distribution of these items over the war's duration. As with national daily press coverage, an initial intense interest was not sustained but the attrition rate was notably more acute in this media sector. For example,

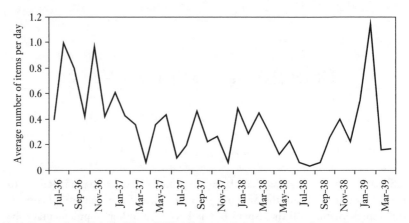

Notes: Based on data included in Aldgate (1979), daily averages are presented to permit comparison between months of different durations. *Averages = total of Spain items produced by all newsreel companies in a calendar month divided by the number of days in the calendar month.*

Figure 7.1 Daily average presence of all newsreel items on Spain by month
(July 1936–April 1939)

only three newsreel items were produced between 16 April and 15 May 1937, whereas this proved a period of considerable national press coverage and comment. Whilst the general reduction can be taken as indicative of a widely shared sense among British news producers that, by 1937, Spain was becoming 'old news', the particularly acute reduction evident in newsreel coverage revealed the very limited carrying capacities these outlets had for news content. This deficiency was noted at the time in an edition of the magazine, *World Film News*, when one commentator, Brian Crosthwaite, remarked:

> The brilliant work of the newsreel companies on the Abyssinian invasion and now on the Spanish Civil War was at first sufficiently sensational in its presentation of the violence and grimness of the modern battlefield to be simply the highspot of every issue. But as time goes on, it is a little depressing to find such material pushed down to the lower level of baby-shows and beauty parades. On such vital situations this banal and negligent treatment should be avoided at all costs. (Crosthwaite, 1937: 41)

A high proportion of footage originated from the Nationalist sector – sixty-six per cent of the 160 items where it is possible to deduce this aspect. This tendency was most pronounced in Gaumont's coverage – seventy-three per cent. What is not clear from the details contained in Aldgate's study is the extent to which the footage was generated by the newsreels companies themselves or provided to them by the Nationalist forces. Nevertheless, these distributions contrast greatly with those in the daily press, in which the large majority of coverage originated in Republican Spain.

Aldgate's analysis shows that the newsreels had only a minor role in breaking news about the war. For example, no newsreel mentioned the intra-Republican conflict in Barcelona and only Gaumont ran a report on the destruction of Guernica and then only ten days after it had occurred. Furthermore, the newsreels mainly maintained a 'strict silence' on the presence of foreign forces in Spain through 1936, even though these matters had been reported extensively in the national press (see ibid.: 135). The first mention of the International Non-Intervention Agreement came in January 1937, six months after it was first brokered. On the rare occasions breaking news was reported, it was often erroneous. For example, Gaumont mistakenly reported the fall of Madrid on 9 November 1936. From this, we can see that newsreels may have been key sites for propaganda and 'a formative element in the creation of public opinion on Spain' (ibid.: 112) but they did so more through illustration rather than information. These trends can be explained to a large extent by the logistical problems in obtaining footage from Spain. But this was not the only factor at work. As will be shown, newsreel companies willingly curtailed what they said and what they showed about the war.

As with the national press, the newsreels paid little attention to Spain before the initial outbreak of the war (see ibid.: 106) and there was some initial confusion about how best to locate, present and interpret the events unfolding. Much of the earliest coverage was, therefore, largely descriptive, although evaluative dimensions quickly emerged. In this emerging frame, a lot of coverage focused on the anarchy, disorder and religious intolerance of Republican Spain and said little about the constitutional authority of the Republican government or its constructive aspirations (see ibid.: 116). At the same time, the Nationalists tended to be portrayed as fighting for traditional Spanish values and, even when footage of atrocities committed by its forces was available, it was generally not used (see ibid.: 119). For example, Pathé Gazette declined to make any use of René Brut's footage of the Nationalist massacre of Republican prisoners in Badajoz on 14 August 1936, even though stills from the footage were distributed widely across other international media (see ibid.). Many newsreels also showed a willingness to portray Franco in a heroic mode. Gaumont delayed a story on the Nationalist relief of Toledo until after Franco's arrival at the scene, thereby conveying the mistaken impression that he was present at the relief and 'giving his role greater symbolic value' (ibid.: 133).

The newsreel company most openly hostile to the Republic was British Movietone News and its editorial stance obviously mirrored that of its proprietor, Lord Rothermere. But a review of newsreel coverage of the war published at the time claimed this was just the most extreme example of a general political bias against the Republic across the sector (see Crosthwaite, 1937: 41). Aldgate concurs with this assessment, observing that what was lacking in most of the early newsreel coverage was 'a sense of balance' (Aldgate, 1979: 116). These partisan tendencies modified somewhat in 1937. For example, the arrival of aerial bombing of Republican towns produced the first 'hint of criticism in the British newsreels of Nationalist infamy' (ibid.: 119). But the shifts in editorial opinion were not as evident as they were in the national press.

However, to focus on the extent to which newsreel coverage favoured Republican or Nationalist forces is to miss the key point about the political orientation of newsreels over Spain. Aldgate shows these news organisations were only tangentially concerned with the internal politics at stake. Rather, their main concerns were pro-British and all events in Spain were defined in these terms. At the start of the war, this involved stressing the self-contained nature of the war in Spain and using its violence and passion to highlight the temperance and rationality of British society. For example, extensive newsreel coverage was given to a speech by the British Prime Minister in November in 1936, in which he contrasted the peace and prosperity of Britain with the chaos in Spain and the rising tensions in Europe. As Aldgate comments, 'It is "Wonderful Britain" all over again, and the opinions of the newsreels are seen to be vindicated by the leading figure in the establishment' (ibid.: 137).

This ethnocentric frame persisted throughout but Aldgate shows that its emphasis changed from 1937 onwards. As the international implications of the conflict deepened and general international tensions grew, the focus on 'stable Britain' shifted to a portrayal of a Britain committed to peace but prepared for war should that necessity arise (ibid.: 156). Within this framework, the newsreels' original policy on intervention and non-intervention of 'the less said, the better' was jettisoned (ibid.: 129). References to non-intervention started to emerge but the overwhelming tenor of coverage emphasised the legitimacy of the policy, its effectiveness and the vital and constructive role that Britain was playing in its observance (see ibid.: 156, 166). Critical viewpoints of British policy struggled to gain any foothold. For example, in February 1938, Paramount invited the Clement Attlee, the Labour party leader, to comment on the resignation of Anthony Eden. The highly critical analysis he provided of British government policy was removed from circulation within hours of its release (see ibid.: 175).

Examples such as this offer a telling insight into the extent to which British national interests and British government interests were seen as indivisible by the newsreel companies. Certainly, the deference and pliability of the newsreels to government wishes contrast with national press responses to the war which, for all their failings, gave far greater vent to awkward questions and critical facts. Aldgate's concluding assessment is damning:

So if the pictures of Spain, and indeed Britain, which they presented were limited and partial, they were deliberately so. If they failed to explain fully the role of Russia, Germany or Italy in the Spanish Civil War, then again it was for a purpose. If, finally, they failed to explain what the Spanish Civil War was about, then there can be no doubt that the newsreels helped to prevent the Spanish situation from being understood. (ibid.: 193–4)

The roots of this passivity and obsequiousness, what Aldgate defines as a reduced 'capacity for an independent and informed opinion' (ibid.: 90), are explained by a range of internal and external factors. These included prorietorial conservatism, the lack of a strong ethos of editorial independence in the sector, a fear or alienating public opinion and concerted official pressures from national and local authorities in Britain.

Seeing and believing – visualising Spain

Aldgate's analysis demonstrates that, in terms of content, newsreel coverage of Spain was threadbare by comparison to the national daily press. Many major stories were marginalised or even completely ignored and, even when attempts were made to report developing events, newsreel coverage could do little but corroborate information that had hit the newsstands days, even weeks, before. Why, therefore, should newsreels be considered to have played such a significant role in the formation of public opinion about Spain? Part of the reason lies in the access they had to the non-newspaper reading public although this was a less significant fraction of the adult population of Britain in the 1930s than it is today. But the main reason lay in the visuality rather topicality of the medium. Newsreels allowed British citizens to see for themselves the conditions and consequences of war and this lent an immediacy to events in Spain that was difficult to conjure through words alone.

The significance of this factor should not be overstated, however, as visual representation was not the sole preserve of newsreels. Newspapers and other current affairs publications also published multitudinous images of the war to accompany the acres of editorial commentary. The late 1930s also saw the emergence of new magazines, like *Life* and *Picture Post*, that centred on photographical essays and created a new mass marketplace for photojournalism. Obviously, these were single not moving images but this did not necessarily mean that newsreel footage could claim a greater drama and immediacy. Newsreel cameras of the day were cumbersome and had to be firmly anchored – plus they were difficult to operate. This meant they were not suited to capturing unstaged action and, in the main, they recorded events that could be predicted and, if necessary, choreographed. In contrast, developments in photographic cameras – improvements in shutter and film speeds, camera size and lens quality – meant that journalists could more readily capture action quickly, dramatically and intimately. One of main reasons Spain was described at the time as ' "the most photogenic war anyone has seen" ' (quoted in Cockburn, 1967) was because it was the first war where the technology had the flexibility and ubiquity to do so effectively. According to Susan Sontag:

> The Spanish Civil War was the first war to be witnessed ('covered') in the modern sense: by a corps of professional photographers at the lines of military engagement and in the towns under bombardment, whose work was immediately seen in newspapers and magazines in Spain and abroad. (1998)

Amateur contributions also added to the volume of photographic images, as ordinary correspondents were encouraged to carry cameras on their travels and newspapers occasionally printed photographs supplied from other sources (for example, 'A Daily Express Woman Reader Took This Picture in Spain', the *Daily Express*, 27 July 1936: 2).

The most comprehensive analysis of photographic representation of the Spanish Civil War is Caroline Brothers' 1997 book *War and Photography*. One of the impressive aspects of this study is its confident grasp of visual theory and the way this is used to deconstruct photographic images in the British and French press. The result is a highly nuanced, cross-national comparison that, in highlighting some important cultural differences in visual representations, demonstrates how photographic images and their relation to textual information did not so much capture the reality of events in Spain as construct them.

Brothers organises her analysis under three thematic groupings to identify ideological differences between and within the British and French photographic media. It is pertinent to this discussion to summarise her main observations with regard to each.

The combatants

Images of combatants in Spain drew on a range of conflictive and contradictory myths. Brothers' analysis begins by examining the visual representation in the French and British press of the Republican militias who took up arms to resist the rebellion. She notes that, while the pro-Republican press in both countries emphasised the popular support for their actions, there were clear differences in the way this public consent was communicated. Within the British press there was a tendency to portray militia members and ordinary citizens as co-operative but separate, whereas the French press had no compunction about reproducing images that illustrated 'the interchangeability of militia-members and civilians, the French seemingly readier to accept the notion of ordinary citizens taking up arms' (ibid.: 41).

Brothers explains this difference in relation to the distinct political cultures and histories of each nation. Revolutionary politics had played a foundational role in the creation of the modern French state, thereby permitting 'unambiguous parallels' to be drawn between events in Spain and France's 'own revolutionary past' (ibid.: 56). No such precedent existed within British political culture, where revolutionary fervour had long been viewed with scepticism. For this reason, images in the pro-Republican press in Britain 'downplayed the movement's spontaneity, implying organisation and containment where none existed' (ibid.: 56). Having said this, the visual representation of the militias in pro-Republican publications in both countries also shared 'a powerful mythology of their representation of soldiers at war' (ibid.: 47), using images that emphasised the discipline, courage and selflessness of the Republican militia.

Predictably, the themes that were valorised in the pro-Republican press were disdained in the pro-Nationalist press in both nations. Publications sympathetic to Franco selected images that demonstrated the political extremism, violent anticlericalism, indiscipline, dishonour, cowardice and stupidity of the Republican militia. But, despite the manifest difference of political intent that motivated the selection of these images, they were nevertheless 'drawn from the same cultural pool' (ibid.: 52).

Theses of courage, honour and discipline, and their antitheses, were also mobilised extensively in the visual representation of the Nationalist forces, which included Moorish troops recruited from Spanish Morocco. However, the deployment of imagery here was not entirely consistent to the representation of the militias. In the pro-insurgent press of both nations, attention was drawn to the quality of the Nationalist soldiery while questions of 'their rapport with the rest of the nation went virtually unexplored' (ibid.: 59). In Brothers' judgement this exposed a 'paternalistic ideology. The army was a class apart; it fought and was unquestionably responsible for the people's own good' (ibid.). Much of this positive imagery also drew on 'a crusader myth', which helped divert attention from the political goals of the rebellion and tapped directly into 'cultural attitudes already well-established in the collective imagination of Britain and France' (ibid.: 74). For this reason, Brothers identifies a far higher degree of consensus in the images selected by the pro-insurgent press in both Britain and France. She also notes that the presence of African Muslims fighting a purportedly 'Christian' war created presentational difficulties for the pro-Nationalist papers, which they countered by selecting images that emphasised the discipline and benevolence of the Moorish soldiery. But, for all these problems, the pro-Republican papers found the crusader myth a difficult one to counter:

> Insurgent courage, discipline, benevolence and popularity were denigrated in photographs of hollow victories in empty towns and of deserters cheerfully going over to the Republican side. More complex politically, but less effective as visual propaganda . . . More usually the pro-Republican press responded to Insurgent propaganda on its own terms, denouncing the holy crusade as hypocritical and the Moors as Nazi dupes: they rarely introduced any more effective counter-propaganda of their own. (ibid.: 75)

Female combatants were popular subjects for photographs, particularly during the initial stages of the rebellion (ibid.: 77). According to Brothers, these representations 'sign-posted deep-felt anxieties over acceptable conduct for women and the effect on society when traditional behaviour patterns broke down under the impact of war' but these concerns played out differently in the British and French press (ibid.: 76). Almost all women warriors fought for the Republic, thereby producing predictable partisan differences in their specific treatment by particular publications. Nevertheless, uncertainties were apparent, even in the pro-Republican press, as to the appropriateness of direct female engagement and these concerns seemed to be more acute in the British press. Brothers notes that pro-Republican publications in Britain stressed the gender of female combatants to emphasise their valour but downplayed their femininity, whereas, in French papers, '[t]he shock juxtaposition of women and weapons gave an edge to their femininity, while their gender was used deliberately to confer legitimacy on the armed struggle' (ibid.: 85). These cultural differences were evident also in the pro-Nationalist press. While in the British press women's involvement in the fighting was 'the very stuff of scandal', it was not extensively discussed in the pro-insurgent press in France (ibid.: 87).

But whether these women were represented as admirable 'Amazons' or crazed 'Carmens', Brothers demonstrates that all visual constructions were underwritten by a male gaze, with coverage emphasising the 'otherness' of these women. Moreover, in her assessment, any greater tolerance of female involvement evident in the French images was not so much indicative of a greater liberality in French society as of the fact that French women were even more disempowered than those in Britain at that time.

The civilians

The second substantive component of Brothers' analysis examines the visual representation of the impact of the war on civilian life and the civilian environment. Inevitably, the shadow of the bomber loomed greatly in such coverage and her analysis begins with a discussion of the 'semiology and the city at war' (ibid: 101–20). Papers in both countries and of all political persuasions published large numbers of images of bombers and planes flying into battle, as well as aerial photographs that provided detached views of the urban environments that had now fallen within the bomb-sights. However, the suspicion of any fetishism and distanciation of the new modes of total warfare evident in these images was balanced by 'an equally insistent counter pulse . . . to investigate the effects of the new technology on the ground and to register its impact on a human scale' (ibid.: 104).

Both pro-Republican and Pro-Nationalist papers published large numbers of images of urban devastation but they did so for different political and ideological reasons. The former used them to demonstrate the sham of non-intervention; the latter sought to foster pacifism within public opinion through them, thereby buttressing the case for non-intervention. But beyond these vested motives, the visual representation of devastated cities connected generally to ill-founded projections about the orderliness and rationality of the urban environment:

> To both peoples the city was by definition a highly organised space of relative functional stability in which sites were geared to specific purposes, and within which even the most insignificant objects had an appropriate place . . . In meticulously detailing the erosion of the concept of the city – its stability, integrity, privacy and security – the French and British press effectively reinforced notions cherished within the collective imagination, defending human values against the absurdity of urban life in war. (ibid.: 120)

The objectification of these 'human values' was manifested in the extensive representation of Spanish civilians. But the 'anthropology of civilian life' thus created was skewed at its core by powerful preconceptions within Britain and France about Spanish society (ibid.: 121). The images of Spanish civilian life during the war were predicated on assumptions about its character before the war – traditional, family orientated, rural and governed by the rituals of the church. Moreover, in visualising the disruptions to this idealised notion of Spanish society – food queues, air raids, the abandonment and politicisation of children, religious desecration – the imagery also connected with deep and anxious projections about what modern war would look like closer to home. For this reason, '[i]t was above all the collective fears, ideals and expectations of societies distant from Spain that were formulated and given substance in these fragile paper signs' (ibid.: 138).

The victims

Concepts of victim-hood were implicit within the visualisation of civilian lives and environment but Brothers' analysis also examines the specific visual picturing of victims in British and French newspapers. In the first part of this section, she examines the copious coverage given to refugees. In national terms, British and French visualisations drew on 'a remarkably similar pool of characteristics' (ibid.: 142). In political terms, there were major differences in their coverage in the pro-insurgent and pro-Republican press. In the former, the emotional and political implications of the refugees were circumscribed: 'These closed narratives, characterised by images of refugees at journey's end, safe in their places of exile, signalled an endeavour to contain the emotive power of their plight and to limit their situation to a matter of practical consideration' (ibid.). In the pro-Republican press, however, the plight of refugees was portrayed as an open narrative, drawing on powerful biblical associations to portray their exodus from danger as a journey into even greater insecurity and uncertainty. But what the representations of both sides shared was a sense of:

> refugee passivity, docility and powerlessness . . . nor was it mere coincidence that they were also widely held as defining qualities of women and children, who more than any other social group were identified with the refugee archetype and were best able to elicit pathos on their behalf. (ibid.: 160)

The second categorisation of victim Brothers examines is the visual record of the casualties of war – the wounded, the dying and the dead. Her analysis shows how such images were sanitised and censored by news editors sensitive to the limits of public sensibilities and that this reluctance was more pronounced in the British press than the French. Only rarely were graphic illustrations of death and mutilation provided – the *Daily Worker*'s publication of children killed by an aerial attack on the Republican town of Getafe in October 1936 is one example – and only then for clear propagandistic purposes. In the main, death was dealt with through 'euphemism, symbol and pathos' or '[i]f the moment, or more commonly, the aftermath of wartime killing were ever shown, this was generally from a distance, or with overtones that sensationalised the photographic act' (ibid.: 184).

Shifting (photo)frames

Detailed consideration of Caroline Brothers' analysis of the trends in photographic representation of the Spanish Civil War is warranted because of the richness and sophistication of the insights it provides. However, there are some issues related to the photographic representation of the war that remain unexplored in the book. Her interest in examining differences between 'pro-insurgent' and 'pro-Republican' newspapers meant her sampling focused on the extremes of press opinion because only those newspapers that could be confidently categorised in one camp or the other were analysed. This means a significant rump of British (and French) coverage is absent from the discussion. (The book's index shows one reference to the *Daily Express* and no references to *The Times*, *Daily Telegraph* or *Daily Mirror*.) Furthermore, it is not easy to deduce the respective prominence of these different images or the extent to which the visual representation of the war altered as events unfolded.

One element of the content analysis of national press coverage of the war described in the previous chapter involved quantifying the frequency of appearance, and subject matter, of photographs and images in British press coverage (see Table 7.1). Although the categorisation of the images is crude compared to the fine-grained deconstructions provided by Brothers, the resulting statistics permit some insights into changes in the visual representation of the war and they also encompass a wider range of press outlets.

The results show that most pictures were published in the earliest weeks of the war despite the considerable logistical difficulties foreign news organisations faced in getting news out of Spain during these early stages. In April–May 1937, their number reduced by sixty-three per cent but increased again in the latter stages of the conflict. In January and February 1939, newspapers carried more than twice as many images relating to the war than they had in 1937.

Many of these images originated in the newsrooms of Britain. Maps were consistently prominent across all sample periods and dominated the first two. At the start of the war, the great majority of these were of the entire Iberian peninsular and these general maps were even more dominant during April–May 1937, although this was largely an artefact of the reduced number of photographs and illustrations, overall. However, more detailed regional maps started to gain a presence in 1937 and, by 1939, were the most frequently used.

At the start of the war, many of these general maps identified the locations of major cities and regions and contained no specific information, such as which forces held which areas (see, for example, the maps published by the *News Chronicle* on 20, 21, 22 and 23 July 1936). This, in part, reflected the general confusion that prevailed in the first weeks but it also suggests that the principal purpose of these maps during the early months of the war was to provide geographic orientation for British audiences and it was only in the later stages that they began to assume an informational function. This is a telling measure of the remoteness of Spain from British perspectives in the 1930s – not only physically but also culturally and experientially (see Shelmerdine, 2006; Moradiellos, 2003).

Although maps were mainly used for informational purposes, there were occa-sions when their design and detail conveyed subtle political associations and pro-jections. For example, as Nationalist forces closed on Barcelona in January 1939, the *Daily Express* superimposed the picture of two bombers over an angled map of Barcelona and the regions surrounding it, labelling it a 'Bomber's eye view' (18 January 1939: 2). The following week, the *News Chronicle* superimposed a map of the British Home Counties on the same area, under the heading 'If London Were Barcelona Franco's Lines Would Be As Shown Here' (25 January 1939: 2).

In terms of photography, far more images were of Republican locations and subjects than Nationalist. Of the occasions where it was possible to deduce this reliably, eighty-one per cent of the photograph images were taken from a Republican vantage point, compared to nineteen per cent from a Nationalist one. This distribution provides a point of contrast with newsreel imagery, where there was less disparity in visual vantage points.

The greater visual presentation of the interior environment of the Republic was undoubtedly a product of the different controls that pertained in both sectors (see previous discussions). However, as Caroline Brothers' analysis so elegantly demonstrates, this cannot be assumed to have worked to the Republic's political and ideological advantage. Images of mobilised, militarised citizens could as readily be used to de-legitimise the Republic as to legitimise it – just as images of urban devastation could be used to support or repudiate Britain's policy of non-intervention. Photographs are inherently polysemic and it is impossible to see the images 'independently from the ways they are framed by the text. Photographs attain meaning only in relation to the settings in which they are encountered' (Becker, 2002: 302).

That said, it is possible to identify two transitions in photographic coverage from these results that may reveal something about the paper's shifting editorial dispositions regarding the Republic. First, extensive imagery of mobilised, mil-itarised (and presumably politicised) Republican citizens that created so much propaganda fodder for the pro-Francoist press and such ambivalence among the pro-Republican press was the sole preserve of the 1936 sample period. However, the representation of 'suffering Republican citizens', but a minor aspect of British coverage at the start, came to dominate the recrudescence of Spain as a visual news story in January–February 1939. Developing Caroline Brothers' analysis, this shift from the portrayal of active citizens to passive non-citizens re-orientated coverage from matters that were symbolically disadvantageous to the Republic to one that threatened the legitimacy of Nationalist actions. Second, at the start of the war, twelve per cent of all images portrayed 'violent death and injury in Republican zones' and '[a]cts of religious desecration'.[1] By April–May 1937, these images had been displaced by images of '[u]rban bomb and shell damage in Republican territory', most of which focused on the devastation of Guernica. Here again, therefore, we can detect a shift in imagery from issues that were ideologically problematic for the Republic to ones that challenged the honourableness of Nationalist conduct.

Table 7.1 Photographs and Illustrations in the British Daily National Press by Year

16 July–15 August 1936	*16 April–15 May 1937*	*16 Jan–15 Feb 1939*
General maps of Spain 29%	General maps of Spain 41%	Suffering Republican citizens 35%
Mobilised Republican citizens 12%	Urban bomb damage in Republican territory 20%	Regional maps 30%
Urban bomb damage in Republican territory 8%	Regional maps 20%	General maps of Spain 12%
Suffering Republican citizens 7%	Suffering Republican citizens 7%	Nationalist military victory/advance 4%
Republican military action (up close) 6%	Military technology 2%	Urban bomb damage (Republican) 3%
Dead/murdered Republican civilians 6%		Nationalist leaders 2%
Religious desecration (Republican zones) 4%		Nationalist military actions (distant) 1%
Nationalist leaders 3%		Republican military actions (distant) 1%
Republican leaders 3%		Mobilised Republican citizens 1%
Regional maps 2%		
All other images 20%	All other images 10%	All other images 11%
(381 photographs and and illustrations)	(142 photographs and illustrations)	(319 photographs illustrations)

Notes: *Daily Mirror, Daily Telegraph, Daily Herald, Manchester Guardian, The Times, News Chronicle, Daily Express, Daily Mail, Daily Worker.* Up to three images could be coded per news item, to cover occasions when multiple visuals were used.

National weekly newspapers and news reviews

This final section of the chapter summarises briefly the editorial responses of other national news publications in Britain to events in Spain. This discussion draws mainly on the review provided by Benny Morris in his broader study of the British weekly press coverage of appeasement (1992).

Morris's analysis conflates two types of news publication under the heading of 'The British Weekly Press' – newspapers proper, whose principal function, like their daily equivalent, was to purvey hard news and information, and news reviews, whose function was to provide interpretation of contemporary affairs (see PEP, 1938: 46). Furthermore, his review is selective as it focuses on 'serious weeklies' (ibid.: 116) and excludes consideration of the editorial responses of popular newspapers such as the *Sunday Express*, the *Sunday Dispatch*, the *Sunday Graphic*, the *Sunday Pictorial* and *Reynolds News*. Nevertheless, the concise analysis provided by Morris provides a valuable contribution to this appraisal of British media responses to the Spanish Civil War. It also provides a clear sense of the contingency and changeability of press opinion which, as discussed in the previous chapter, has been insufficiently appreciated to date.

Table 7.2 itemises the papers and journals covered in his discussion. Several of these remain leading publications to this day (*The Observer*, *New Statesman*, *The Sunday Times*, *The Economist*, *The Spectator*); some others still exist but have become less influential in public debates (*The Tablet*, *Tribune*); and others have since sunk into historical obscurity (*The Saturday Review*, *Time and Tide*). Table 7.2 also summarises Morris's assessment of: (a) the positions these publications assumed in relation to the antagonists in the war; and (b) the policy of international non-intervention. In summarising the latter, I have related Morris's distinction to the typology utilised in the previous chapter between 'strong non-intervention' (the robust international enforcement of the agreement), 'weak non-intervention' (national observation of the agreement), 'weak intervention' (the lifting of arms embargos) and 'strong intervention' (direct military involvement in support of one side).

The detail in Table 7.2 shows there was a strong correlation between the party-political orientation of papers and their affiliations to the antagonists. Almost all Labour and Liberal publications strongly endorsed the Republican cause, *The Spectator* proving the sole exception. In the main, pro-Conservative papers backed Franco – however, there was greater variability in this camp. *The Sunday Times* was unaligned for the first months of the war and only became more receptive to the Nationalist cause in mid 1937, after the paper's acquisition by Lord Camrose, who was a close political ally of Chamberlain (ibid.: 107). *The Saturday Review* began as strongly pro-Nationalist but 'Fascist atrocities and the spectacle of Britain enduring humiliation led to a dampening of its pro-Franco ardour' (ibid: 109).

There was, however, a strong cross-party consensus with regards to non-intervention. Only *Tribune* advanced the case for weak intervention consistently, although the *Economist* came to share this view towards the end of 1937. The *New Statesman*'s position on this is particularly intriguing, not least because it lends an interesting perspective to one of the most infamous editorial controversies sparked by the war. In mid 1937, George Orwell submitted an article to the *New Statesman* titled 'Eye-Witness in Barcelona' in which he argued, on the basis of his experiences fighting for the POUM in Spain, that the Communists in Spain were pursuing a repressive, counter-revolutionary agenda. The article was rejected by the journal's editor, Kingsley Martin, but he offered Orwell the

Table 7.2 Weekly newspaper stances on Spain

	General Political orientation	*Position on antagonists in Spain*	*Position on Non-Intervention*
The Observer	Conservative	Strongly pro-Nationalist (see Morris, 1992: 107)	Consistently endorsed weak non-intervention (see ibid.: 108–9)
The Sunday Times	Conservative	From July 1936 to mid 1937 the paper was equally condemnatory of both Republican and Nationalist causes. From mid 1937 to the end of the war it acquired a 'pro-Nationalist tilt' following the paper's acquisition by Lord Camrose, who was a close political ally of Chamberlain (ibid.: 107).	Consistently endorsed weak non intervention – 'unwaveringly supported' (ibid.: 111)
The Spectator	Liberal	'While always flaunting its liberal and democratic credentials, the journal only reluctantly and, at times, equivocally expressed sympathy for the Republican cause' (ibid.: 112).	Recognised the threat a Nationalist victory posed to British strategic interests but supported weak non-intervention 'through thick and thin' because of its wider concerns about German and Italian counter-measures that could be provoked by its abandonment (ibid.: 112).
Tribune	Labour	Consistently pro-Republican – the paper was created in January 1937 to mobilise public support for the Republic.	Endorsed weak intervention throughout (see ibid.: 120)
The Economist	Liberal	'From the first, *The Economist* came out clearly and unequivocally in support of the Republic' (ibid.: 115).	Initially came close to supporting weak intervention but soon endorsed weak non-intervention for the sake of European peace, albeit with increasing reluctance.

Table 7.2 (continued)

	General Political orientation	*Position on antagonists in Spain*	*Position on Non-Intervention*
			By late 1937–early 1938, its editorial stance shifted towards supporting weak intervention – 'the firmest anti-appeasement advocate amongst the serious weeklies' (ibid.: 116).
The Tablet	Non-aligned with Conservative sympathies	Strongly Pro-Nationalist (see ibid.: 107)	Pro-weak non-intervention, 1936–1937 (see ibid.: 107)
New Statesman and Nation	Labour with Communist sympathies	Strongly Pro-Republican (see ibid.: 117)	From August 1936–June 1937 supported weak non-intervention largely out of dread of a wider war (see ibid.: 117–8). In July 1937 there was extensive debate within the paper about shifting editorial support to weak intervention but, after that period, the paper 'continued, through its silence, to consent to non-intervention' (ibid.: 119).
The Saturday Review	Liberal Conservative	July 1936, strongly pro-Nationalist, justified by concerns about anti-Communism. By April 1937, 'Fascist atrocities and the spectacle of Britain enduring humiliation led to a dampening of its pro-Franco ardour' (ibid.: 109).	Unclear In November 1937, it criticised the British government for its anti-Nationalist neutrality and urged that belligerent rights be conferred on the insurgents (see ibid.: 109).
Time and Tide	Liberal	Strongly pro-Republican	In August 1936, advocated strong non-intervention but quickly

Table 7.2 (continued)

General Political orientation	Position on antagonists in Spain	Position on Non-Intervention
		back-pedalled to support weak non-intervention. The attack on Guernica in 1937 created some uncertainty in the paper's support for this position but it reaffirmed its commitment by July 1937 in the interests of wider European peace. (see ibid.: 116–17). In late1938–early 1939 its position shifted towards endorsing weak intervention, albeit unconvincingly (see ibid.: 117).
The Truth Conservative	From July–December 1936, '[i]mplicit sympathy for the Republic pervaded its pages' (ibid.: 109) From January 1937, there was 'muted support for Franco' (ibid.: 110) '*Truth* found the Spanish conflict a conscience-tormenting episode: espousal of appeasement towards Germany and Italy clashed with its appreciation of Britain's interest in the Mediterranean, fear of Communism with abhorrence of Fascist mores and ideals, compassion for an embattled democracy with a desire to support the Conservative government' (ibid.: 109).	Up until November 1936, it supported weak non-intervention. By December, it was criticising the policy as a 'grim joke' and seemed to be moving towards advocating 'strong non-intervention' or complete disengagement (thus implicitly condoning weak intervention). However 'this ambivalent advocacy of British firmness proved short-lived' (ibid.: 110). By April 1937, it was reasserting the case for weak non-intervention.

opportunity to review Franz Borkenau's book *The Spanish Cockpit*. This review was again rejected by Martin and, on this occasion, he explained in writing that the reason lay in Orwell's reiteration that the rising influence of the Communists ' "had pulled [the Republic] to the right" ' (quoted in Shelden, 1991: 305). His rejection letter stated:

> 'I am sorry that it is not possible for us to use your review of *The Spanish Cockpit*. The reason is simply that it controverts the political policy of the paper. It is very uncompromisingly said and implies that our Spanish Correspondents are all wrong.' (29 July 1937, quoted in ibid.: 305)

Orwell was incensed and took the rejection as further evidence of the pernicious influence the Communists exerted over the left-wing press of the day, which he deemed more damaging than the hysterical atrocity propaganda of the reactionary press. However, if there was justification to Orwell's suspicions, Morris's analysis shows that the extent of Communist influence was not consistent across the left-wing press. For, although the *New Statesman* was not alone in deciding that the pragmatic concerns about avoiding a European war should outweigh matters of political principle, in pursuing this line it contradicted the international Communist line at the time, which opposed non-intervention and sought to recruit democracies in an anti-Fascist alliance.

Overall, Morris's findings suggest there was less volatility in weekly press opinion over the war and the question of non-intervention than has been shown in the national daily press. Furthermore, there seemed to be no equivalent to the consistent trend noted in the daily press, which saw increasingly sympathetic coverage of the Republic emerging as the war unfolded. Indeed, two weekly publications became more pro-Nationalist during the course of the conflict (*The Truth* and *The Sunday Times*).

Concluding remarks

This chapter has examined other significant avenues of Spanish news in Britain during the 1930s – specifically, newsreels, photojournalism and the weekly press. The detail of the discussion highlights points of similarity and distinction to those identified in the review of daily press coverage in the previous chapter.

As with national press coverage, a process of attrition was evident in levels of newsreel and photographic coverage as the war progressed, although the endgame stimulated a final flurry of attention. Indeed, the marginalisation of Spain as news happened more quickly and dramatically in both instances with the significant reduction in visual representation of the conflict in early 1937 presaging the wider relegation in the news value of events in the country by several months. The British public lost sight of the war before they stopped reading about it.

Despite this transitory aspect, visual media were significant because they apparently allowed the British public 'a special form of witnessing' of the drama and tragedy of the Spanish War (Turner, 2004: 82). However, any notion that these gave more meaningful insights into the reality of the war is, of course, mistaken. As Anthony Aldgate and Caroline Brothers respectively demonstrate, the visualisation of the war was highly selective and politicised and it drew on powerful parochial preconceptions. The British media saw what they expected to see in Spain. Furthermore, the images were always and inescapably subordinated to the linguistic realm, as, in the final instance, it is words that explain and frame the meaning of images (Hall, 1973).

A further issue related to the visual representation of the war was the dominance of the photographic still over the moving image. Debate continues to this day as to which holds the ascendancy (see, for example, Sontag, 1998) but innovations in photographic technology in the 1930s, coupled with enduring limitations of newsreel technology, ensured that it was, paradoxically, the static modes of representation that brought viewers closer to action and the immediacy of experience. In the final reckoning, newsreels were purveyors of reportage rather than reporting.

The use of imagery in the British press confirms the trend noted in the previous chapter that saw the British press became more sympathetic in their treatment of the Republic as the war progressed. Contentious and problematic imagery related to the Republic was prominent at the start – for example, depictions of armed civilians, religious desecration and Republic dead – but then receded, to be replaced by images that challenged the legitimacy and humanity of Nationalist actions – urban bomb damage and suffering refugees, for example. However, it was not possible to discern a similar and consistent trend in newsreel coverage or in the weekly papers. While the most overtly anti-Republican content of some newsreels reduced as the war unfolded, most coverage unquestioningly accepted the probity and advisability of British neutrality and connived in the suppression of inconvenient matters related to foreign intervention in the war. And although there was a greater presence of pro-Republican sentiment in the weekly press, most accepted that non-intervention was the least worst, if not the only, feasible policy that Britain could pursue in relation to the war.

Note

1. It is interesting to note that, although the *Daily Mail* gave greatest coverage to allegations of Republican killings during this period, it only published one photograph of a dead person in Republican territory ('Patriot Officer Shot Dead in Valencia', 8 August 1936: 16). The visual proof it provided of Republican atrocities was overwhelmingly focused on images of religious desecration (for example, 'These pictures from Spain vividly illustrate the horrors of Red rule', 3 August 1936: 10; 'More Pictures of Red Sacrilege in Spain', 5 August 1936: 16; 'Reds' War on Religion', 6 August 1936: 16; 'Reds' Skull Display in Madrid Church', 7 August 1936: 16; 'Reds' Havoc in Cathedral', 11 August 1936: 16). It is unlikely that this emphasis is explained by the paper's lack of access to images of death and injury in the Republican zone – such images were published elsewhere in other national newspapers (for example,

'Grimmest picture from Spain since the revolt. Montana barracks after the surrender – and massacre', the *Daily Express*, 28 September 1936: 16; 'Shot down and left to die in the gutter – bodies of two revolutionaries beside a car in Barcelona', the *Daily Mirror*, 23 July 1936: 1; 'Girl Victim of War is Led to Hospital', the *Daily Express*, 29 July 1936: 2). The *Mail*'s visual focus on images of religious desecration was probably because it was seen as a less ambiguous topic and more likely to offend 'respectable' opinion, both in relation to the act itself and because of the imputations it readily provoked about the transgressions of personal freedom. In contrast, images of death and injury were innately more ambiguous as it was less easy to differentiate between the legitimate targets and innocent victims.

8

Journalists, Spain and the Propaganda State

Antony Beevor has observed that '[h]istory is usually written by the winners, but in the case of the Spanish Civil War it has mostly been written on behalf of the defeated' (2003: 250). In his view, this inversion of the normal course of events is explained by the impact of the global conflict that began five months after the end of the Civil War. Franco's pre-war alliance with Hitler and Mussolini irreparably destroyed his reputation, even though Spain remained neutral in the Second World War and had considerable strategic value to the West in the Cold War that followed. However, if we accept that media representations are both a litmus paper of public opinion and a key element in its formation, then the details of this book suggest that the denunciation of Franco started before the Second World War. The sympathies of pro-Republican news organisations strengthened as the war progressed and, by the end, several that had originally baulked at the idea of British intervention in its defence were firmly recommending this action. In the pro-Nationalist and non-aligned media, changes in the emphasis and tone of their coverage revealed growing reservations about Franco and the implications of his victory. At the same time, the opprobrium the right-wing media heaped on the Republic at the beginning dwindled, to be replaced by more than a modicum of compassion for those fleeing the Nationalists' advance and admiration for the endurance of those who persisted in the struggle in the face of overwhelming odds. At the start of the war, newspapers like the *Daily Mail* were vilifying all loyalists as 'Reds' but, by its end, they were calling them 'Republicans'.

The reasons for this change in media attitudes are complicated. There were the specific, media-related factors. The Republic had technical advantages in communicating internationally; its management of the foreign press was less oppressive and more sophisticated than the Nationalists'; and the greater freedom it gave to journalists to explore its interior life both helped to publicise the suffering of its citizens and challenge simplistic stereotypes about Red Terror and Soviet domination. Changes in British media attitudes were also influenced by wider political and military developments in the conflict. By late 1937, centralised political and military authority had established within the Republic and the unsanctioned killings in the urban areas and the revolutionary components and aspirations of the Republic that so disturbed international media opinion had been curbed. At the same time, growing evidence of the rebels' military ruthlessness and the scale of Italo-German involvement fatally compromised claims that their rebellion was a Christian crusade to defend the integrity and identity of Spanish nationhood. More generally, the tide of international affairs had opened up divisions within elite opinion in Britain about non-intervention and appeasement generally. Thus, evaluative changes in the media coverage of Spain both expressed and amplified broader societal transitions. As Brian Shelmerdine's recent research shows, there was a marked shift in British political opinion and cultural attitudes as the war developed and, from mid 1937, fervent Francoism in Britain became increasingly isolated to 'a dwindling constituency of the like-minded' (Shelmerdine, 2006: 173).

However, in noting the change in media evaluations, particularly among centre-right organisations, it is important not to overstate it. It was more pronounced in the daily press than newsreels and weeklies but, even there, the shift was often subtle and accretive and had little discernible impact on many papers' view of Britain's foreign policy in the war. Despite their less aggressive stance towards the Republic, most maintained their support for British non-intervention. Additionally, this re-evaluation occurred as Spain moved to the margins of the mainstream news agenda.

On these bases, we can conclude that the Republic may have won the propaganda war in the British media but, as it was fighting for much higher stakes than its enemies, the scale of its victory was insufficient. The purpose of its propaganda strategy was to mobilise Britain and other democracies to intervene in its defence, whereas all the Nationalists needed to do was to relativise perceptions sufficiently to preserve the inertia that guaranteed victory and this minimal objective was achieved.

Nevertheless, these changes show that British media responses to Spain were not as static and passive as has been suggested by previous accounts and that their formation needs to be understood in processual terms – as being affected by, and affecting, the dynamic evolution of political events and debates. This study has also shown that media analysis should move beyond basic evaluative questions about which side commanded most support to address the *interpretative* dimensions of coverage. This means considering 'what is included and what is excluded, what is foregrounded and what is backgrounded, what is thematized and what is unthematized, what process types and categories are drawn upon to represent events, and so on' (Fairclough, 1995: 103–4).

Particular news media emphasised different issues at different times and their news agendas often offered a telling indication of their editorial stance on the war. But, for all these differences, they operated within a restricted range. British coverage was dominated by three broad structures of interpretation. The first was the 'defence of democracy' interpretation, which emphasised the democratic credentials of the Republic and located the war as part of the international anti-fascist struggle. The second was the 'legitimate reaction' interpretation that saw the Nationalists' rebellion as justified in the light of local left-wing extremism and the growing threat of Soviet expansionism. The third was the 'British interests/ British values' interpretation, which prioritised the needs of the British nation and valorised domestic political and cultural values by emphasising the distance and 'otherness' of the war in Spain. All of these interpretative structures deployed simplistic dichotomies to define the war – between 'Fascists' and 'Anti-Fascists', 'Communists' and 'Anti-Communists' and 'Them' and 'Us' – which inhibited media attention to differences and tensions *within* the opposing camps. The social revolutionary aspects of the war, in particular, were conspicuously and consistently neglected and, even when events in Catalonia in spring 1937 forced this matter to their attention, new dichotomies were introduced that diverted discussion from the deeper issues at stake – between 'disorder' and 'order', 'extremism' and 'moderation', 'lawlessness' and 'lawfulness', for example.

A range of factors produced this cognitive compression – dichotomies helped to dramatise coverage and fitted more comfortably with the narratology of news; the combatants themselves prohibited discussion of internal disunity and promoted the undifferentiated stigmatisation of their enemies; official sources in Britain emphasised national strategic considerations and discouraged debate about wider matters of political and ideological principle; and media proprietors and senior news editors gave full rein to their political prejudices in their pursuit of profitability.

As the war progressed, the 'defence of democracy' interpretation gained credence over the 'legitimate reaction' interpretation within the British media but it was the 'British interests/British values' interpretation that dominated most British coverage. Perceptions of Spain, both in the media and more generally, were constructed around British concerns, stereotypes and assumptions (see Buchanan, 1993; Moradiellos, 2003; Shelmerdine, 2006: 174–7) and the increased sympathy towards the Republic within the centre-right media is, to a large extent, explained by a growing unease that Franco's victory would contravene the strategic interests of the nation.

The impact of media coverage

By accepting that media responses cannot be divorced from the wider social and political context from within which they were emerged, one might conclude, on this basis, that news organisations were mainly dependent variables in public and political debate about Spain, reflecting rather than setting the wider agenda. Although it is important to be cautious of media-centrism and of claiming a spurious causality, I think there are at least two reasons why the British media can be seen to have played a much more active role in the emergence, maintenance and management of wider debates about the Spanish Civil War, both within Britain and internationally.

First, there were several instances when media reporting set the terms of international debate. For example, if one was forced to identify a tipping point in British attitudes towards the Nationalists, it was the aerial destruction of Guernica in April 1937, which would never have achieved its political and symbolic notoriety but for the chance proximity of four foreign journalists who witnessed its immediate aftermath.

Second, the media mattered because powerful political sources assumed that they mattered. During the 1920s and 1930s political elites in many nations became obsessed with propaganda, both in the opportunities it offered and the threats that it posed. Lacking any corrective from audience research, public attitudes and behaviour were assumed to be highly susceptible to manipulation. As Harold Lasswell put it in the late 1920s:

> Collective attitudes are amenable to many modes of alteration. They may be shattered before an onslaught of violent intimidation or disintegrated by economic coercion. They may be reaffirmed in the muscular regimentation of the drill. But their arrangement and rearrangement occurs principally under the impetus of significant symbols: and the technique of using significant symbols for this purpose is propaganda. (1927: 628)

Such presumptions of power meant that all sources connected with the conflict kept a close eye on the media, particularly those in Britain, under the assumption that, if they controlled media attitudes, they would control public attitudes. As Tom Buchanan notes:

> In the 1930s 'public opinion' was conventionally regarded as being the public view of opinion-formers, who interpreted the sentiments of their voiceless fellow-citizens. Considerable power was seen to reside in the editorial columns of leading newspapers, especially *The Times* – hence the attempts by government to manage their views on sensitive issues such as appeasement. Public opinion was not an entity to be scientifically tested, but rather an amorphous public morality, to be interpreted and moulded by politicians and journalists. (1997: 22)

But what evidence is there that the media in fact exerted influence on public beliefs and attitudes? Establishing retrospectively the actual effect of media coverage on public opinion about Spain is highly problematic. It is a paradox of history that, as archives open up and memoirs are published, we come to know more and more about the actions, motives and beliefs of political elites, but less and less about the thoughts, preferences and concerns of ordinary people, despite their ubiquity and availability at the moment of their emergence. Fortuitously, the Spanish Civil War coincided with the first systematic polling on public opinion in Britain and several of the first polls assessed public attitudes to the war.

Their results suggest that public hostility to Franco was far greater than media hostility at the start of the war. For example, a British Institute of Public Opinion poll in January 1937 found that only fourteen per cent believed that 'Franco's junta' should be seen as the legal government of Spain (although the choice of phrasing here may have affected the distribution of responses). Subsequent polls showed that support for the Republic increased as the war progressed, from fifty-seven per cent in March 1938 to seventy-two per cent in January 1939 (Shelmerdine, 2006: 174). Particularly significant was the near halving of the 'no preference' response, from thirty-six to nineteen per cent.

From this limited evidence, it would seem that media and public attitudes in Britain diverged and then converged over Spain, although it is impossible, on the basis of this evidence, to deduce whether this revealed confluence rather than influence and, if it was the latter, which was the independent variable.

However, trying to identify media influence from attitudinal data is a notoriously futile exercise. Numerous studies of media agenda setting have shown that media influence is not likely to be found in what people think (attitudes) but in what they think about (cognitions). (For a discussion and example of these processes, see Deacon and Golding, 1994: 190–7.) Unfortunately, no evidence was collected during the 1930s that measured changes in public perceptions of the salience of Spain as an issue, so we can only speculate on this aspect. But it is pertinent to note that media agenda-setting effects have been most consistently found in the reporting of 'high-threshold issues' – that is, matters that are beyond the direct experiences and personal knowledge of large sections of the population, which in turn creates a higher 'need for orientation' among news consumers (see, for example, Leff et al., 1986; McCombs, 2004; Weaver, 1980). The Spanish Civil War fulfilled both of these criteria and, when considered alongside the public furore that followed press exposés of the attack on Guernica, it seems reasonable to conclude that the media probably had a considerable influence in drawing public attention to the conflict and drawing it away from it.

History lessons

Consideration of British media representations of Spain and the factors that shaped them is justified, I believe, for its intrinsic historical importance. However, an additional rationale for the study was to gain historical perspective on some contemporary debates about the political role of the media, particularly during international conflicts.

Making comparisons and drawing connections between the present and the past is, I appreciate, a risky enterprise, particularly with events that are now very distant in time. As Leslie Poles Hartley famously put it, 'The past is a foreign country: they do things differently there' ([1953] 2000). Nevertheless, we share borders with this foreign country and to abandon any attempt to draw historical connections and to analyse the cross-border traffic can only lead to 'a narcissistic presentism, or a drastic loss of engagement with historical time' (Pickering and Keightley, 2006: 924). In the final section of this book I set out what I believe to be some points of continuity and discontinuity between the conditions in the 1930s and in contemporary conditions.

The British media and 'the devil's decade'

Many of the most influential analyses of the changing political role of the media in Britain take the end of the Second World War as their starting point and, on this basis, several have identified periodic shifts in the relationship between the media and political systems caused by changes in both (see, for example, Blumler and Kavanagh, 1999; Norris et al., 2001; Seymour-Ure, 1991). Overall, the transformation is seen as entropic: with the stability of the immediate post-war consensus fragmenting as a result of the converging impact of political de-alignment and media proliferation, innovation and competition. It is this narrative that forms the back-story to current laments about the dominance of 'spin', disengagement, trivialisation and cynicism in political communication processes.

However, the immediate post war period was a highly untypical period in British political history, and therefore a questionable departure point for any historical review. The experience of the war years forged an unprecedented national unity in Britain and distaste for partisan political rhetoric (Seymour-Ure, 1991). Media organisations were emerging from several years of tight government control and were well trained in sublimating their independence to the demands of the national interest. Newsprint remained rationed for several years after the war and the newspapers of the immediate post-war period were stunted and limited creations (Wieten, 1988). But, once the historical remit is extended to the pre-Second World War period, a different perspective emerges and the narrative of 'stability to instability' is disrupted.

By the mid 1930s, a consumer boom had partially resuscitated the British economy but the country remained divided politically and socially and this was exacerbated by economic ongoing exclusions and inequalities. According to Claud Cockburn:

> [i]t was at this period that the image of Them and Us first became widely recognised in Britain . . . All that was universally known among Us about Them was that They were out to bilk, mislead, confuse and thwart Us at every turn. (1973: 99–100)

In this context and as international tensions grew, the British state began to re-structure its propaganda apparatuses, decommissioned after the First World War, but official uncertainty remained as to what form they should take. The British government wanted to exert its authority over mainstream media activities but it was still undecided as to how best to do so. At the same time, the news industry was experiencing a period of expansion and intense competition. Many newspapers were extending their structure and content to survive in this highly competitive commercial environment and new forms of mass communication, radio in particular, were establishing their presence with all the uncertainty and excitement that innovations of this kind entail.

Within this changing unstable environment some striking continuities with modern-day Britain are evident. For example, contemporary concerns about how commercial pressures are leading to news media to disengage from public affairs were also evident in the pre-war period. The 1930s may or may not have been a 'golden era' of foreign *reporting* as was claimed by some (see, for example, Maxwell-Hamilton, 2005; Cox, 1999) but foreign *coverage* was hard hit as intense competition for audience share and advertising revenue encouraged insularity in many news outlets, shifting the editorial emphasis towards human interest and celebrity news stories and life-style features (see Gannon, 1971: 1–2). In his last message to his editor, before his death, Louis Delaprée of *Paris Match* wrote bitterly about his paper's preoccupation with the abdication crisis in Britain, saying, 'You make me work for nothing but the paper-basket. Thanks . . . The massacre of a hundred Spanish children is less interesting than a Mrs. Simpson's sigh' (1937: 47). Although directed at a French news editor, his sentiment was one that many of his British colleagues at the time would have shared.

Even within professional journalist debates, some striking continuities are evident. For example, the major disagreements within the international press corps in Spain as to where their professional obligations ended and their political responsibilities began anticipated, by some six decades, modern debates about the legitimacy of a 'journalism of attachment' in which reporters set aside their pretence at objectivity and side instead with the victims of violence and conflict (see Bell, 1998).

Of course, it would be misleading to suggest that there have not been profound changes in changes in the organisation, transmission and funding of foreign correspondence over the last seventy years but, at the very least, these similarities challenge the entropic model of political change contained within many accounts of historical developments in political communication since the end of the Second World War. They also demonstrate the need to remain alert to areas of continuity as well as discontinuity in historical change (Deacon et al., 2007: 170–1). To provide an example of what I mean, I shall end this book by speculating on what this study of the mediation of the Spanish Civil War might reveal about the broader evolution of media–state relations in Britain.

The Propaganda State

In the early 1990s, Peter Golding and I used the phrase 'the Public Relations State' to describe the increased promotional sensibilities and activities of the British government in the late twentieth century (see Deacon and Golding, 1994: 5–7). Since then, the term has gained a modest currency to describe this ongoing and intensifying process, both in the UK and abroad (see, for example, Wring, 2005; Ward, 2003; Moloney, 2000).

One might conclude from the detail of this book that the Public Relations State had a longer lineage than we appreciated. For example, there was increased strategic investment and planning in official publicity in the late 1930s, a centralisation and 'presidentialisation' of news management, an assiduous cultivation of media contacts, close media monitoring and a disturbing tendency to conflate the political self-interests of the incumbent administration with general public interest (Cockett, 1989: 7). Despite these similarities, however, I believe there are sufficient dissimilarities to require another term to capture the distinctiveness of state promotionalism in Britain during the 1930s. The label I propose is 'the Propaganda State'.

I must acknowledge that I am not to first to use this term. John Pilger (2005) and Nancy Snow and Philip Taylor (2006) have used it to criticise the domestic and international communication strategies of the USA in its prosecution of the War on Terror. The term has also been used by Peter Kenez (1985) and Daniel Lynch (1999) to describe the historical formation and transition of totalitarian systems in the Soviet Union and China. The difference in my use of 'the Propaganda State' here is that it is divested of negative connotations and applied in a more localised and historically precise sense.

A basic reason for adopting the term 'propaganda' to describe state promotionalism in Britain in 1930s is that this is the term that would have been used at the time (see Mackenzie, 1938; Blanco-White, 1939; Irwin, 1936). 'Public Relations' had no equivalent public currency during the 1930s and, although negative connotations were beginning to cluster around the term 'propaganda', it was still often used in a descriptive manner to describe any kind of promotional discourse. But beyond its historical appropriateness, it is its semantic distinctiveness from 'Public Relations' that helps tease out important historical differences.

In the contemporary professional literature on PR, 'Public Relations' is often defined as a form of mutual, dialogic communication. Other authors have dismissed this claim, arguing that it is a mode of communication that is intrinsically governed by the intention to manage and manipulate perceptions and attitudes for material and political advantage (see, for example, Manning, 2001; Miller and Dinan, 2007). Nevertheless, the term does imply that it is an activity that seeks to establish common ground between communicators and recipients and create at least the impression of reciprocity between them. In comparison, 'Propaganda' is understood as a more assertive, monologic form of communication – talking *to* mass audiences, rather than talking *with* discrete publics.

This distinction encapsulates a major difference between official publicity activities in 1930s Britain and today. In our contemporary situation, much official communication is directed towards self-legitimisation – explaining, promoting and justifying the state's own structures, functions and 'fitness for purpose' (to employ modern managerialist argot). This emphasis on reflexive impression management is necessitated by a range of interlocking factors. Globalisation has compromised the stability and sovereignty of the nation state and created a range of pressures that have radically redefined its powers and role. In Britain, major state retrenchments over the last thirty years have required extensive use of public relations in both selling-off public assets and redefining public expectations of the social contract (Miller and Dinan, 2000). This has all occurred in a context of wider political and cultural instability and change – national identities are not as homogenous as they were and new social movements have redefined the terms and locations of political life. At the same time, the media complex has become more central to the conduct of political business – some would say it now defines it with its logic – but, here again, there is evidence of fragmentation, diversification and transformation facilitated by rapid technological innovations. In the 24/7, multichannel, multimedia world, 'the Public Relations State' needs to work harder than ever to explain and defend itself, whilst still pursuing its political and ideological objectives.

The Propaganda State of the 1930s also developed as a response to uncertainty and change but uncertainty and change of a very different nature. Hostile foreign powers were threatening national values and strategic interests through propagandistic and military aggression. Changes in the political franchise coupled with growing public frustration over the inadequacy of existing social welfare provision were increasing internal pressures for an expansion of the executive's role. At the same time, new forms of mass communication were emerging and established forms were expanding their reach. All of these factors necessitated increased planning and investment in official communication. Nevertheless, there remained a deep surety in the rectitude and resilience of the British political establishment that does not exist today. The Propaganda State of the 1930s recognised the need to legitimise its policies but felt little need to legitimise itself. Thus, its approach was fundamentally didactic. Confident in its intrinsic authority, it sought to educate and instruct public opinion in instrumental ways. Whereas modern political communicators apply sophisticated marketing techniques to segment and target influential sections of the electorate, the Propaganda State sought to engage and change public opinion en masse, to marshal the nation's energies to face the military and economic dangers that were increasing (Taylor, 1999). Furthermore, although unsettled by new forms of mass communication, officials retained confidence in the essential subordination of the media system to the political system. The Propaganda State was thus a creature of a mediated, rather than mediatised, political system. This is not to say it lacked sophistication in its methods and strategies (see, for example, Ian Aitken's 1990 study of the Documentary Film Movement) but it was constructed on high modernist principles that were very different from the contingencies that vitiate the Public Relations State of the late-modern era.

Coda

The last words of this book have to be about Spain. I recently revisited Madrid to take a proper look at the imposing Telefónica building that still dominates the top of the Gran Via. Although an obvious target for Franco's artillery, its robust concrete walls were sufficiently thick to provide protection to refugees, arms caches and soldiers. But its greatest significance was the access it provided to the international telephone network. Without this link and the others controlled by the Republic in Valencia and Barcelona, the international media coverage of the conflict would have been very different. As I moved across the street to photograph the building, I noticed the garish front of a mobile phone shop sheltering below it, offering telecommunication possibilities that would have been unimaginable during the war. That the Spanish Civil War is almost beyond the reach of living memory is a self-evident fact but this was the moment when the scale of the temporal distance of this event hit me most profoundly and intuitively.

And, yet, the Spanish Civil War still matters deeply to many people. Indeed, in Spain it has recently started to matter more than it has for decades, as the *pacto del olvido*, the 'pact of forgetting', forged after Franco's death has begun to crumble (Tremlett, 2007: 69–95). But the war also resonates powerfully in far-removed countries, none more so than Britain. Around the time I started writing this book, I attended a lecture at the Imperial War Museum in London organised by the International Brigade Memorial Trust. The event was packed and, from scanning the room, it was clear that people from all generations and backgrounds were present. Their knowledge of, and passion for, the memory of this long-finished conflict was almost palpable. Afterwards, as I walked back to Waterloo Station in the early spring sunshine, passing billboards with bright orange posters advertising bargain flights to Barcelona, Malaga and Madrid, I found myself reflecting upon the origins of that interest and the role that the mainstream news media may have played in initiating international identification with events in 'a far away country of which we know nothing' (Buchanan, 1993: 1).

Picasso's *Guernica* is not only recognised as the outstanding piece of art inspired by the Spanish Civil War but also one of the supreme artistic achievements of the twentieth century. In Caroline Brothers' view, the painting captured the terrors of total war more insightfully, poignantly and accurately than any of the photographic images published at the time and, because of this, retains political relevance to this day (see Brothers, 1997: 200). The perceptiveness of the latter point was demonstrated in February 2003 when the replica of the painting housed in the United Nations building in New York was covered with a blue drape as the US Secretary of State presented the case for a military invasion of Iraq to the Security Council. Accounts differ as to whether the cover-up was at the behest of television producers worried about the visual disruption of their camera feeds or spin doctors fearing the connotative incongruities it might create but, whatever the motive, the profound symbolism of the act was the subject of considerable comment at the time.

However, *Guernica* also shows the need to be wary of overstating the distinctiveness of great art from perishable journalism for, in the painting's monochrome colours and the linear hatching effect on the hind quarters of the dying horse at the centre of the picture, Picasso acknowledges the crucial role newspapers, newsreels and photographs played in creating awareness and understanding of this distant atrocity. Thus further irony is added to the UN's decision to cover it up for the cameras in 2003 because *Guernica* offers not only testament to the material suffering created by mechanised warfare but also commentary upon its mass mediation.

Bibliography

A Journalist (1937), *Foreign Journalists Under Franco's Terror*, London: United Editorial Ltd.

Ackelsberg, Martha A. (2005), *Free Women of Spain: Anarchism and the Struggle for the Emancipation of Women*, Oakland, CA: AK Press.

Adamthwaite, Anthony (1983), 'The British Government and the Media, 1937–1938', *Journal of Contemporary History* 18(2): 281–97.

Aitken, Ian (1990), *Film and Reform: John Grierson and the Documentary Film Movement*, London: Routledge.

Aldgate, Anthony (1979), *Cinema and History: British Newsreels and the Spanish Civil War*, London: Scolar Press.

Allan, Stuart (2003), *News Culture*, Second Edition, Maidenhead: Open University Press.

Ayerst, David (1971), *'Guardian': Biography of a Newspaper*, London: Collins.

Bialer, Uri (1980), *The Shadow of the Bomber: The Fear of Air Attack and British Politics, 1932–1939*, London: Royal Historical Society.

Bartlett, Vernon (1941), *This is My Life*, London: Evergreen Books.

Batchelor, Denzil (1961), *Babbled of Green Fields*, London: Hutchinson.

Becker, Karin (2002), 'Photojournalism and the Tabloid Press', in Liz Wells (ed.), *The Photography Reader*, London: Routledge, pp. 297–308.

Beevor, Antony (2003), *The Spanish Civil War*, London: Cassell Military Paperbacks.

Beevor, Antony (2007), *The Battle for Spain: The Spanish Civil War 1936–1939*, London: Phoenix Books.

Bell, Martin (1998), 'The Journalism of Attachment', in Matthew Kieran (ed.), *Media Ethics*, London: Routledge, pp. 15–22.

Bingham, Adrian (2004), 'Monitoring the Popular Press: an Historical Perspective', *History and Policy* www.historyandpolicy.org/papers/policy-paper-27.html (accessed 5 November 2007).

Blair, Tony (2007), 'Public Life', lecture given at Reuters International, London, 12 June 2007, www.number10.gov.uk/output/Page11923.asp (accessed 23 April 2008).

Blanco-White, Amber (1939), *The New Propaganda*, London: Victor Gollancz.

Blumler, Jay and Dennis Kavanagh (1999), 'The Third Age of Political Communication: Influences and Features', *Political Communication* 16(3): 209–30.

Bolín, Luis (1967), *Spain: the Vital Years*, Philadelphia and New York: J. B. Lippincott Company.

Borkenau, Franz ([1937] 2000), *The Spanish Cockpit*, London: Phoenix Press.

Brennen, Bonnie (2003), 'Sweat not Melodrama: Reading the Structure of Feeling in *All the President's Men*', *Journalism* 4(1): 115–31.

Brothers, Caroline (1997), *War and Photography: A Cultural History*, London: Routledge.

Buchanan, Tom (1993), ' "A Far Away Country of which We Know Nothing"?: Perceptions of Spain and its Civil War in Britain, 1936–1939', *Twentieth Century British History* 4(1): 1–24.

Buchanan, Tom (1997), *Britain and The Spanish Civil War*, Cambridge: Cambridge University Press.

Buchanan, Tom (2007), *The Impact of the Spanish Civil War on Britain: War, Loss and Memory*, Brighton: Sussex Academic Press.

Buckley, Henry (1940), *The Life and Death of the Spanish Republic*, London: Hamish Hamilton.

Cardozo, Harold (1937), *March of a Nation*, London: The Right Book Club.

Carr, Raymond (2001), *Modern Spain: 1875–1980*, Oxford: Oxford University Press.

Carter, Cynthia, Gill Branston and Stuart Allan (eds) (1998), *News, Gender and Power*, London: Routledge.

Cesarani, David (1999), *Arthur Koestler: the Homeless Mind*, New York: The Free Press.

Chalaby, Jean (1998), *The Invention of Journalism*, Basingstoke: Macmillan.

Chapman, Jane (2005), *Comparative Media History*, Cambridge: Polity.

Chisholm, Anne (1979), *Nancy Cunard*, London: Penguin.

Chomsky, Noam (1968), *American Power and the New Mandarins*, London: Penguin.

Churchill, Winston (1948), *The Gathering Storm*, London: Cassell.

Cockburn, Claud, (1958), *Crossing the Line*, London: MacGibbon and Kee.

Cockburn, Claud (1967), *I, Claud*, London: Penguin.

Cockburn, Claud (1973), *The Devil's Decade: The Thirties*, New York: Mason and Lipscomb.

Cockett, Richard (1989), *Twilight of Truth: Chamberlain, Appeasement and the Manipulation of the Press*, London: Weidenfeld and Nicolson.

Cockett, Richard (1990), 'The Foreign Office News Department and the Struggle Against Appeasement', *Historical Research* February 1990, 63: 73–85.

Combs, James (1993), 'From the Great War to the Gulf War: Popular Entertainment and the Legitimation of Warfare' in Robert Denton (ed.), *The Media and the Persian Gulf War*, Westport, CT: Praeger, pp. 257–84.

Conlon, Eddie (2001), *The Spanish Civil War: Anarchism in Action*, Workers Solidarity Movement, June 2001, http://struggle.ws/pdfs/spain.pdf (accessed 5 July 2007).

Constantine, Stephen (1983), *Social Conditions in Britain 1918–1939*, London: Methuen.

Corner, John (2007), 'Mediated Politics, Promotional Culture and the Idea of "Propaganda"', *Media, Culture and Society* 29(4): 669–77.

Cottle, Simon (2007), 'Ethnography and News Production: New(s) Developments in the Field', *Sociology Compass* 1(1): 1–16.

Cowles, Virginia (1941), *Looking For Trouble*, New York and London: Harper & Brothers.

Cox, Geoffrey (1937), *The Defence of Madrid*, London: Victor Gollancz.

Cox, Geoffrey (1999), *Eyewitness: A Memoir of Europe in the 1930s*, Otago: University of Otago Press.

Crosthwaite, Brian (1937), 'Newsreels Show Political Bias: Editing of Spanish War Scenes Discloses Partisan Views', *World Film News & Television Progress* 1(7), October 1937, p. 41.

Crozier, Brian (2001), 'Guernica Myths', *The Independent* 23 October 2001, p. 2.

Cudlipp, Hugh (1980), *The Prerogative of the Harlot: Press Barons and Power*, London: Bodley Head.

Curran, James and Jean Seaton (2003), *Power Without Responsibility: the Press and Broadcasting in Britain*, London: Routledge.

Davies, Alan (1999), 'The First Radio War: Broadcasting in the Spanish Civil War, 1936–1939', *Historical Journal of Film, Radio and Television* 19(4): 473–513.

Davis, Aeron (2001), *Public Relations Democracy: Public Relations, Politics and the Mass Media in Britain*, Manchester: Manchester University Press.

Davis, Aeron (2002), *Public Relations Democracy: Public Relations, Politics and the Mass Media in Britain*, Manchester: Manchester University Press.

Davis, Frances (1940), *My Shadow in the Sun*, New York: Carrick & Evans.

Davis, Frances (1981), *A Fearful Innocence*, Ohio: Kent State University Press.

de la Mora, Constancia (1939), *In Place of Splendor: The Autobiography of a Spanish Woman*, New York: Harcourt, Brace and Company.

de los Rios, Fernando (1937), *What is Happening in Spain?*, London: Press Department of the Spanish Embassy.

Deacon, David and Peter Golding (1994), *Taxation and Representation: The Media, Political Communication and the Poll Tax*, London: John Libbey.

Deacon, David and Dominic Wring (2002), 'Partisan Dealignment and the British Press', in J. Bartle, R. Mortimore and S. Atkinson (eds), *Political Communications: the British General Election of 2001*, London: Frank Cass, pp. 197–211.

Deacon, David, Michael Pickering, Peter Golding and Graham Murdock, (2007) *Researching Communications: A Practical Guide to Methods in Media and Cultural Analysis*, London: Arnold.

Delaprée, Louis (1937), *The Martyrdom of Madrid: Inedited Witnesses* (no named publisher).

Delmer, Sefton (1961), *Trial Sinister: An Autobiography*, London: Secker and Warburg.

Dick, Alan (1943), *Inside Story*, London: George Allen and Unwin.

Driberg, Tom (1956), *Beaverbrook*, London: Weidenfeld & Nicolson.

Duff, Sheila Grant (1982), *The Parting of Ways*, London: Peter Owen.

Duff, Sheila Grant (1976), 'A Very Brief Visit', in P. Toynbee (ed.), *The Distant Drum: Reflections on the Spanish Civil War*, London: Sidgwick and Jackson.

Durham, Meenakshi (1998), 'On the Relevance of Standpoint Epistemology to the Practice of Journalism: The Case for "Strong Objectivity"', *Communication Theory* 8(2): 117–40.

Edwards, Jill (1979), *The British Government and the Spanish Civil War*, Basingstoke: Macmillan.

Ellwood, Sheelagh (1994), *Franco*, London: Longman.

Evans, Harold (2004), 'Propaganda versus professionalism', *British Journalism Review* 15(1): 35–42.

Fairclough, Norman, (1995), *Media Discourse*, London: Edward Arnold.

Fenby, Charles (1937), 'British Public Opinion on Spain', *The Political Quarterly* 8(2): 248–58

Fernsworth, Lawrence (1939), 'Revolution on the Ramblas', in Frank Hanighen (ed.) *Nothing But Danger*, New York: National Travel Club, pp. 13–47.

Fischer, Louis (1941), *Men and Politics: an Autobiography*, New York: Duell, Sloan and Pearce.

Fleay, C. and M. L. Sanders (1985), 'The Labour Spain Committee: Labour Party Policy and The Spanish Civil War', *The Historical Journal* 28(1): 187–97.

Flint, James (1987), ' "Must God Go Fascist?": English Catholic Opinion and the Spanish Civil War', *Church History* 56(3): 364–74.

Fryth, Jim (1986), *The Signal Was Spain: The Spanish Aid Movement in Britain, 1936–1939*, London: St Martin's Press.

Gannon, Franklin Reid (1971), *The British Press and Germany: 1936–1939*, Oxford: Clarendon.

Gauthier, Gilles (2005), 'A Realist Point of View on News Journalism', *Journalism Studies* 6(1): 51–60.

Gerahty, Cecil (1937), *The Road to Madrid*, London: Hutchinson.

Gerbner, George (1969), 'Institutional Pressures Upon Mass Communicators', *The Sociological Review Monograph* 13: 205–48.

Gilligan, Carol (1982), *In a Different Voice: Psychological Theory and Women's Development*, London: Harvard University Press.

Gitlin, Todd (1980), *The Whole World Is Watching*, Berkeley: University of California Press.

Graham, Frank (1999), *Volunteer for Liberty: Battles of the Brunete and the Aragon*, Newcastle: no publisher (ISBN 0–85983–148–5).

Gramling, Oliver (1940), *AP: The Story of News*, New York: Farrar & Rinehart.

Graves, Robert and Alan Hodge (1940), *The Long Weekend, 1918–1939*, London: Faber and Faber.

Hall, Stuart (1973), 'The Determination of News Photographs', in S. Cohen and J. Young (eds), *The Manufacture of News*, Beverly Hills, CA: Sage, pp. 176–90.

Hamilton, John (2005, 'A Remembrance of Foreign Reporting', *Nieman Reports* 59(2), Summer 2005, pp. 62–3.

Hargreaves, Ian (2003), 'Poisonous Pens Write Media Out Of Picture', *Times Higher Education Supplement* 21 March 2003, No. 1581: 18–19.

Hart, Jeffery (1973), 'The Great Guernica Fraud', *National Review* 5 January 1973: 27–9.

Hartley, L. P. ([1953] 2000), *The Go-Between*, London: Penguin Modern Classics.

Haworth, Bryan (1981), 'The British Broadcasting Corporation, Nazi Germany and the Foreign Office', *Historical Journal of Film, Radio and Television* 1(1): 47–55.

Herbst, Josephine (1991), *The Starched Blue Sky of Spain*, New York: Harper Perennial.

Herman, Ed and Noam Chomsky (1988), *Manufacturing Consent: The Political Economy of the Mass Media*, New York: Pantheon Books.

Holguín, Sandie (2002), *Creating Spaniards: Culture and National Identity in Republican Spain*, Madison: University of Wisconsin Press.

Holme, Christopher (1995), 'The Reporter at Guernica', *British Journalism Review* 6(2): 46–51.

Hubble, Nick (2005), *Mass Observation and Everyday Life: Culture, History, Theory*, Basingstoke: Palgrave Macmillan.

Inglis, Fred (2002), *People's Witness: the Journalist in Modern Politics*, New Haven and London: Yale University Press.

Irwin, Will (1936), *Propaganda and the News or What Makes You Think So?*, New York: McGraw Hill.

Jackson, Angela (2002), *British Women and the Spanish Civil War*, London: Routledge.

Jackson, Gabriel (1972), *The Spanish Civil War*, Chicago: Quadrangle Books.

Jensen, Geoffrey (2002), *Irrational Triumph: Cultural Despair, Military Nationalism, and the Ideological Origins of Franco's Spain*, Reno: University of Nevada Press.

Kaltenborn, Hans von (1937), *Kaltenborn Edits the News*, New Hampshire: Gold Seal Books.

Kaltenborn, Hans von (1950), *Fifty Fabulous Years 1900–1950: A Personal Review*, New York: G. P. Putnam's Sons.

Keeble, Richard (1997), *Secret State, Silent Press: New Militarism, the Gulf and the Modern Image of Warfare*, Luton: John Libbey Media.

Kenez, Peter (1985), *The Birth of the Propaganda State: Soviet Method of Mass Mobilization, 1917–1929*, Cambridge: Cambridge University Press.

Kerbel, Matthew (1999), *Remote and Controlled: Media Politics in a Cynical Age*, Boulder, CO: Westview Press.

Kershaw, Alex (2002), *Blood and Champagne: The Life and Times of Robert Capa*, Basingstoke: Macmillan.

Knickerbocker, Hubert (1936), *The Siege of Alcazar: A Warlog of the Spanish Revolution*, Philadelphia: David McKay Company.

Knightley, Phillip (1975), *The First Casualty: The War Correspondent as Hero, Propagandist, and Myth Maker from the Crimea to Vietnam*, London: Andre Deutsch.

Knoblaugh, H. Edward (1937), *Correspondent in Spain*, London and New York: Sheed & Ward.

Koestler, Arthur (1937), *Spanish Testament*, London: Gollancz.

Koestler, Arthur (1954), *The Invisible Writing: Autobiography*, London: Collins with Hamish Hamilton.

Koestler, Arthur (1966), *Dialogue with Death*, The Danube Edition, London: Hutchinson.

Koss, Stephen (1990), *The Rise and Fall of the Political Press in Britain*, London: Fontana.

Lasswell, Harold (1927), 'The Theory of Political Propaganda', *The American Political Science Review* 21(3): 627–31.

Lee, Laurie (1991), *A Moment of War*, London: Viking.

Leff, Donna, David Protess and Stephen Brooks (1986), 'Crusading Journalism: Changing Public Attitudes and Policy-Making Agendas', *Public Opinion Quarterly* 50: 300–15.

Lemish, Dafna (2005), 'The Media Gendering of War and Conflict', *Feminist Media Studies* 5(3): 275–80.

Leys, C. (2001), *Market Driven Politics: Neoliberal Democracy and the Public Interest*, London: Verso.

Lichtenberg, Judith (2000), 'In Defense of Objectivity Revisited', in J. Curran and M. Gurevitch (eds), *Mass Media and Society* (3rd edn), London: Edward Arnold.

Lister, Ruth (2003), *Citizenship: Feminist Perspectives*, Basingstoke: Palgrave Macmillan.

Little, Douglas (1979), 'Twenty Years of Turmoil: ITT, The State Department, and Spain, 1924–1944', *Business History Review* 53(4): 449–72.

Little, Douglas (1988), 'Red Scare 1936: Anti-Bolshevism and the Origins of British Non-Intervention in the Spanish Civil War', *Journal of Contemporary History* 23(2): 291–311.

Lynch, Daniel (1999), *After the Propaganda State: Media, Politics, and 'Thought Work' in Reformed China*, Stanford: Stanford University Press.

MacColl, René (1956), *Deadline and Dateline*, London: Oldbourne Press.

McCombs, Maxwell (2004), *Setting the Agenda: the News Media and Public Opinion*, Cambridge: Polity.

McCullagh, Francis (1937), *In Franco's Spain*, London: Burns Oates & Washbourne Ltd.

Mackenzie, Alexander (1938), *The Propaganda Boom*, London: Right Book Club.

McLachlan, Donald (1971), *In the Chair: Barrington-Ward of 'The Times', 1927–1948*, London: Weidenfeld & Nicolson.

McLaughlin, Greg (2002), *The War Correspondent*, London: Pluto.

Manning, Paul (2001), *News and News Sources*, London: Sage.

Matthews, Herbert (1938), *Two Wars and More to Come*, New York: Carrick & Evans.

Matthews, Herbert (1946), *The Education of a Correspondent*, New York: Harcourt, Brace and Company.

Matthews, Herbert (1972), *A World in Revolution*, New York: Charles Scribner's Sons.

Mazzoleni, Gianpietro and Winfried Schulz (1999), ' "Mediatization" of Politics: A Challenge for Democracy?', *Political Communication* 16: 247–61.

MBC (Museum of Broadcast Communication) (2007) www.museum.tv/archives/etv/S/htmlS/spain/spain.htm (accessed 14 June 2007).

Miller, David and William Dinan (2000), 'The Rise of the PR Industry in Britain 1979–1998, *European Journal of Communication* 15(1): 5–35.

Miller, David and William Dinan (2007), *A Century of Spin: How Public Relations Became the Cutting Edge of Corporate Power*, London: Pluto.

Minifie, James (1976), *Expatriate*, Toronto: Macmillan.

Moloney, Kevin (2000), *Rethinking Public Relations*, London: Routledge.

Monks, Noel (1955), *Eyewitness*, London: Frank Muller.

Moorehead, Caroline (2003), *Martha Gellhorn: A Life*, London: Vintage.

Moradiellos, Enrique (1999), 'The British Government and the Spanish Civil War', *International Journal of Iberian Studies* 12(1): 4–13.

Moradiellos, Enrique (2002), 'The British Image of Spain and the Civil War', *International Journal of Iberian Studies* 15(1): 4–13.

Morris, Benny (1992), *The Roots of Appeasement: The British Weekly Press and Nazi Germany During the 1930s*, London: Frank Cass.

Nash, Mary (1995), *Defying Male Civilization: Women in the Spanish Civil War*, Denver: Arden Press.

Negrine, Ralph (1989), *Politics and the Mass Media in Britain*, London: Routledge.

Negrine, Ralph and Darren Lilleker (2002), 'The Professionalization of Political Communication: Continuities and Change in Media Practices', *European Journal of Communication* 17(3): 305–23.

Norris, Pippa, John Curtice, David Sanders, Margaret Scammell and Holli Semetko (2001), *On Message: Communicating the Campaign*, London: Sage.

North, Joseph (1958), *No Men Are Strangers*, New York: International Publishers.

Oakley, Ann (1998), 'Gender, Methodology and People's Ways of Knowing: Some Problems with Feminism and the Paradigm Debate in Social Science', *Sociology* 32(4): 707–31.

Oborne, Peter (1999), *Alastair Campbell: New Labour and the Rise of the Media Class*, London: Aurum.

Orwell, George (1938), *Homage to Catalonia*, London: Secker and Warburg.

Orwell, George ([1943] 2001), 'Looking Back on the Spanish War', in Peter Davidson (ed.), *Orwell in Spain*, London: Penguin Classics.

Padelford, Norman (1937), 'The International Non-Intervention Agreement and the Spanish Civil War', *The American Journal of International Law* 31(4): 578–603.

PEP (Political and Economic Planning) (1938), *Report on the British Press*, London: PEP.

Peters, Anthony R. (1986), *Anthony Eden at the Foreign Office 1931–1938*, Aldershot: Gower Press.

Pickering, Michael and Emily Keightley (2006), 'The Modalities of Nostalgia', *Current Sociology* 54(6): 919–41.

Pilger, John (2005), 'The Propaganda State', www.lewrockwell.com/pilger/pilger27.html (accessed 15 July 2008).

Pitcairn, Frank (1936), *Reporter in Spain*, London: Lawrence & Wishart Ltd.

Preston, Paul (1993), *Franco: A Biography*, London: HarperCollins.

Preston, Paul (2004), 'The Answer Lies in the Sewers: Captain Aguilera and the Mentality of the Francoist Officer Corps', *Science & Society* 68(3): 277–312.

Purcell, Hugh (2004), *The Last English Revolutionary: Tom Wintringham 1898–1949*, Gloucester: Sutton Press.

Rankin, Nicholas (2003), *Telegram from Guernica: The Extraordinary Life of George Steer, War Correspondent*, London: Faber & Faber.

Read, Anthony and David Fisher (1984), *Colonel Z: the Secret Life of Master Spies*, London: Hodder and Stoughton.

Read, Donald (1999), *The Power of News: the History of Reuters*, Oxford: Oxford University Press.

Reed, Douglas (1938), *Insanity Fair*, London: Jonathon Cape.

Rogers, F. Theobald (1937), *Spain: A Tragic Journey*, New York: The Macaulay Company.

Romeiser, John (1982), 'The Limits of Objective War Reporting: Louis Delaprée and *Paris Soir*', in John Romeiser (ed.), *Red Flags, Black Flags: Critical Essays on the Literature of the Spanish Civil War*, Madrid: Studia Humanitatis, Ediciones José Porrúa.

Romilly, Esmond ([1937]1971), *Boadilla*, London: Macmillan and Co.

Rose, Norman (1982), 'The Resignation of Anthony Eden', *The Historical Journal* 25(4): 911–31.

Rosen, Jay (1993), 'Beyond Objectivity', *Nieman Reports* 47(4): 48–53.

Ruiz, Julius (2007), 'Defending the Republic: The García Atadell Brigade in Madrid, 1936', *Journal of Contemporary History* 42(1): 97–115.

Scannell, Paddy and David Cardiff (1991), *A Social History of British Broadcasting, Volume One 1922–1939: Serving the Nation*, Oxford: Blackwell.

Schlesinger, Philip (1989) 'From Production to Propaganda?' *Media, Culture & Society* 11(3): 283–306.

Schlesinger, Philip (1990), 'Rethinking the Sociology of Journalism: Source Strategies and the Limits of Media-Centrism', in M. Ferguson (ed.), *Public Communication – The New Imperatives*, London: Sage, pp. 61–83.

Schudson, Michael (1991), 'The Sociology of News Revisited', in James Curran and Michael Gurevitch (eds), *Mass Media and Society*, 1st edn, London: Edward Arnold.

Schudson, Michael (2001), 'The objectivity norm in American journalism', *Journalism* 2(2): 149–70.

Scott-Watson, Keith (1937), *Single to Spain*, New York: E. P. Dutton & Company.

Scott-Watson, Keith (1939), 'Escape from Disaster', in Frank Hanighen (ed.), *Nothing But Danger*, New York: National Travel Club, pp. 243–85.

Sebba, Anne (1994), *Battling for News: the Rise of the Woman Reporter*, London: Hodder & Stoughton.

Segel, Harold (ed.) (1997), *Egon Erwin Kisch, The Raging Reporter: A Bio-Anthology*, Lafayette, IN: Purdue University Press.

Seldes, George (1987), *Witness to a Century: Encounters with the Noted, the Notorious, and the Three SOBs*, New York: Ballantine Books.

Seymour-Ure, Colin (1987), 'Leaders and the Media', in J. Seaton and B. Pimlott (eds), *The Media in British Politics*, Aldershot: Gower, pp. 3–24.

Seymour-Ure, Colin (1991), *The British Press and Broadcasting Since 1945*, Oxford: Blackwell.

Sheean, Vincent (1939), *Not Peace But a Sword*, New York: Doubleday, Doran & Company.

Shelley, Robert (1960), 'The Philatelic Aspects of the Spanish Civil War 1936–1939', *Stamp Lover* August/September 1960: 1–4.

Shelden, Michael (1991), *Orwell: The Authorized Biography*, New York: HarperCollins.

Shelmerdine, Brian (2002), 'The Experiences of British Holidaymakers and Expatriate Residents in Pre-Civil War Spain', *European History Quarterly* 32(3): 367–90.

Shelmerdine, Brian (2006), *British Representations of the Spanish Civil War*, Manchester: Manchester University Press.

Simons, Marlise (1998), 'Fascism's Prey: Now Healing and a Quest for Truth', *The New York Times* 12 May 1998, Section A: 4.

Skelton, Robin (1964), *Poetry of the Thirties*, London: Penguin.

Snow, Nancy and Philip Taylor (2006), 'The Revival of the Propaganda State: US Propaganda at Home and Abroad Since 9/11', *International Communication Gazette* 68(5–6): 389–487.

Sontag, Susan (1998), 'Looking at War: Photography's View of Devastation and Death', *The New Yorker* 78(38): 82–98.

Sorel, Nancy (1999), *The Women Who Wrote the War*, Philadelphia: Arcade Publishing.

Southworth, Herbert (1977), *Guernica! Guernica! A Study of Journalism, Diplomacy, Propaganda and History*, Berkeley: University of California Press.

Southworth, Herbert (1999), *Conspiracy and the Spanish Civil War: The Brainwashing of Francisco Franco*, London: Routledge.

Steer, George (1937), *The Tree of Gernika: A Field Study of Modern War*, London: Hodder and Stoughton Ltd.

Stenton, Michael (1980), 'British Propaganda and Raison d'Etat 1935–40', *European History Quarterly* 10(1): 47–74.

Stradling, Robert (2008), *Your Children Will Be Next: Bombing and Propaganda in the Spanish Civil War*, Cardiff: University of Wales Press.

Straw, Jack (2003), Speech to the Newspaper Society Annual Lunch, 1 April 2003, www.newspapersoc.org.uk/news-reports/pr2003/Jack-Straw-speech.html (accessed 2 July 2003).

Taylor, Edmond (1939), 'Assignment in Hell', in Frank Hanighen (ed.), *Nothing But Danger*, New York: National Travel Club, pp. 49–73.

Taylor, Philip (1999), *British Propaganda in the Twentieth Century*, Edinburgh: Edinburgh University Press.

The Times (1952), *The History of* The Times, *Volume 4, 1912–1948*, London: The Times.

Thomas, Hugh (2003), *The Spanish Civil War*, London: Penguin.

Thomas, James (2004), 'A cloak of apathy: political disengagement, popular politics and the *Daily Mirror*' 1940–1945, *Journalism Studies* 5(4): 469–82.

Tiltman, Hessell (1938), *Nightmares Must End*, London: Jarrolds.

Tremlett, Giles (2007), *Ghosts of Spain: Travels Through a Country's Hidden Past*, London: Faber and Faber.

Tuchman, Gaye (1972), 'Objectivity as Strategic Ritual: An Examination of Newsmen's Notions of Objectivity', *American Journal of Sociology* 77(4): 660–79.

Tunstall, Jeremy (1996), *Newspaper Power: The New National Press in Britain*, Oxford: Oxford University Press.

Turner, Leigh (2004), 'Warfare, Photojournalism and Witnessing', *Canadian Medical Association Journal* 170(1): 82–3.

Tusan, Michelle (2005), *Women Making News: Gender and Journalism in Modern Britain*, Urbana and Chicago: University of Illinois Press.

unknown author (1937), *Intellectuals and the Spanish Military Rebellion*, London: Press Department of the Spanish Embassy.

Vergara, Alexander (1998), 'Images of Revolution', introduction to *The Visual Front: Posters of the Spanish Civil War*, Herbert Southworth Collection, University of California: San Diego, USA – http://orpheus.ucsd.edu/speccoll/visfront/intro.html (accessed 2 April 2008).

Voigt, Frederick (1938), *Unto Caesar*, London: Constable and Company.

Voigt, Frederick (1949a), *Pax Britannica*, London: Constable and Company.

Voigt, Frederick (1949b), *The Greek Sedition*, London: Hollis and Carter.

Walton, John (1994), 'British Perceptions of Spain and their Impact on Attitudes to the Spanish Civil War: Some Additional Evidence', *Twentieth Century British History* 5(3): 283–99.

Ward, Ian (2003), 'An Australian PR state?', *Australian Journal of Communication* 30(1): 25–42.

Watkins, K. W. (1963), *Britain Divided: The Effect of the Spanish Civil War on British Public Opinion*, London: Nelson.

Weaver, David (1980), 'Audience Need for Orientation and Media Effects', *Communication Research* 7(3): 361–73.

Weaver, Denis (1939), 'Through the Enemy's Lines', in Frank Hanighen (ed.), *Nothing But Danger*, New York: National Travel Club, pp. 95–116.

Wernik, Andrew (1991), *Promotional Culture*, London: Sage.

Whelan, Richard (2002), 'Proving that Robert Capa's "Falling Soldier" is Genuine: a Detective Story', *Aperture Magazine*, 166, Spring 2002, www.pbs.org/wnet/american-masters/database/capa_r.html (accessed 1 May 2008).

Whelan, Richard (2000), 'Robert Capa and the Spanish Civil War: Courage, Loyalty and Empathy', *Media Studies Journal* 14(2), Spring/Summer 2000, www.freedomforum.org/publications/msj/courage.summer2000/y07.html (accessed 22 April 2008).

Whitaker, John (1943), *We Cannot Escape History*, New York: The Macmillan Company.

Wieten, Jan (1988), 'The press the papers wanted? The case of post-war newsprint rationing in the Netherlands and Britain', *European Journal of Communication* 3(4): 431–55.

Willcox, Templee (1983), 'Projection or Publicity? Rival Concepts in the Pre-War Planning of the British Ministry of Information', *Journal of Contemporary History* 18(1): 97–116.

Williams, Kevin (1998), *Get Me a Murder a Day! A History of Mass Communication in Britain*, London: Arnold.

Williams, Raymond (1977), *Marxism and Literature*, Oxford: Oxford University Press.

Wrench, Evelyn (1955), *Geoffrey Dawson and Our Times*, London: Hutchinson.

Wring, Dominic (1996), 'Political marketing and party development in Britain: a "secret" history', *European Journal of Marketing* 30(10/11): 100–11.

Wring, Dominic (2005), 'Politics and the Media: The Hutton Inquiry, the Public Relations State, and Crisis at the BBC', *Parliamentary Affairs* 58(2): 380–93.

Wurtzel, David (2006), 'A Newspaperman in Madrid', *History Today*, August 2006, 56, pp. 48–9.

Wybrow, Robert (1986), *Britain Speaks Out, 1937–1987*, Basingstoke: Macmillan.

Yindrich, Jan (1939), 'Seen from a Skyscraper', in Frank Hanighen (ed.), *Nothing But Danger*, New York: National Travel Club, pp. 143–60.

Index